BAGAN
AND THE
WORLD

The **ISEAS – Yusof Ishak Institute** (formerly Institute of Southeast Asian Studies) is an autonomous organization established in 1968. It is a regional centre dedicated to the study of socio-political, security, and economic trends and developments in Southeast Asia and its wider geostrategic and economic environment. The Institute's research programmes are grouped under Regional Economic Studies (RES), Regional Strategic and Political Studies (RSPS), and Regional Social and Cultural Studies (RSCS). The Institute is also home to the ASEAN Studies Centre (ASC), the Nalanda-Sriwijaya Centre (NSC), and the Singapore APEC Study Centre.

ISEAS Publishing, an established academic press, has issued more than two thousand books and journals. It is the largest scholarly publisher of research about Southeast Asia from within the region. ISEAS Publishing works with many other academic and trade publishers and distributors to disseminate important research and analyses from and about Southeast Asia to the rest of the world.

BAGAN
AND THE
WORLD

Early Myanmar and Its Global Connections

EDITED BY

GOH GEOK YIAN

JOHN N. MIKSIC

MICHAEL AUNG-THWIN

ISEAS YUSOF ISHAK
INSTITUTE

First published in Singapore in 2018 by ISEAS Publishing
30 Heng Mui Keng Terrace
Singapore 119614
E-mail: publish@iseas.edu.sg
Website: <http://bookshop.iseas.edu.sg>

The responsibility for facts and opinions in this publication rests exclusively with the authors and their interpretations do not necessarily reflect the views or the policy of the publishers or their supporters.

ISEAS Library Cataloguing-in-Publication Data

Bagan and the World : Early Myanmar and Its Global Connections / edited by Goh Geok Yian, John N. Miksic and Michael Aung-Thwin.
  1. Burma—History—Pagan period, 849–1287.
  2. Pagan (Burma)—History.
  I. Goh, Geok Yian.
  II. Miksic, John N.
  III. Aung-Thwin, Michael.
DS529.2 B21   2018

ISBN 978-981-4786-02-7 (soft cover)
ISBN 978-981-4786-65-2 (e-book, PDF)

Cover image: Mural from Temple 1026 in Bagan depicting a journey by water. The temple is undated but probably was constructed in the 12th or 13th century. Photo Credit: Goh Geok Yian.

Typeset by Superskill Graphics Pte Ltd
Printed in Singapore by Markono Print Media Pte Ltd

Contents

Preface

This book was inspired by a conference in Bagan, sponsored by the Nalanda-Sriwijaya Centre, ISEAS, in 2012. Participants in the conference were invited to submit chapters for a book about ancient Bagan's connections with the rest of Asia. This book contains ten chapters, each by a respected expert in early Myanmar history. The publication of this volume marks an important step forward in reintroducing scholarship on Myanmar and Myanmar scholars to the rest of the world. Four of the authors are Myanmarese academics, and one of the three author-editors is of Myanmar ancestry.

The conference sought to gather evidence with which to dispel the myth that Myanmar has always been a hermit kingdom or nation. This book presents abundant evidence that the kingdom of Bagan, which flourished from around 1000 to 1300, played a major role in the development of the economy, religion, art and technology in the area which stretches from India to China.

At the time the conference was conceived, Myanmar was just re-establishing contact with the outside world. The publication of this book demonstrates that Myanmar's growing integration into the international community does not signify a new relationship; Myanmar has more often been a catalyst for development and communication between West Asia, South Asia, East Asia, and Southeast Asia than a passive bystander. Buddhism formed one of the major contexts in which Myanmar exerted considerable influence over early Asian civilization. Bagan was also an economic power, and one of Southeast Asia's oldest and largest urban cultures. Myanmar is now resuming its role as an integral part of Asia which it played a thousand years ago.

The editors and authors would like to pay tribute to the late Pamela Gutman, who passed away during the interval between the conference and the publication of this book. She is greatly missed by all scholars with an interest in Myanmar. Her publications will long remain important contributions to the study of this fascinating nation. We would like to dedicate this volume to her memory.

Contributors

Michael Aung-Thwin is Professor of Asian Studies at the University of Hawai'i at Manoa, Honolulu, United States.

Olga Deshpande is an art historian in the Oriental Department, State Hermitage Museum, Saint-Petersburg, Russia.

Goh Geok Yian is Associate Professor in the School of Humanities and Social Sciences, Nanyang Technological University, Singapore.

The late **Pamela Gutman** was Honorary Associate with the Department of Art History, University of Sydney, Australia.

Bob Hudson is with the Asian Studies Program, University of Sydney, Australia. He is Adviser to UNESCO and the Myanmar Ministry of Religious Affairs and Culture, Bagan and Pyu Ancient Cities World Heritage Bids; an Open Society Foundations Visiting Fellow, Yangon University, Myanmar; a Visiting Lecturer with the Field School of Archaeology, Pyay, Myanmar; and Adviser to the Prince Claus Fund for Culture and Development, Amsterdam.

Kyaw Lat is an architect and town planner.

John N. Miksic is Professor in the Department of Southeast Asian Studies, National University of Singapore.

Elizabeth Moore is Professor in the School of Oriental and African Studies, University of London and Visiting Researcher at the Nalanda-Sriwijaya Centre, ISEAS – Yusof Ishak Institute, Singapore.

Rila Mukherjee is Director of Institut de Chandemagore, West Bengal and Professor of History at the University of Hyderabad, India.

Mya Oo is Director of the National Library of Myanmar, Department of Archaeology, National Museum and Library, Ministry of Culture, Republic of the Union of Myanmar.

Pyiet Phyo Kyaw is a lecturer in the Department of Archaeology, University of Yangon, Myanmar.

Win Maung (Tampawaddy) is a traditional architect and an independent scholar.

1

Keynote: The Myth of "Splendid Isolation"

Michael Aung-Thwin

Thank you for honouring me as keynote speaker for this marvellous occasion, especially since it is an international conference being held in Myanmar Pyi, and of all places, at Pagan. I could not have imagined as a *Yangon tha* ("son of Yangon") growing up in Yan Kin (and South India) that one day I would be back to give such a keynote address. That reminds me of the time when I was a young lad in Yan Kin during *thingyan*, when people would build floats, and go around town reciting the poetry they had composed in front of judges who gave them scores for originality and "importance". Much of the poetry was social satire. I remember a few stanzas of one of these composed by nearby high school students:

ရန်ကင်းမြို့မှာ နွေအခါ, ရေ မလာလို့. ချွေး တလုံးလုံး,
သုံးထပ်, လေးထပ် အခန်းတွေ, အခက်ပေါတာ, ထက်လိုက်ဆင်းလိုက်,
Duplex က ဆရာတွေ, ပန်းပင်တွေကာ ရေတရှဲရှဲ။

That's all I remember. For those who don't know Burmese, much will be lost in translation because of the metre, rhyme and context. But let me try anyway:

At Yan Kin in summer, with no running water, beads of sweat,
Three- and four-storey apartments, difficult to go up and down,
The *sayas* in the Duplexes, their flowers are awash with water.

So, it is indeed an honour, from Yan Kin *cha teik* (young whippersnapper) to keynote speaker. Now, to bite the hand that feeds me.

The conference premise states: "It has often been the case that the history of the ancient cities of Myanmar has been examined in splendid isolation, without sufficient reference to their external links", and so "it is this aspect of regional and broader connectivities of Myanmar polities which we hope to underline through this conference". The conference will attempt to produce an "overview of the relations between historical Myanmar polities and other Mainland Southeast Asian political and cultural centres, including those of the Tai, Thai, Mon and Khmer, as well as with the polities of India, China and maritime Southeast Asia … [to] … examine the external linkages of the major Myanmar polities and their urban centres prior to the 16th century".

I have no quibble with the *goals* of the conference and its attempts to demonstrate these external linkages. But I do have a quibble with the *premise* that the study of Myanmar's ancient cities has been done in "splendid isolation".

First of all, since the period under discussion extends to the 16th century, it includes not only the earlier cities of the so-called "Pyu period" but later ones such as Pagan, Inwa, Bago, Muttama and Toungoo, all predating the 16th century. The contention, therefore, is that all these cities have been examined in "splendid isolation". Second, and perhaps the more important aspect of my quibble, there is the question of what we mean when we say "city". I don't want to debate whether or not a city is orthogenetic or heterogenetic and all that John Miksic has to say about that subject, just to ask the following: Are we referring *only to the physical entity* outlined by its brick walls? Or does the word "city" include the "stuff" inside it? Are we talking about just the "box", or the "contents" of the box as well?

I can't imagine that by "city" all we mean is the "box" and not its "contents": the peoples, the languages, the products (such as literature, art, artefacts, architecture), the conceptual system including notions of power, legitimacy and authority, along with the symbolic dimensions of the city itself. How can one talk about the city of Pagan, for instance, without talking about its rulers, its people, its art and architecture, its symbolic dimensions, its wealth and power, its political and cultural role, its significance to the country's history? All these are legitimate parts of the discussion, so the question is whether they too have been examined in "splendid isolation"? My answer is for the most part, "no", with an important exception which I'll get to later. The issue is thus much broader, so that the premise of the conference must be expanded to deal not only with the city per se but the "stuff" inside the city as well.

The Myth

If one looks at the existing scholarship, both in terms of the *periods* under discussion — pre-historic, urban, classical, and early modern — as well as in terms of the *disciplines* that have contributed to the study of those periods — archaeology, epigraphy, history, anthropology, art history, and so on — it is clearly *not true* that Myanmar's urban history has been examined in "splendid isolation". Scholarship on Myanmar's Palaeolithic and Neolithic cultures, its bronze and iron civilizations (relevant here because they provided the very foundations of our "ancient cities"), the urban civilization that followed (here we get the true "city", best represented by Pagan, Ava, Bago and Toungoo) have *not* been studied in "splendid isolation". On the contrary, nearly all the scholars who have dealt with these latter cities and the "stuff" inside them have been quite cognizant of the larger context in which they existed. Let us take a look at the work done on the subject heretofore.

There's no reason not to begin with scholars such as Thilawuntha, U Kala and Twinthin, the three most influential and important chroniclers of the pre-colonial era. Although admittedly not focused just on the city, note that only about ten per cent of Thilawuntha's *Yazawinkyaw* is about Myanma Pyi; the rest is about his understanding of the "holy land" — in this case, Buddhist South Asia. Not only was it *not written* in isolation, his work actually gave "agency" to the *external*, not the *internal* world. It is true that U Kala's *Mahayazawingyi* is primarily about Myanma Pyi. But then, that was his subject matter; he chose to write about it. Even then, he was very much influenced by Sri Lanka's *vamsa* tradition; in fact, the title of his work was taken from the *Mahavamsa*, while his long prologue dealt with Buddhist mythology. When he got to the actual history of Myanmar he was always cognizant of the kingdoms, countries and peripheral areas surrounding Myanma Pyi, using over seventy different texts, some of them representing these regions. China was always in the story, as were Siam and Cambodia, and in terms of religion and culture, Buddhist South Asia and Sri Lanka were the models par excellence. As for Twinthin, it is true that his section on Buddhist South Asia and its linkages to Myanmar are very short, while most of his work is on Myanmar itself, hence his original title, *Myanma Yazawinthit* — NOT *Mahayazawinthit*. I don't want to get into a debate here over whether it was originally titled *Myanma Yazawinthit* or *Maha Yazawinthit*; but, like U Kala's work, his subject matter focused on the country deliberately. In other words, if you *choose* to write about the American Civil War, I can't really criticize you for not including European history, can I?

Beyond these early indigenous historians, if you glance at the 19th-century *Pitakat Thamaing*, which represents many different scholars and generations, and its 2047 distinct titles, you will find in the list treatises about regional states and cities: Ayudhaya, Chiangmai, Sri Lanka, India and China. Then, if you look at the list of manuscripts microfilmed by Kagoshima University in the early 1970s — particularly those that were not included in the *Pitakat Thamaing* — you will find accounts written by indigenous scholars of Portugal, Italy, France, and even Iran.[1] How many people in Southeast Asia at the time even knew that such a place as Iran existed, let alone write about it? To me, that these works were even written suggests that the outside world was not unknown or ignored by Myanmar scholarship. And this attitude continued during the late 19th and 20th centuries as well. Let's look at the latter, which I will organize around the periods that they represent in Myanmar's history.

Prehistory

The late 19th and early 20th-century geologists and prehistorians (Fritz Noetling, G.E. Grimes, E.H. Pascoe, G. Cotter, D.L. Stamp, E.I.C. Clegg, P. Evans, C.A. Samson, and Chhibber, along with the more famous Movius, de Terra, T.O. Morris, and Anderson) had linked (rightly or wrongly) both Myanmar's geologic periods and Stone Age sites (precursors to, and foundations of, our "ancient cities") and their artefacts (the "stuff" inside the cities) to regions outside Myanmar: particularly Africa, Europe, India, China, and Southeast Asia while using external periodization schemes: Palaeolithic, Neolithic, Chalcolithic. The use of such terms in itself shows that these authors did not assess the data in isolation. It's true that they gave agency to Europe, particularly von Heine-Geldern who theorized that bronze was brought to Southeast Asia by Europeans via China and

Vietnam. But whether they were right or wrong is not at issue; rather, whether the scholarship was done in isolation.

This pattern of looking at the larger context was continued by local scholars like U Myint Aung and U Aung Thaw in their works on Myanmar's geology and prehistory, along with those of Wilhelm G. Solheim II in the 1960s. More specifically, domesticated agriculture, pottery and bronze artefacts were linked to Spirit Cave, Hoa Binh, Dong Son, Arikamedu, Ban Chiang, and other places in South and Southeast Asia. Subsequently, and more recently, Bob Hudson and the late Pam Gutman connected the Myanmar "Neolithic" in Western Myanmar with the rest of Southeast Asia. In fact, they wrote their chapter as part of a general volume on prehistory of the region, linking these cultures in Myanmar to what was also found in the rest of the region. Even the late Than Tun, who was not a prehistorian, in the earlier chapters of his *Nay Hle Yazawin* made similar, broader connections between what was in the country and what was outside.

Early History

In terms of early history — that is, the era just prior to the true Urban Period with the "Pyu" — U Win Maung and Elizabeth Moore continued this way of looking at internal things with external references by placing Myanmar's "River Valley Civilizations" in a broader context, particularly when they dealt with the metal cultures of the Samon, Mu, Irrawaddy, Chindwin, Sittaung and Thanlwin. There is a clear realization in their work, especially that of the Samon River Valley Civilization, not only that it had cultural ties to the Dian Culture of Yunnan but that they were also pre-Buddhist. (Both are very important conclusions, providing the rest of us the wherewithal to pursue it even further with our own scholarship.) The evidence that they gathered — beads, bronze and iron weapons and implements, pottery shards, stone and metal figurines — reminds us of many other sites in Southeast Asia — so that *even without an explicit statement about linkages* to external regions, the evidence they provided itself did the linking that was far from being done "in splendid isolation".

Urban Period

When we get to the Urban Period proper (what we call the "Pyu period", let's say the thousand years between the last half of the millennium BCE and the first half of the millennium CE), the scholarship remains aware of external studies. Most scholars who have researched this culture and period were cognizant of what was happening in especially South India and Sri Lanka — particularly the sites of Nagarjunakonda and Polonnaruwa. U Aung Thaw showed these connections, as did Janice Stargardt, not to mention several before either of them: Blagden, Duroiselle, Ray, Taw Sein Ko, U Tha Mya, and Luce. In more recent years we have Paul Wheatley and once again the late Pamela Gutman's thesis on Arakan and Bob Hudson's on the Pyu, and Elizabeth Moore and U Win Maung's works of the same period. And don't forget our younger and newer, in-country scholars like Maung Maung Swe, Htwe Htwe Win, U Myo Nyunt Aung, U Kyaw Lat, amongst others; they all dealt with this period as well. All their works are cognizant of the entire region of Asia and beyond; some more, some less. Are you telling me that all of the above worked in "splendid isolation"?

In short, the period from the Stone and Metal Ages settlements to the early urban age in Myanmar has seen many scholars who have been quite aware of the cultures around Myanmar and have not been as parochial as implied. Let's now investigate the historical phases.

"Classical" and Early Modern Periods

When we get to the "classical" and "Early Modern Periods", realization of Myanmar's external context was not only continued but accelerated. The ancient cities, especially Pagan, along with the "stuff" it contained, were rarely examined without the context that was India. Everyone who has written on Pagan, from some of the first colonial writers (such as Henry Yule and Michael Symes) to Phayre, Taw Sein Kho, Duroiselle, Blagden, Chen Yi Sein, G.H. Luce, invariably had India, China and (even if wrongly) Europe in mind, not only in their explicit analyses but also in their general conclusions. This is particularly true of the art historiography of these sites. Now, whether the studies were mainly accurate or not is, once again, *not* at issue; it is whether they saw little or nothing beyond Myanmar Pyi, conceptually and empirically.

Let us examine in greater detail just a few of those external influences concerning one of those cities: the ground plans, vaulting techniques and symbolism of the Pagan temples. That question (the ground plans and vaulting) has vexed art historians since the beginning, with travellers like Henry Yule, whose sentiments were articulated by his travelling companion, a Mr Oldham. They thought that the ground plan of the four-sided Pagan temples (such as the Ananda) represented a Greek Cross, so to them it suggested Christian influences in the design. He wrote that "so strongly unlike all other Burman buildings, can these have owed their origin to the skill of a Western Christian or Missionary? May not the true cross-like plan of the Ananda be thus symbolical, and may he not, in the long-trusting hope of a zealous worshipper of Christ, have looked forward to the time when this noble pile might be turned from the worship of an unknown god to the service of the Most High? I can't think any Burman ever designed or planned such buildings".[2] Even though obviously wrong, he was *not* thinking in "splendid isolation" either; in fact, *non-isolation* — that is, his assumption of the universalism and truth of Christianity — was what caused his faulty conclusion.

In terms of Pagan vaulting techniques, serious and competent art historians invariably invoked China, the Romans, East India, and other parts of Southeast Asia when assessing that phenomenon. Although none of these explanations is entirely satisfactory, the point is that they were *not* done in isolation. Pierre Pichard's work on the vaulting — perhaps the closest we are going to get to their origins — was done with a broad knowledge of engineering techniques and examples found outside of Myanmar.

The *symbolic dimensions* of the stupa-temples and related issues — their alignments, their doctrinal bases, their everyday functions, their iconography, their art work — that have been raised by art historians and Buddhist scholars, have *not* been done in "splendid isolation" either. U Ba Shin, Sergei Oshsegove, Lily Handlin, Daw Nyunt Nyunt Swe and others have scrutinized the information regarding and gleaned from individual temples that have sought links outside Pagan in the larger Buddhist world. Apart from the temples per se, the symbolism of some of these cities themselves, particularly those that were capitals/centres (Sriksetra, Pagan, Inwa, Toungoo and Bago), were also a subject of discussion by scholars who took the analysis outside Myanmar, especially to India. Particularly the way in which the capital cities were placed in the context of a larger Buddhist–Hindu cosmology, linking it with *Tavatimsa*, the abode of Sakka/Thagya (Indra), a Vedic deity. Such symbolic dimensions are truer of Sriksetra, Pagan, Toungoo and Mandalay, and less so of Amarapura, Inwa and Bago. Bago's design, especially Bayinnaung's capital, was more secular than it was religious, while Inwa's had Sinic elements in it. Both sites need further study for sure, but the current scholarship has not been done in "splendid isolation".

Beyond the contents and symbolism of these cities, even the question regarding the *origins* of cities was not done in isolation; the subject is invariably part of conceptual and theoretical studies enmeshed in the issues surrounding "the origins of the state", for the city itself is believed (by the best historical geographers like the late Paul Wheatley) to have been the foundation of the state, a subject that is quite broad and found nearly everywhere in academia. To reiterate: all the above studies pertinent to the conference question of "ancient cities" and its contents were not done in splendid isolation.

In terms of the discipline of history, my generation certainly did not write in "splendid isolation" when we dealt with Pagan, Inwa or Toungoo. In fact we went even further in terms of using the influence of Western social science theory in our studies, by listening to anthropology and (god forbid) even to postmodernism. Consider my own dissertation, resulting in *Pagan: the Origins of Modern Burma*. It certainly was not written in "splendid isolation", even if I personally felt isolated in cold, Ann Arbor, Michigan and Elmira, New York. Consider also Vic Lieberman's recent works. Has he worked on Myanmar history in "splendid isolation"? Not even close: he is probably the one who has linked the field of Myanmar Studies (and Southeast Asian) history to a far larger world than anyone else had done before, placing Myanmar's history not only in the context of world history but in the context of world climate, world demography, and world disease.

The generation of historians that followed ours continued that tradition as well. Consider all the historians who wrote chapters in Jos Gommans and Jacques Leider's edition of *The Maritime Frontiers of Burma*. The entire volume was intended to place Myanmar — whether its cities or its commerce — in a larger Bay of Bengal context. Similarly, the scholarship of younger historians who followed them, represented by one of the newest and youngest Pagan scholars in the audience (Geok Yian Goh), also placed her thesis on Pagan in a much larger intellectual Theravada Buddhist context of South Asia.

How can we say, then, that these are examples of scholarship done in "splendid isolation"? There are many others (such as Bob Taylor, Maitrii Aung-Thwin, the late Kris Lehman, Juliana Schober, Erik Braun, Pat Pranke, Alicia Turner, Alexey Kirichenko, Pat McCormick, to name just a few) whose works I haven't mentioned because their disciplines and foci lie outside the general period of time with which this basically historical conference is concerned: that is, up to the 16th century. These works were anything but done in "splendid isolation", empirically or conceptually. In fact, just the opposite!

Why Then?

The more interesting question for me is why are we saying this? Why are we saying that we have been parochial, working in "splendid isolation"? Why are we needlessly beating ourselves up? I think a plausible answer may be that we have (unfortunately) begun to believe what everyone outside has been hammering away at for the past two decades: that we are isolated, parochial, inward looking, xenophobic. The last, xenophobia, is an accusation that has been around for over a century. And we want desperately to disprove this by showing that we are quite cognizant of the "global" as well. This more recent pressure from, and fetish with, "globalization" (academically anyway) has also been in part responsible for the contention that we have been heretofore "isolated'.

There are *historical and political reasons* for creating this myth of isolation. The outside, especially the Western world, has always considered the coasts of Myanmar to be the "front door" of the country, for that is where *they* entered. It must have been the front door, for they would never stoop to enter via the back door. Historically, however, the coasts of Lower Myanmar were not the country's "front door" but its "back door". The *north* was the country's "front door". For most of the country's history, China has been most important politically, while India (call it the "side door" if you wish) has been the most important culturally. Lower Myanmar was the "frontier" — the "boondocks".

So when the West entered Myanmar Pyi by the back door and found the Burmese looking the other way — to the north towards China or sideways towards India — and away from *them*, they took that as looking "inward'; hence, the terms parochialism, isolationism, xenophobia. In other words, this whole notion regarding the direction of Myanmar's gaze has contributed to the myth of "isolation". (Most Western news reports continue this image: the BBC, AP, VOA invariably characterize the country as "isolated", even with the tremendous transformations that have occurred during the last two years. The reason is that this notion of "isolation" gives "agency" to forces *outside* the country, not the forces *inside* the country, so that the Burmese people are seen as passive recipients and beneficiaries, *not actors and agents of change*, a self-fulfilling argument. The outside world has the perception that unless *they* do something, nothing gets done inside. That's largely untrue, as has been proved by the political events that have transpired in the past two or three years.

To use one example, but outside of academia — that is, in politics, perhaps the most *difficult* area to transform in any society — the reason there has been a warming of relations between some of the most intransigent Western countries such as the United States and the United Kingdom and Myanmar is *not* because of what *they* did; it's because of what *you* did. You, the people and government of Myanmar, held the line and "stayed the course" under tremendous political and economic pressures, both external and internal.

It is because *you* were successful in implementing multiparty democracy as promised in 1987 — despite tremendous odds, trials and tribulations, natural disasters, economic sanctions and relentless political pressure perpetrated by the strongest and wealthiest corporations and nations on earth to affect the kind of change *they* wanted. Despite that, we have the situation today that we have. It is not because of *them* but because of *you*. You successfully ended the half-century of civil war by 2000 (if not earlier), implemented the seven-step road map to democracy initiated in 2004, wrote the new Constitution in 2008, held free and fair elections in 2010, seated the Hluttaw in 2011, dissolved military rule in March of the same year (as promised) and held by-elections subsequently. It is because of these *internal actions* that we have the current state of affairs.

The outside world did very little to help. In fact they were an obstruction nearly every time something positive was about to occur. (I have an acquaintance at the Foreign Correspondents Club in Bangkok who told me in confidence that any positive news that came out of Myanmar during the past twenty-five years, they suppressed, as their "contribution". To what, I'm not quite sure; certainly not freedom of the press!) Some even wished an "Arab Spring" on Myanmar Pyi! (I guess they really don't care much about the country or its people.)

So, it is not *because* of them but *despite* them that these changes have taken place. *You* did most of the hard work to make that happen. So don't let them tell you it was because of their generosity, magnanimity, goodwill and so on that led to these better relations. If *you* hadn't done what you did over the past twenty years, they wouldn't have even considered it. (Of course, there were other, broader geopolitical reasons that were also factors, but I won't get into them here.)

Now, how is all that related to our conference premise of "splendid isolation"? In the following way: what had happened politically during the past twenty-five years within Myanmar had internationalized Myanmar Studies, so that the country was being scrutinized by the outside world far more closely than it ever had been previously, but only with regard to a very narrow range of select subjects. In other words, it was another kind of "splendid isolation" — isolation of external people from the country: its local events, its languages, its priorities, its post-colonial history, its political values. Put another way, some academic (but mainly journalism's) treatment of Myanmar was almost totally unrelated to what was most important to most of the people living inside it. Without even stepping into Myanmar in many instances — or in others, just barely, in order to legitimize one's research, to say "I've been there" — nearly everything in Myanmar's past was reinterpreted to fit that imagined *present*, to be commensurate with one's current *image* of it. That *external* form of "splendid isolation" did much more damage to Myanmar scholarship than any internal "splendid isolation" might have done. The point I'm trying to make here is that "splendid isolation" can work both ways — you can be as isolated *from* the country as *in* the country.

More specifically, if you look at early Burmese history (even art history) written *before* the riots of 1988 and *after* the riots of 1988, you'll notice a clear difference. The dissertations, books and articles published *after* 1988 were invariably characterized by a "sub-text" that was *binary* in nature, that posited authoritarian against democratic values. Even earlier works that had been influenced by Karl Witfogel's "Oriental Despotism" (and long put to rest in academia) reared their ugly head after 1988, with unequivocal statements about the tyranny and despotism of Myanmar's *past*. And yet, the evidence itself had not changed: the Old Burmese inscriptions, the chronicles, the art and architecture of the Pagan Temples had not changed. What *had* changed was the *way Burmese society was being reinterpreted* by the outside world *because of 1988*.

It is true that such influences by political events were mostly the domain of those in more "present-oriented" fields, such as political science and journalism, although there were, I'm afraid, some scholars who also succumbed to the political winds of the time and jumped on the bandwagon in fields as non-political as art history. My point is that what happened *politically* had an important impact on the historiography (even art historiography) of Myanmar Pyi. And unless we are cognizant of this kind of influence on our scholarship and are on guard for it all the time, we will be working in another kind of (external) "splendid isolation".

The Reality

So much for the myth of "splendid isolation"; let us now deal with the *reality* of "splendid isolation" in Myanmar scholarship. And that reality, in one particular respect at least, is that we *have* indeed been working in "splendid isolation" — in the *conceptual and theoretical arena.*

The Theoretical Arena

I know that many, especially older, academics in Myanmar look at theory with some scepticism. But let me assure you that not only am I an older academic but also that theory is *not the opposite* of empiricism. Rather, it enhances empiricism. It is really a particular way of thinking about things. It raises issues that would not be raised if all we were concerned about were "the facts". A theoretical approach asks particular kinds of questions about those facts and problematizes them. If we don't, we will never progress beyond a certain point. And once these questions are asked and the issues raised, the answers must not only make sense, they still must be supported by "the facts" anyway. So, theory and empiricism are not contradictory but complimentary.

This is an area where some of my respected predecessors have failed: they had the facts — in some cases, better than I had — but the most famous ones did not know what to do with them. They did not ask the kinds of theoretical questions of those facts; that is, what these facts meant or their significance in a broader theoretical and conceptual framework. And that's because Myanmar Studies lacked a theoretical component. Theory includes epistemology, which asks the question "how do we know what we know", as well as methodology, which asks the question "how do we approach that subject". These are questions that Myanmar scholarship up to the mid-20th century rarely asked of itself or its data. In *that* sense I would concede that Myanmar Studies in general was conducted in "splendid isolation".

But it is a problem that can be redressed, and where much progress can be made. Myanmar scholars, with their language skills and in-depth knowledge of the country and culture, but using the kinds of theoretically sophisticated analyses and approaches to the study of the country found outside it, can contribute immensely to the field. The reverse isn't always true: no matter how long and hard non-native scholars study the language, they cannot acquire the kinds of language skills that you have — with some exceptions like Saya John Okell and a few others. Take advantage of that: combine the language and cultural knowledge with what the outside has to offer in terms of theory.

But do it on your own terms. In the same way that Myanmar has been the main agent in successfully bringing in the outside world politically in recent years — on its own terms — we can do the same academically by providing the *internal* wherewithal for such success. We will have to do the work that will allow people (with more money) who sincerely want to help us in this endeavour. In the long run though, the definitive prehistory, early history and early modern history of Myanmar must be, and will be, written by scholars who know the country's languages and cultures best, who have lived here for years, who know the people, who have *experienced* rather than just observed Myanmar from the outside.

In order to implement this, one can use different strategies. Just to suggest one, we should start thinking about working towards adding another component to the kinds of projects that translated Burmese materials into English (such as Dr Than Tun's "Royal Orders" or, in the China field, Geoff Wade's work on the Ming sources into English). Perhaps we should do the reverse: start translating into Burmese the most important *theoretical and conceptual* works in English and other languages for Myanmar scholars, and make sure that they have easy and inexpensive access to them.

So far, we on the outside have taken, taken and taken, and not given back much to the country. Oh sure, we've left our old cameras, flash units, old motorcycles and bicycles for those who worked with us, but what about something more substantial? What about creating a centre in Myanmar that is academically linked to the Nalanda-Srivijaya project of ISEAS, to help implement this and other future goals? We can start on a small scale and see where it goes. I cannot think of a better Buddhist country today than Myanmar and a more appropriate place than Pagan with which to link the Nalanda-Srivijaya project, given its stated objectives. Can you?

Conclusion

Finally, and to end this keynote address, let me reiterate that although I don't think Myanmar's history up to the "early modern period" — even if focused narrowly on ancient cities — has been carried out in "splendid isolation", the *goals* of this conference are in fact to demonstrate that external linkages *did exist* between Myanmar polities and centres outside them. Thus, although the premise of the conference may be a bit faulty, its *goals* *continue* the tradition begun by our predecessors rather than depart from it.

Notes

1. *The Catalogue of Materials on Myanmar History in Microfilms Deposited in the Center for East Asian Cultural Studies*, vol. 1, edited by Thu Nandar, p. 12, reels 43 and 44. These are *Italian Than Yauk Sa Tan* and *Iran Than Yauk Sa Tan*, both parabuiks.
2. See Michael Aung-Thwin, *The Mists of Ramanna* (Honolulu, University of Hawai'i Press, 2005), p. 203.

2

Analysis of Construction Techniques in Pyu Cities and Bagan

Kyaw Lat

A remarkable fact about Bagan is that presently over three thousand monuments are found concentrated in an area of forty-two square kilometres (sixteen square miles). An Inwa dynasty king, Moe-Nyin-Thado, recorded 4,474 structures there in the 15th century. There are presently 3,122 monuments and mounds in the list of the archaeological department. If there were over 4,400 monuments in the 15th century, it is possible that approximately a thousand monuments are no longer standing, either in scattered ruins, rebuilt into new structures not listed in the inventory, or possibly eroded away by the Ayeyarwady River over the past five centuries.

This chapter examines the construction techniques utilized at the Pyu sites such as Sriksetra and Bagan and compares these construction techniques with selected historical sites in Southeast Asia from the period between the beginning of the first millennium CE and the 14th century. This period starts with incipient urbanization and concludes with the end of Bagan in Myanmar history.

Overview of Ancient Civilizations in East Asia

The earliest complex societies in Asia were found in the Indus Valley and the Yellow River and Yangtze River valleys. These societies developed parallel to the civilizations of ancient Egypt, Mesopotamia and Crete.

The Yellow River and Yangtze River valleys were two core regions from where the Shang dynasty drew influences. Traditional records mention a series of legendary pre-Shang rulers, such as the Yellow Lord (Huang Di), who invented the key features of civilization like agriculture, the family, boats, carts, bows and arrows, and the calendar. It is believed that these rulers existed before the 22nd century BCE. They were superseded by the Shang dynasty (1570–1045 BCE), which coincided with the beginning of written and archaeological records. Chinese accounts of the Shang rulers match inscriptions on animal bones and tortoise shells that date from the 20th century BCE at the city of Anyang in the valley of the Huang He (Yellow River) (Lawler 2009; Long and Taylor 2015).[1]

The remains of settlements belonging to Harappa culture are found throughout the Indus River Valley in Pakistan, India's northwestern states as far east as New Delhi, and reaching up to the Oxus River in northern Afghanistan. The Indus Valley civilization which emerged around 2500 BCE and abruptly terminated sometime around 1700 BCE encompasses one of the largest geographical areas covered by a single Bronze Age culture; the reasons for its strange disappearance are not fully understood by scholars.

The sudden end of Harappa was followed by an interval of about a thousand years during which no large-scale complex societies are known to have evolved in South Asia. Historians do not know why there were no or very few sites comparable to the Harappan sites in the Indian subcontinent between 1700 BCE and the 7th century BCE. By the 7th century BCE, the kingdom of Magadha emerged centred at Pataliputra, near Patna in the state of Bihar. Chandragupta Maurya was the first ruler of the Mauryan dynasty; the third king, his grandson Asoka, became king around 269 BCE and expanded his empire until it stretched from the Kashmir region in the north to modern Karnataka state in the south, and from the Ganges delta in the east to southern and eastern Afghanistan in the northwest. King Asoka sponsored the production of numerous inscriptions about Buddhist teachings and other edicts found in various parts of the Indian subcontinent.

The 1st century CE witnessed the start of a process of proliferation of polities in Southeast Asia which embraced political ideologies and religious belief systems influenced by Hinduism and Buddhism. In northern Vietnam, Confucius-Chinese culture had a more entrenched influence. Chinese dynasties, beginning from the Han, ruled northern Vietnam under its commandery system. During the next millennium, China lost, re-established, and lost control of Vietnam, until a polity known as Nam Viet became independent.

Rakhine, in the southwest part of Myanmar, was one of the first localities to adopt Buddhist and Hindu beliefs and Indic writing systems and political ideas. In central Myanmar, indigenous inscriptions, later Burmese chronicles, and Chinese records refer to a people or an archaeological culture as "Pyu", which is a language. Artefacts associated with this archaeological culture are found at towns like Halin, Tagaung, Sriksetra (Tharehkettara) and Pinle; this culture covers a wide area ranging from Shwebo district in upper Myanmar to Pyay in southern Myanmar. These sites appear to form part of the same archaeological culture.[2] They began as walled sites which were constructed around the 1st century BCE/CE; some Burmese scholars suggested an earlier date of the 3rd century BCE (Nyunt Han et al. 2007). The final phase of "Pyu" culture probably ended around the 9th century when the "Pyu" people purportedly became assimilated by populations presently known as Myanmar, although the Pyu language appeared in epigraphy until the Myazedi inscription of 1113;[3] in contrast, Rakhine culture appears to represent a continuous tradition from proto-history through today.

An Overview of Building Technologies in Southeast Asia

Early sites in middle Myanmar like Beikthano, Halin, Sriksetra and others started building with brick by the turn of the first millennium BCE/CE. The following provides an overview on the usage of the main building materials, brick or stone, in the Southeast Asian region:

1. In India, early permanent Buddhist structures were rock-cut caves, temples and monasteries hewn into the hills. Later freestanding structures were constructed with brick as well as stone.
2. All middle Myanmar sites used mainly brick.
3. Shan, Kayah and Kachin areas in the north and northeastern regions of Myanmar also used primarily brick.
4. Rakhine structures were built with brick during the early periods.

By the zenith period of the 16th and 17th centuries in Myohaung, natural stone was mainly used; this stone was cut to almost uniform size and used in a way similar to brick.

5. Khmer sites in Cambodia and Dvaravati sites in central Thailand used a combination of laterite and sandstone.
6. Thailand, beginning in the Sukhothai period of the 13th century, used both stone and brick.
7. The southeast areas of Myanmar (Ramaññadesa) also used natural materials, consisting mainly of laterite (a form of clay which hardens into rock on exposure to the atmosphere), similar to the Dvaravati sites in the Chao Phraya valley.
8. Borobudur in Java, constructed in the 9th century, was built of natural stone.

This broad overview of brick- and stone-based cultures in the Southeast Asian region focuses on the construction of religious buildings, which are meant to be long-lasting. Timber was mainly used for residential buildings, and the environment offers various timber species; the perishability of timber also means that no ancient palaces survived in Southeast Asia.

Historical Sites in Myanmar

The oldest sites with architecture in Myanmar comprise "Pyu" sites in the north and central Ayeyarwady valley, Rakhine in the southwest coastal regions, and "Mon" sites in the southeast regions. Most of these sites can be dated to the period between the 1st century BCE and the late first millennium CE. The oldest sites with architectural remains are "Pyu" sites: Beikthano, Tagaung, Halin and Sriksetra. The building remains from Mon sites date from a few centuries later. The oldest inscriptions, sculpture and architectural remains from Rakhine can be dated to the early first millennium CE. It is probable that Rakhine buildings of an earlier period were constructed using timber.

Building Technology in Myanmar before Bagan

Beikthano

The oldest remains of buildings extant in Beikthano, Halin and Sriksetra are primarily stupas, monasteries, temples and a few residential buildings for the elite. The foundations of a number of stupas found at Beikthano suggest that they had circular plans. These structures are circumscribed by rectangular or circular walls, which bear strong resemblance to the Andhra (dome-shaped) type of stupas at Amaravati and Nagarjunakonda in India, which were built originally in the 2nd century BCE. It is plausible that the earliest structures at Beikthano could also be dated to the period within a century or two on either side of the beginning of the first millennium CE. Radiocarbon dating appears to support this hypothesis (Aung Thaw 1968, p. 18).

Two buildings excavated at Beikthano have rectangular plans; they are presumably large temples. The inner dimensions of both buildings are close to each other: 11.68 by 22.88 metres (38'4" × 75'1") for KKG 9 and 11.88 by 23.87 metres (39' × 78'4") for KKG 11. The walls of these structures were constructed using brick; two rows of timber columns inside the room allowed these buildings to have wider hallways. The combined usage of brick and wood suggests that the architects and builders were not in a position to construct entirely with brick and had to utilize other perishable materials. This also suggests that the buildings in Beikthano were representative of transitional architecture which marked the shift from building with timber to building with masonry materials.

Sri-Khitara (Sriksetra)

In Sri-Khitara (Sriksetra), such temples with brick walls and timber roofs were constructed at the beginning of occupation at the site, but later, in about the 7th century, the first temples with true scientific vaults covering inner spaces were constructed completely of brick. Architectural historians who specialize in Southeast Asian architecture aver that Bagan is the only place in Southeast Asia where true scientific vaults were used before the 11th century. In India, only mosques constructed after the 13th century began to apply this construction technology, which was introduced together with Islamic culture from the Middle East. Other areas in the Southeast Asian region, such as the Angkor kingdom or the Dvaravati sites of Thailand, did not use the true vault.

There are examples which demonstrate that the construction of true arches and vaults was developed in Sriksetra and transferred to Bagan. If the builders in Bagan had adopted this technology from Sriksetra, they were fortunate, because it would have been impossible to build thousands

FIGURE 2.1   Comparison of building technology in Southeast Asian cultures: **A** Borobudur, Central Java; **B** Angkor Wat, Suryavarman II (r. 1111–1150); **C** Po Nagar, Champa, Vietnam; **D** Wat Sri Savaya, Sukhothai; **E** Prasai Hin, Phimai.
Source: John N. Miksic.

FIGURE 2.2 Foundation for a stupa, Beikthano, Site 3.
Source: John N. Miksic.

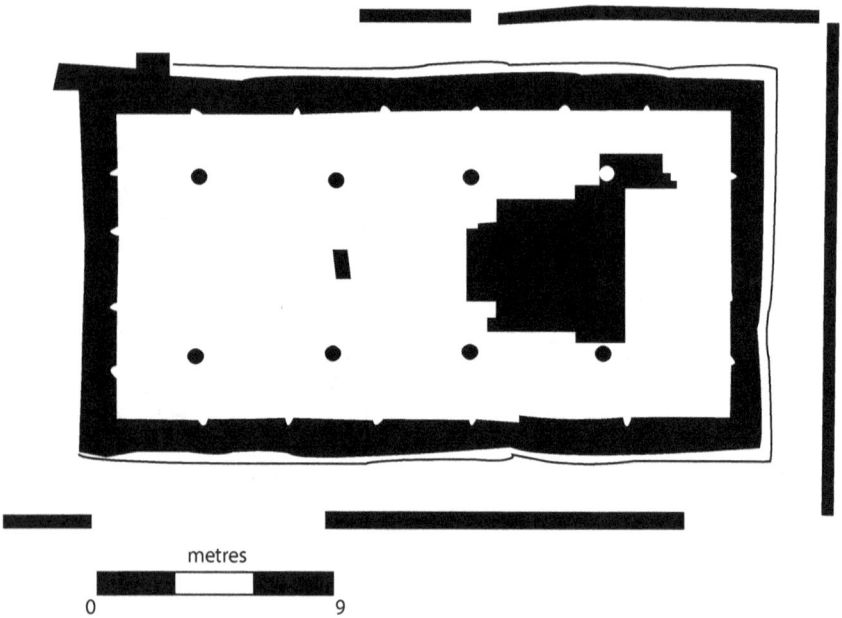

metres

0   9

FIGURE 2.3 Plan of a Temple at Beikthano, Site 3. Redrawn by Goh Geok Yian.

of the structures in Bagan without utilizing the arch and vault. Vaulting was an important development in the history of building technology: in early periods it would have been easy to construct walls with brick or stone, but to cover all rooms and openings with brick and stone would have posed a problem for which not all ancient civilizations had solutions.

The Egyptians applied stone beams or slabs to cover the inner spaces of their temples; this method is time-consuming and labour intensive (Brown 1959). At Mohenjo-Daro and Harappa, the people built advanced cities with roads and drainage systems arranged in grid patterns between 2500 BCE and about 1500 BCE, but they did not develop the true arch and vault. The builders used timber roofs to cover the inner spaces of their buildings and timber lintels for the openings, but this is not a perfect solution. On one hand, the builders of Harappa built masonry structures to be long-lasting, but on the other, this intention was not achieved because timber could only last for a few hundred years, compared to brick, which can last millennia. Brick structures are however more vulnerable to earthquake damage, and hence may not be suitable for areas such as the Indus Valley, where tremors of sizeable magnitude are frequent.

FIGURE 2.4   Temples of Sriksetra: **A** Yahanda Gu; **B** Hpaya-Taung; **C** Le Myet Hna.
Source: John N. Miksic.

In India, Hindu and Buddhist structures used stone beams or, in some cases, corbelled arches. Corbelled arches are not scientific arches; they were constructed using large brick slabs, and each horizontal layer was laid with a slight offset inward as it rises to the ridge (Brown 1959). The main disadvantage of this method is that the spans are narrow and they cannot withstand heavy loads, which are normally required for the temples that are topped with sikharas, or square-based towers, where relics are enshrined.

The structural principle of a true arch is "the resolution of forces": the forces from both sides of the opening meet at the centre of the top of the opening, and the result of the two opposite forces acts to project pressure vertically upwards. For this reason, a keystone, or central *voussoir*, which is larger than the other stones, must be placed exactly at the centre to act vertically downwards in the opposite direction to the resultant force. The weight of the keystone and other loads (of walls, roofs, etc.) act downwards on the arch, which stands with two forces together from both sides. In other words, the two forces together must bear the forces acting vertically downward.

In Sriksetra there are a few temples that can be called prototypes of Bagan temples: Bebe Gu, East Zegu and Le Myet Hna. These are simple brick structures with true vaults. In terms of design and structure, they are basically similar to Bagan temples. These examples with true scientific vaults were constructed during a later period in Sriksetra,[4] but a few structures may represent transitional structures before the builders began to utilize true vaults.[5] These structures, Baw-Baw-Gyi Stupa and a very small temple called Yahanda Gu, share a feature: a passageway (tunnel) where corbelled vaults were applied as in India. Later builders developed the technique of making true vaults and constructed two types of temple: a simple single shrine temple covered with a cross vault and a second type which comprised a pillar in the middle forming a passage in the shrine. These two types became the basic prototypes for Bagan temples: all Bagan temples evolved from these two structural types. After the 10th century, the structures increased in size and some design innovations were also developed.

Some archaeologists in Myanmar have suggested that the Baw-Baw-Gyi was constructed about the 6th or 7th century (Sein Maung Oo 1969, p. 207), while temples like Ashe Zegu, Bebe Gu and Le Myet Hna could be dated to the 7th century. These are estimates based on the Buddha

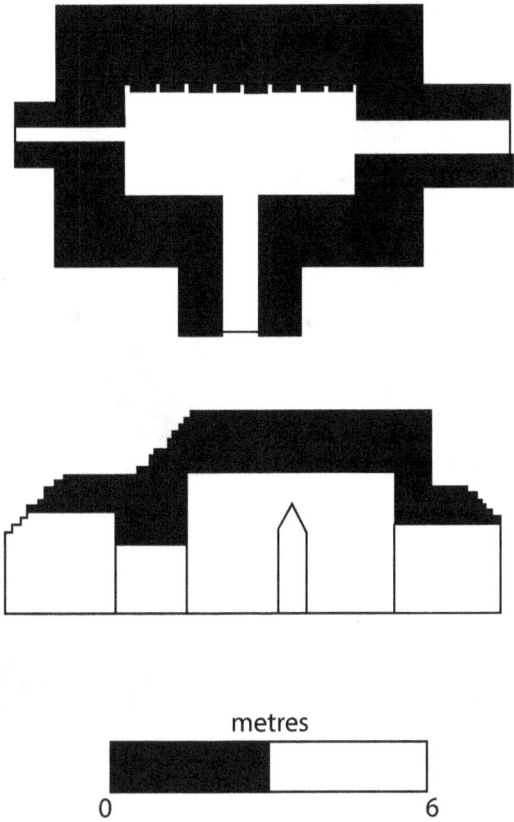

metres

0   6

FIGURE 2.5   Plan of Yahanda gu, constructed with corbelled vault. Redrawn by Goh Geok Yian.

images in those temples (Marshal 1907–8, p. 42). However, these estimates based on Buddha images are extremely problematic; more recent scholars suggest that the Bagan period did not predate the 10th or 11th centuries (Pichard 1994; Strachan 1989; Stadtner 2005).

It is argued here that the builders in Sriksetra developed the method of building scientific vaults and arches which was later transferred to Bagan. The two temple types in Sriksetra, a simple shrine covered with cross vault, such as the Bebe Gu or Ashe Zegu, and a shrine with a solid pillar in the centre surrounded by a passage, like Le Myet Hna, are the two prototypes for later Bagan temples.

FIGURE 2.6 **A** Hpaya-Mar; **B** Baw-Baw-Gyi.
Source: John N. Miksic.

Bebe Gu   Le Myet Hna

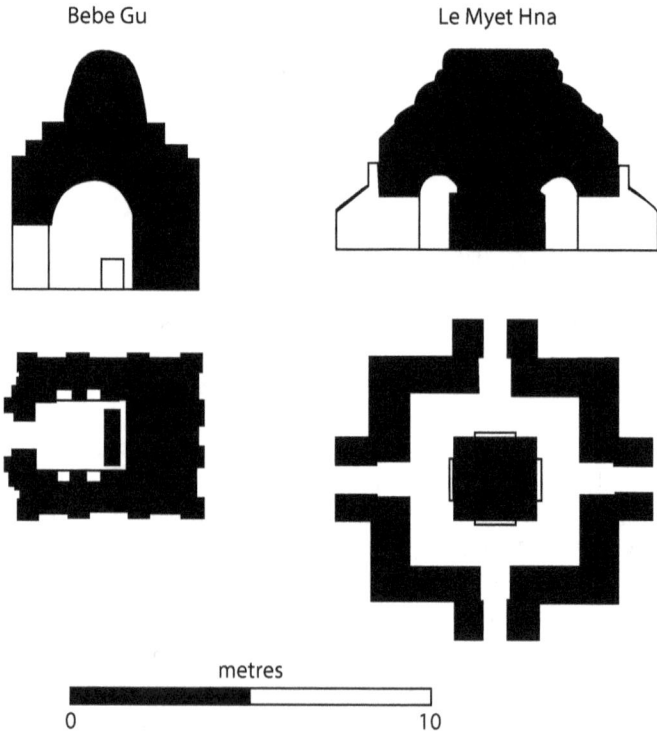

metres
0   10

FIGURE 2.7 Temples with scientific vaults in Sri Khitara. Redrawn by Goh Geok Yian.

Architecture of Bagan

Urban Design Principles in Bagan

The road system and layout of Bagan give the impression that there was no systematic road alignment or urban design for the walled city. This opinion is predicated on current perceptions and comparison with other capitals in Asia and Myanmar that reflected systematic rectangular grid plans, such as Beijing, Chang An, Inwa and Mandalay. It is important to note here that these were not necessarily contemporaries of Bagan.

The author used data derived from *parabaiks* (traditional manuscripts) and existing physical structures to reconstruct the layout of old Bagan from the middle of the 12th century. The aim was to reproduce a plan of Bagan according to the design King Pyin Bya used in building structures in the 9th century; some of these structures continued to be built until the middle of the 12th century.

Based on this author's reconstructed plan, the area in the city wall is approximately 152 hectares, or about 374 acres, sufficient for about two thousand families, or roughly a population of ten thousand.[6] The area

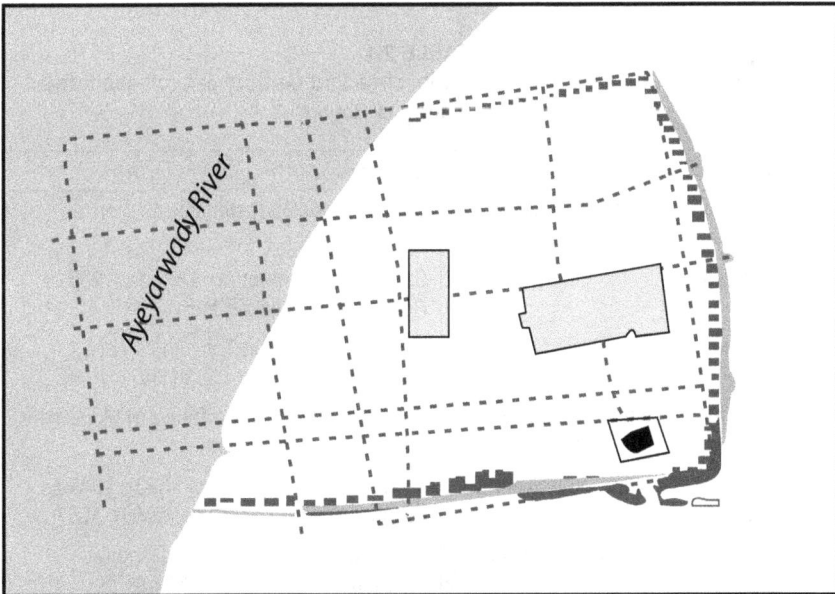

FIGURE 2.8 Reconstructed plan of Bagan. Redrawn by Goh Geok Yian.

within the walls was probably meant only for the royal family and their immediate entourage who resided in close proximity.

Stupas

Architecture in Bagan can be broadly divided into two major categories: stupas and temples. The earliest stupas from India were dome-shaped structures. The foundations of similar dome-shaped stupas have also been found in ancient sites of Myanmar, like Beikthano, Halin and Sriksetra. The form of the stupas appears to follow a particular path of development: stupas constructed in more recent periods have elongated shapes, which can be attributed to the desires of builders and sponsors to create taller structures, reflecting the sacredness of stupas.

Temples

The function and construction techniques of Buddhist temples evolved new forms from the 2nd century BCE in India to the present. One major transformation was the transition from constructing large halls to that of separate shrines and vestibules. Another technological change was the

TABLE 2.1
Evolution of Stupas: From Beikthano, circa 2nd Century CE until about the 13th Century in Bagan

	Main Stupa Types	Examples
1.	Andhara/Amaravati influence	Beikthano KKG3 (estimated 2nd or 3rd century CE).
2.	Gupta style	Sapada (monument no. 187) ca. 1285 CE. Revival of Sri Lankan form.
3.	Bulbous shape (Pyu)	Hpaya-Mar, Sri-Khit-Tra (6th or 7th c.); Nga Kywe Nadaung 1603 (11th c.).
4.	Tall cylindrical stupa on circular base (Pyu)	Baw-Baw-gyi 6–7th c.; Taung-Bi Monument 1973, Bagan (est. 8–9th c.).
5.	Tall cylindrical stupa on polygonal base	Myinkaba (monument no. 1323), 1045 CE; Lokananda (monument no. 1568), 1057 CE.
6.	Tall cylindrical stupa on multiple terraces	Shwezigon, 1090 CE; Shwe Sandaw (monument no. 1568), 1057 CE.

FIGURE 2.9
Nga Kywe Nadaung, Bagan (monument number 1603; date unknown).
Source: John N. Miksic.

FIGURE 2.10
Lokananda, Bagan (monument number 1023; built circa 1050 CE).
Source: John N. Miksic.

FIGURE 2.11 Shwezigon, Bagan (monument number 001; Built in 1090 CE).
Source: John N. Miksic.

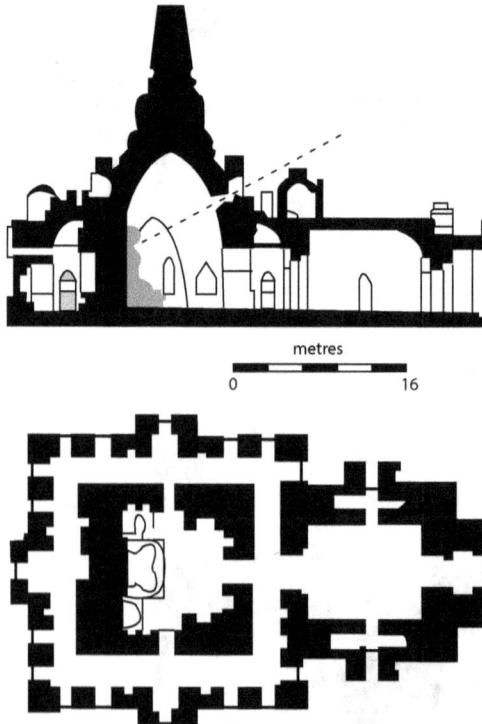

metres

0   16

FIGURE 2.12 Plan and section of Pahto Thamar Temple (monument number 1080).
Redrawn by Goh Geok Yian.

shift from "rock-cut temples" hewn into the hills to freestanding temples (Khin Maung Gyi 1987). This change took place in Gupta India around the 4th century, which was also the time when the first freestanding temples with durable materials were found in India (Brown 1959). The first examples of these freestanding temples were small single-room temples enclosing a shrine.

In Myanmar, hall type temples were found in Beikthano and Sriksetra, probably beginning around the 6th or 7th centuries, which gradually were replaced by single-room shrine types, such as Yahanda Gu and Bebe Gu. The single-shrine temples and the second type with pillars inside the shrine were the basic prototypes appropriated by later Bagan builders. While the first prototype of single-shrine temples experienced limited changes, such as having a separate extended vestibule and then multiple vestibules and entrances, the second type of temples, with the pillar as the load-bearing element, went through six different phases of development.

The first stage of development involved the construction of niches for images. This was achieved by extracting space from the pillars. Examples of such temples are Gubyauk-Nge (no. 1391) and Hlan-Kya (no. 1269).

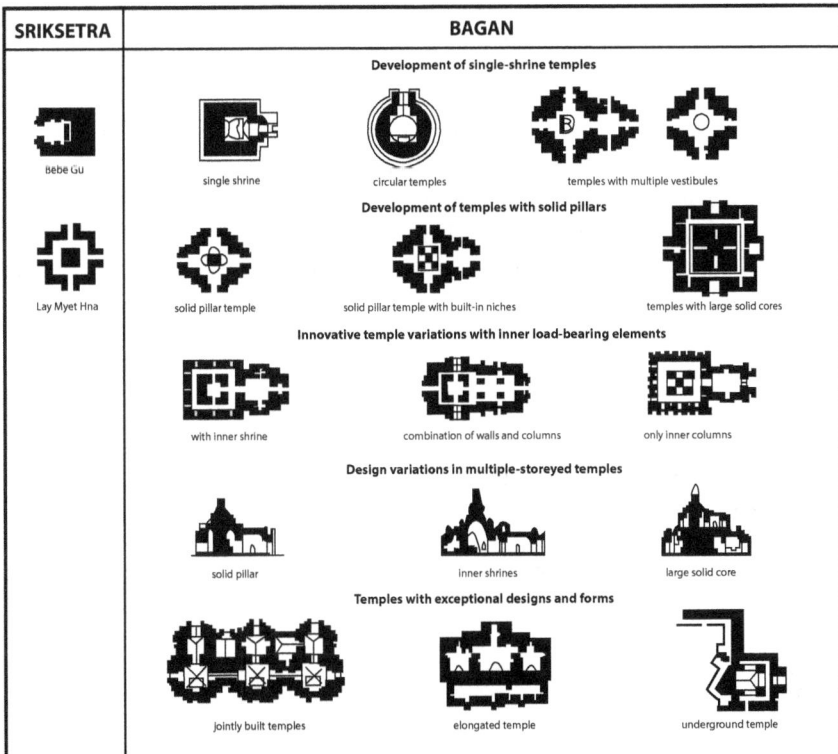

FIGURE 2.13 Development of temples from Sriksetra to Bagan. Redrawn by Goh Geok Yian.

FIGURE 2.14 Hlan-Kya Temple, Bagan (monument number 1269).
Source: John N. Miksic.

The second phase saw the construction of a large solid core in the shrine. The core is a central pillar built according to structural engineering principles. This system of construction, which supported very tall structures like That Byin Nyu, has a broad and tall solid core. This allowed for the expansion of a temple's passage width to more than ten times that of an average building in Bagan (in Htilo Minlo, 11.2 times; Sula Mani, 13.8 times; That Byin Nyu, 18.3 times). The ratio compared to ordinary solid pillar temples in Bagan is between one and four times (Kubyauk Nge in Myinkaba, 1.2 times; Hlan Kya Paya, 3.6 times).

The third stage was the development of inner shrines. The four walls of the inner shrine replaced the structural function of the pillar, and the corridor was separated from the inner shrine. Examples of such temples are Pahto Tha Mya (no. 1605) and Kubyauk-Gyi in Myinkaba.

The fourth level of development involved two layers of corridors circumscribing the core, reflected in the famous Ananda Temple and That Byin Nyu.

FIGURE 2.15   That Byin Nyu Temple, Bagan (monument number 1597).
Source: John N. Miksic.

The fifth phase of development involved four columns in the shrine that took over the load-bearing function. The image in the centre received full light and ventilation. An example is Nan Hpaya in Myinkaba (monument no. 1239).

The sixth phase is a variation on the same structural system of having a pillar as the load-bearing element, but with different design plans. For example, there are temples with polygonal plans, five-sided or eight-sided polygons where the pillars also have polygonal shapes and five or eight Buddha images are placed against the pillars. The original square pillars and four images signified devotion to the four past Buddhas of this earth; the five images refer to the four past Buddhas and the future and last Buddha, Maitreya.

An important requirement of temple construction was to provide sufficient lighting for the inner shrines; they should be dim but not dark. There had to be sufficient light to be able to see the images and to move

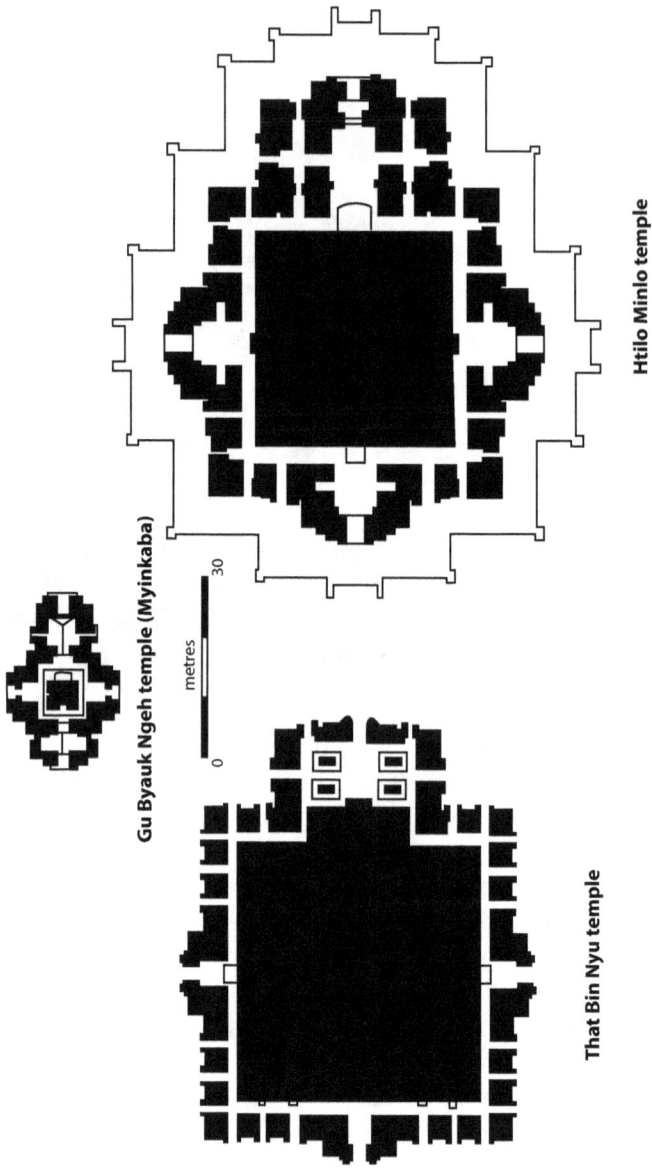

Htilo Minlo temple

Gu Byauk Ngeh temple (Myinkaba)

metres

0   30

That Bin Nyu temple

FIGURE 2.16 Temple plans with large columns. Redrawn by Goh Geok Yian.

FIGURE 2.17 Ananda Temple, Bagan.
Source: John N. Miksic.

around the shrine. This problem was solved with the placement of light wells, like those in the Ananda Temple. This design feature was not new; it was applied first at other smaller temples like Pahto Tha Mya and Nagayon before it was implemented at Ananda. This design element achieved vibrancy through the contrasts achieved in the inner spaces that resulted from the changing effects of darkness and light admitted through the skylight. A number of temples constructed between the 11th and 12th centuries began to utilize this design feature. Such innovations are comparable to Baroque churches of the 17th and 18th centuries in Europe. The advent of electricity, however, ruined these effects.

Temples in Bagan that possess these design features — inner shrines and light wells — are Pahto Tha Mya, Nagayon (monument no. 1192), Kubyauk Gyi in Myinkaba (monument no. 1323), Kubyauk Nge in Wet Kyi In (monument no. 285) and a few others. Pahto Tha Mya probably was constructed at the end of the 10th century according to traditional design. This temple is small but has a remarkable structure exhibiting

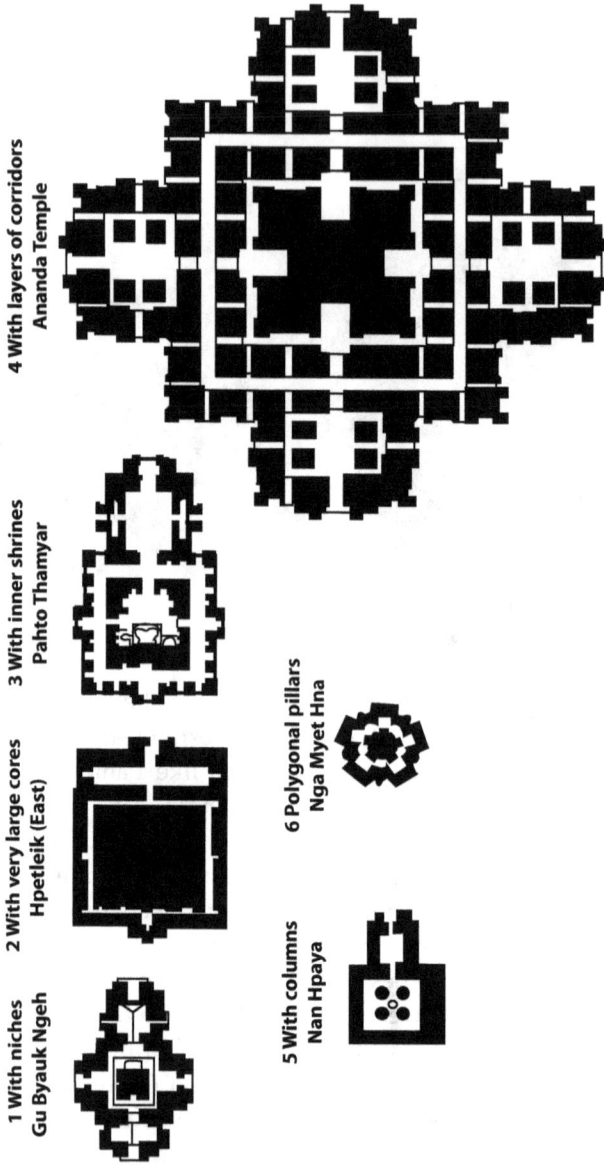

1 With niches
Gu Byauk Ngeh

2 With very large cores
Hpetleik (East)

3 With inner shrines
Pahto Thamyar

4 With layers of corridors
Ananda Temple

5 With columns
Nan Hpaya

6 Polygonal pillars
Nga Myet Hna

FIGURE 2.18   Evolution of Bagan temples. Redrawn by Goh Geok Yian.

FIGURE 2.19 Nagayon, Bagan (monument number 1192).
Source: John N. Miksic.

minute attention to detail. The inner shrine was intentionally designed to be dim. The temple faces east, and the daylight admitted through the perforated windows in the southern and northern exterior walls and through the openings of interior walls provides just enough illumination to be able to move around during evening hours. A part of the roof in the east has a light well constructed according to the angle of the morning sun, allowing sunlight to shine on the image in the inner shrine. Anyone in the shrine before dawn can observe the image suddenly smile at people a few minutes after sunrise. Another innovation introduced in this temple was the omission of the main pillar and the inner walls; the load-bearing function was fulfilled by the four columns. This idea was implemented in a later phase at the end of the 12th century at Nan Hpaya (monument 1239). It allows for a well-ventilated shrine, integrating the passage and the main image.

The above temple types are commonly found in Bagan. But in addition to these, there are also temples featuring other layouts — elongated temples, temples constructed jointly, underground temples, and temples with encased stupas.

Technology and Structural Systems in Bagan

A general observation of Bagan's building technology suggests that approximately four thousand buildings were constructed within a period of about four hundred years. It is likely that this work was achieved using intensive skilled labour, with limited utilization of unskilled manpower. The main building material used was brick. The construction of stupas is relatively quicker and easier than that of more complex structures like two-storey temples, because stupas are solid structures. The construction of buildings with inner spaces entailed more complex technology such as a system of load-bearing walls and supporting vaults and arches. This would have required expert architects and skilled labour. For example, trained skilled manpower was required to make timber frames for vaults and for bricklaying. Unskilled labourers were employed only to carry bricks.

It is probable that a majority of the structures in Bagan, probably eighty per cent, were built within a period of two hundred years between the 12th and 13th centuries. An inscription by Alaung Sithu at Shwe Gu Gyi temple (monument no. 1589) gives an indication of the time taken to build the temple. Construction started on 7 May 1131 and was completed on 17 December 1131; it took a little over seven months. It is hence estimated that the average time of construction for a medium-sized temple could be about one to two years; the construction of stupas would require a shorter period.

The construction of European churches typically required a few centuries, based on the example of Cologne cathedral in Germany, for which construction began in 1248 and was completed in 1880 — taking over six hundred years. There are obviously other factors in addition to technical ones that determine the time required to build a monument. For example, religious attitudes are an important consideration. In a Buddhist society, the donation of a pagoda is a merit-making enterprise, and a person can obtain benefits in the form of favourable subsequent incarnations. A Buddhist would wish to complete such an important task within one lifetime. In comparison, in the Christian community, the contribution of labour and materials to the construction of churches is considered devotion to God, and prolonged works would provide opportunities for more people to participate. The relative complexity of the building design also would have an influence on the construction time required. Most cathedrals in

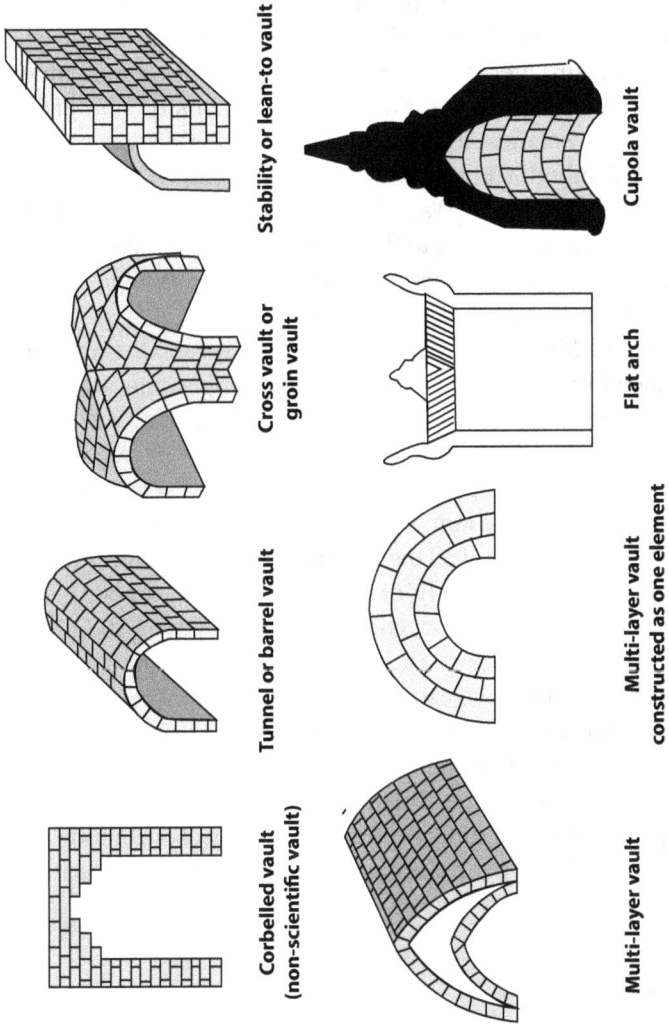

FIGURE 2.20 Types of vaults found in Bagan. Redrawn by Goh Geok Yian.

Europe are very high, at over ninety metres (three hundred feet), whereas the highest building in Bagan, That-Byin-Nyu, is only sixty metres (two hundred feet).

The building materials employed are also an important factor to consider. The main building material used in Bagan was brick. Other ancient civilizations used stone. Compared to brick, natural stone has some advantages: it is stronger and much more durable. However, a much longer time was required to use natural stone in the construction of buildings, such as in the case of most Indian temples, Egyptian structures, and Khmer buildings in Cambodia. For instance, scholars estimate that it took around forty years to build Angkor Wat. The stone had to be quarried, transported to the site of construction, cut to the appropriate size and shape, and lifted and fixed in the required places. The process would have taken a much longer time than that of constructions using brick.

In Bagan the king would donate a few pagodas and the royal entourage and the wealthy would participate in building some structures. This usually resulted in the construction of several pagodas during the reign of a king. Even by today's standards, a span of one or two years to build a medium-sized temple appears to be very short — it can take about two years to complete a single family house if prefabrication techniques are not employed. It is obvious that all the planning, such as architectural drawings and logistics — for the supply of water, bricks and timber — had to be prepared before actual construction began. Moreover, the coordination between the different trades must also have been well planned. For example, in order to build vaults the carpenters must first construct the temporary frameworks that hold the *voussoir*s before the masons lay the bricks on them, after which the keystone must be placed and the timber structures dismantled at the right time. This process requires coordination between different practitioners of different trades, and this coordination must have gone well to facilitate the building of roughly a dozen structures yearly for three centuries.

Building Materials

Brick comprised the main construction material used in Bagan, but natural stone was also used in places where it had a practical advantage. Stone blocks are stronger and they were often utilized as corner stones for strengthening and joining elements like imposts at the joints between vaults and walls. Another reason why stone might have been used is that it was available in large sizes. The stone was cut into slabs and used as perforated windows, floor slabs, sockets for timber columns, and water overflow gutters on roofs, et cetera. In general, stone had the advantage of hardness and availability in large sizes, but it was rarely used as decorative elements. There are two exceptions, in the form of two interesting temples: Nan-Hpaya and Kyauk-Ku-Umin; at these temples, natural stone was used as a decorative material. Other than these, there are very few structures built of stone; there is Shwe Zigon stupa, which was constructed of stone blocks, and Than Daw Kyar (monument no. 1592), which was built of a green stone extracted from Popa Mountain.

The people at Bagan used stone quite differently from the people in the Dvaravati area of central Thailand or the Angkor kingdom of Cambodia. In Dvaravati and Angkor Wat, the people used large slabs of stone, each cut to a different shape. The stone was cut to form corner stones, roofing stones, wall elements, et cetera, as desired. Figures were also frequently hewn from stone blocks as reliefs on walls. In comparison, the stone used in the construction of Shwe Zigon was cut into equal sizes and used as bricks. This suggests that stone was used only as a substitute for brick, probably because the builders of Bagan architecture were used to building with bricks.

Why did the builders of Bagan make very little use of natural stone, even though there are various metamorphic and igneous rocks around Mount Popa, an extinct volcano? I suggest that the builders of Bagan had grown very accustomed to using brick. Bricks inscribed with names of villages are found in the ruins of old structures, which suggests that the millions of bricks needed for construction were baked at various places along the Ayeyarwady River and transported to Bagan by bamboo rafts. Another factor pertains to a folk belief which old people around this area held: according to them, there were many ingyin hardwood trees around Bagan until the 20th century. Most of these trees were cut and used as fuel when the Irrawaddy Flotilla Company began operating in the early 1900s, and old people said that Nyaung Oo was used as their depot for firewood.

In addition to masonry technology, timber buildings formed an important type of Burmese architecture. According to traditional practices of the 18th and 19th centuries, all residential buildings, including palaces, were constructed using timber. These buildings vanished during the last centuries, and a rough impression of these can only be extracted from mural paintings at Bagan. It is possible that major portions of palaces and many residential dwellings were constructed of timber. The details of joinery, construction methods and timber decorations of the Bagan period are unfortunately lost forever, and can never be reconstructed.

Conclusion

This chapter has provided a general overview of the construction technologies utilized in Myanmar from the pre-Bagan through the Bagan periods and compared these techniques with those used in other parts of the Southeast Asian region at the same time. Whereas the architecture of Angkor Wat is noted for its monumentality, complex layout and proportions that fit appropriately to the environment, Bagan architecture is remarkable for its technology, especially the utilization of the true arch and vault which allowed for the building of taller and larger structures. Bagan architecture also exhibits greater diversity in the designs and types of temple structures. The approximately four thousand structures in Bagan were constructed within a period of about three hundred years. This amount of work could only be accomplished with expert builders and other skilled labourers, aided by more limited usage of unskilled manpower. The use of brick as the main building material also allowed for shorter construction periods.

Notes

1. Recent research, including environmental and palaeobotanical studies, has demonstrated that the origins of Chinese complex society were multiple, not single. Earlier Neolithic cultures in the Yangtze and Yellow Rivers and areas such as Inner Mongolia contributed to the establishment of later Yangtze and Yellow River complex societies, such as Liangzhu and Majiabang.
2. For discussion on the "Pyu" and archaeological culture, refer to Miksic and Goh (2016).
3. This is indicated in the Burmese chronicles, such as the *Mahayazawingyi*, *Yazawinthit*, and *Hmannan Yazawindawgyi*.
4. It is also possible that these particular buildings were built much later during the Bagan period, between the 11th and 14th centuries. Sriksetra continued to function as a religious and possibly administrative and habitation site following the 9th century, when Sriksetra ceased to be the core polity or centre of the Myanmar region.

5.   The author believes that transitional architecture is characterized by structures which represent the point of departure in the search for means to cover enclosed spaces.
6.   It is important to note that it is problematic to correlate the area of a site with the density of its population. This estimate depends on several assumptions that cannot yet be verified.

References

Aung Thaw. *Excavations at Beikthano*. Yangon: Ministry of Culture, 1968.

————. *Historical Sites of Burma*. Yangon: Ministry of Culture, 1972.

Brown, Percy. *Indian Architecture (Buddhist and Hindu Period)*. Bombay: Taraporavala, 1959.

Fletcher, Banister. *A History of Architecture on the Comparative Method*. London: Batsford, 1905.

Gutman, Pamela, and Bob Hudson. "The Archaeology of Burma (Myanmar) from the Neolithic to Pagan". In *Southeast Asia from Prehistory to History*, edited by Ian Glover and Peter Bellwood, pp. 149–76. Abingdon: RoutledgeCurzon, 2004.

Khin Maung Gyi (Yangon University). *Bagan Hpaya Mya Thamine hnint Ei Lan Nyun*. Yangon: Pan Shwe Pyi Press, 1996.

Knapp, Ronald. *Chinese Bridges*. Oxford: Oxford University Press, 1993.

Kyaw Lat. *History and Theory of Art and Architecture*. Yangon: Yaung Sone, 2005.

Lawler, Andrew. "Beyond the Yellow River: How China became China". *Science* 325 (2009): 930–35.

Long Tengwen and David Taylor. "A Revised Chronology for the Archaeology of the Lower Yangtze, China, Based on Bayesian Statistical Modelling". *Journal of Archaeological Science* 63 (2015): 115–21.

Maung Maung. *Bagan Zedi Pahti Myar*. Yangon: Popa, 2002.

Miksic, John N., and Goh Geok Yian. *Ancient Southeast Asia*. London: Routledge, 2016.

Nyunt Han, Aung Kyaing, Chit San Win, and Thein Lwin. "Kharit Mataingmi Pawhtun khetdaw Tagaung Halin Beikthano Thareketthaya Maingmaw Shehaung Myohaung Myodaw myar hma athit twet shehaung thutethana bya" [New archaeological finds at prehistoric Tagaung, Halin, Beikthano, Thayekhittara, and Maingmaw ancient cities]. *Shehaung Myodaw Myar* [Myanmar archaeology], 19–20 January 2006, Yangon University Research Paper Reading, pp. 1–22. Yangon: Ministry of Culture, 2007

Pichard, Pierre. *Inventory of Monuments at Pagan*. Paris: UNESCO, 1994.

Po Lat. *Report of Archaeological Survey of Burma, 1959–60*. Rangoon: Ministry of Culture, 1962.

Rowland, Benjamin. *The Art and Architecture of India*. Harmondsworth: Penguin Books, 1970.

Sein Maung Oo. "Theyekhitya Myo Haung" [Old City Sri-khit-tra]. *Pyin Nya Padethar Sa Saung* 3 (1967).

Stadtner, Donald. *Ancient Pagan: Buddhist Plain of Merit*. Bangkok: River Books, 2005.

Strachan, Paul. *Pagan: Art and Architecture of Old Burma*. Whiting Bay, Arran: Kiscadale, 1989.

Vickery, Michael. "Champa Revised". In *The Cham of Vietnam: History, Society and Art*, edited by K.P. Tran and B.M, pp. 362–402. Lockhart. Singapore: NUS Press, 2011.

Wheatley, Paul. *Nagara and Commandery: Origins of the Southeast Asian Urban Traditions*. Chicago: University of Chicago Department of Geography, 1983.

Win Maung. "Evolution of Stupas (1st to 19th century AD)". Paper presented at International Buddhist Conference, May 2007, Bangkok, Thailand, 2007.

3

Khraung-kaik Pitaka-taik: 16th-Century Repositories for Buddhist Scriptures in Mrauk-U

Mya Oo

To study Myanmar history, we need to examine chronicles, archaeological evidence, historical reports and studies, surveys and interviews with local people, among other sources. The Rakhine region is part of an ancient civilization which comprised several flourishing city states rich in cultural heritage. Chronicles mentioned that the Rakhine kingdoms, contemporaries of Burmese polities, were settled systematically by kings since the first century CE. An example was Dhanyawadi City. Rakhine kingdoms existed prior to the Mrauk-U period, which ended in 1785 CE. Each dynasty left an invaluable cultural heritage which showcased its glory and prosperity. This chapter examines the establishment of libraries in Mrauk-U connected with the propagation of Buddhism in the region between the 15th and 18th centuries.

A Brief History of Mrauk-U

Mrauk-U city is the most important archaeological heritage of the Rakhine people. Mrauk-U, which means "plentifully perceived foremost to be completely successful", was Rakhine's last powerful kingdom. It represented the zenith of cultural values for the Rakhine people, and flourished from 1430 to 1785 CE (Rakhine State People Council 1988, p. 7).

The golden age of Mrauk-U was the 16th and 17th centuries, contemporary with the Tudor kings, Queen Elizabeth I and Shakespeare in England, the Moghuls in India, the Ayutthaya kings in Siam, and the kingdoms of Ava (lnwa), Taungngu and Hanthawaddy of Myanmar (Rakhine State People Council 1988, p. 8). U May Oung provides a chronology of Myanmar kingdoms based on various historical accounts of Myanmar and archaeological reports (May Oung 1912, p. 9).

Archaeological evidence from excavations of Dhanyawadi city provides much information on the period beginning with the 1st century CE. Excavations revealed irregular circular brick city walls, a moat, and the palace site. After Dhanyawadi, the Chandra Dynasty established the Vesali kingdom in the middle of the fourth century CE. U Pandi's *Dhanyawadi Yazawinthit* (New Dhanyawadi history) states that Vesali was founded in 790 CE, several decades before Bagan was built in 849 CE. Archaeological evidence from the Vesali site includes Buddha images, stupas, metal materials, inscriptions, et cetera. During the reign of the last Chandra king, Sula Chandra, Vesali became weak and was succeeded by a kingdom centred in the Lemro valley (Rakhine State People Council 1988, p. 8).

In 1404 CE, during the reign of Min Saw Mon at Launggret, the great grandchild of King Min Hti, the political situation in Rakhine became complicated. Wars between Ava and Hanthawaddy extended to Rakhine. The Ava king conquered Launggret in 1406 CE and Min Saw Mon fled to Bengal. After the king's brother Min Khari, who allied himself with Hanthawaddy, stabilized the political situation, King Min Saw Mon returned to Rakhine. In 1430 CE, King Min Saw Mon established Mrauk-U as the capital of the last unified Rakhine kingdom. By the early 17th century the city had attained a population of 160,000. Forty-nine kings ruled at the capital of Mrauk-U until its conquest by the Konbaung Dynasty in 1784 (Rakhine State People's Council 1988, p. 8).

Mrauk-U and its External Relations

Rakhine reached its zenith of political unity and power during the Mrauk-U period. Mrauk-U's external relations were mainly concerned with religion, politics and military affairs, as well as trade with its contemporaries. Some religious architectural techniques were likely introduced to Mrauk-U through its contact with the outside world (Mrauk-U Tha 2008, p. 95). King Min Saw Mon's descendants expanded the Mrauk-U Empire to Bengal by occupying Panwa (or Ramu) and other states from Bengal to Chittagong. They appropriated Indian titles and inscribed their names on the coins produced to facilitate trade (Mrauk-U Tha 2008, p. 98).[1]

The architecture of the Mrauk-U period appropriated new techniques from India and Bengal. The kings sponsored the construction of pagodas and temples in stone, which made them stronger than those built during the Lemro period. The ancient monuments in Mrauk-U are material evidence reflecting the high level of architectural construction techniques (Mrauk-U Tha 2008, p. 98).

The Portuguese traders were the earliest people from Europe to ply their trade in Rakhine. They exported household goods and weapons. Merchants from India, the Maldives, Africa and Persia also came to Mrauk-U. During the middle of the Mrauk-U period, after King Min Ba-gyi (1531–53) conquered Chittagong and Goa, disputes erupted between the rulers of Mrauk-U and the Portuguese, who tried to attack in 1534 CE. The Portuguese were unsuccessful, but King Min Ba-gyi began to employ them in his defence force in order to build up the Rakhine navy and artillery. During the reign of King Min Phalong (1571–93), the Rakhine kingdom was at its military peak. He also strengthened Mrauk-U politically, economically and socially (Mrauk-U Tha 2008, p. 99).

Between the 15th and 18th centuries, Mrauk-U developed relations with Ava and Hanthawaddy. Min Kha-ri of Mrauk-U and King Narapati of Ava met in 1454 CE to settle boundary disputes. In 1547 CE, King Tabin Shwe Hti of Hanthawaddy tried to invade Mrauk-U, but failed (May Oung 1912, pp. 23–25). During King Min Razargyi's reign (1593–1612), Rakhine conquered Hanthawaddy and expanded its boundaries to Dhaka and the Bay of Bengal to the west and the coastal region of Mawlamyaing to the southeast (Rakhine State People's Council 1988, p. 11). Fra Manrique, who travelled to Mrauk-U in the 17th century, described Mrauk-U city as crowded with foreign visitors and merchants from Siam, Burma, India, the Bay of Bengal, and the islands south of the bay (Collis 1943, p. 255).

Buddhism in Mrauk-U

Research on stone inscriptions in Rakhine State demonstrates that Rakhine Buddhism was a form of southern Buddhism. The earliest stone inscription is the Taung-pauk-gyi inscription near Taung-pauk-gyi village in Kyauk-taw. The inscription, written in Brahmi script and Pali language, states that the Lord Buddha stopped a while at Kyauk-taw Hill. Researchers have determined that the style of the script dates the inscription to the 3rd century CE.

Another source is a Buddha image which was excavated from the ancient pagoda of Mrauk-U; the back of the image was inscribed with Brahmi script. The writing on the stone slab is dated to the 4th or 5th centuries CE and contains the word "guardian". Small stupas in the Kyauk-taw region showed that Buddhist art in Rakhine flourished around the 4th and 5th centuries. The Ananda Chandra stone inscription is a comprehensive source on Rakhine Buddhism in the 2nd–3rd centuries CE and the rulers of the Chandra Dynasty (Saw Win 1994, pp. 47–52).

The languages used in Rakhine inscriptions are Sanskrit and Pali. Scholars have argued that Rakhine was influenced by Sri Lanka during the Chandra period. During the reign of King Ananda Chandra, religious relations with Sri Lanka expanded (San Tha Aung 1979, p. 23). According to research, particularly on Ananda Chandra stone inscriptions, the king sent groups to Sri Lanka to copy Buddhist scriptures and give offerings to monks (San Tha Aung 1979, p. 23). The chronicles record that Sri Lanka invited Rakhine to send four religious missions to assist in the purification of its sangha during the Mrauk-U period. Venerable monks from Rakhine led these missions, which managed the ordination ceremonies and the propagation of Buddhism in Sri Lanka (Seik-keln-da 2000, p. 79).

Several inscriptions contain abstract ideas conveyed in the Buddha's teachings. The script used can be dated to the 5th and 6th centuries CE; it resembles scripts from the Gupta period in India. Buddhist sculptures similar to Gupta and Pala styles were also found in Rakhine (San Tha Aung 1979, p. 23).

The stone pagodas in Mrauk-U were built using heavy stone blocks which were fitted compactly and joined with cement intended to resist the penetration of roots into the building and reduce moisture in the buildings' fabric (Rakhine State People's Council 1988, p. 17; Shwe Zan 1995, p. 21). One of the unique arts of Mrauk-U consists of floral arabesques on the temple walls (ခြုံးပန်းခြုံးနွယ်). Temples and pagodas are topped with stone umbrellas, another architectural element which distinguishes Rakhine architecture from that of central Myanmar.

Repositories (Libraries) of the Mrauk-U Period

The *Rakhine Yazawinthit* states that the kings of Mrauk-U supported the propagation of Buddhism throughout Rakhine to ensure its survival in the region. They built pagodas, temples, monasteries, and repositories for religious texts. By donating scriptures, Rakhine kings aimed not only to make merit; they also wanted to encourage monks and the common people to study the teachings of Buddha (Sandarmarlar Lingarra 1997).

The Rakhine chronicles and inscriptions suggested that there were thirty large monasteries in Mrauk-U (see list in Appendix A) (Saw Win 1994, pp. 109–12), with an additional 3,700 satellite monasteries to which forty-eight depositories (*pitaka-taik*, or libraries) were attached for storing Buddhist literature. The *pitaka-taik* were built in the compounds of pagodas or temples and monasteries. The Rakhine kings hoped to rule a powerful and prosperous kingdom through merit-making activities, fair rule of the country and by safeguarding the persons and properties of their people. The kings were important sponsors of the Buddhist religion; they usually built a supreme pagoda at the forepart of their royal palace, and also monasteries commemorating their ascension to the throne. One of the old monasteries donated during the Mrauk-U period is Phara-paw, which is located close to the west side of Phaya-paw Pagoda. This monastery was constructed of wood without using any iron nails.

Pitakat-taik represent a few of the buildings which survive from the Mrauk-U period (see Appendix B for a list of these library repositories) (Saw Min New 1993–94, p. 50). Most of the *pitaka-taik* were destroyed due to natural causes, treasure hunters and wars. Local researchers who conducted surveys at Mrauk-U provided a list of several extant libraries, which included the following:

1. Mahamuni Pitaka-taik. This building is located at the west corner of the lowest terrace of Mahamuni Pagoda; Min Kha-ri donated a library to it in 1439.
2. Shwe-gu-taung Pitaka-taik. When King Min Saw Mon founded a palace in Mrauk-U, he built Shwe-gu-taung Pagoda to the east of the palace site and a monastery near the pagoda. In the compound of the monastery stands a brick library built on a square base. The base measures thirteen and a half metres square, the body is six metres high, and it has entrances on three sides. The upper part of the library

has been destroyed. The chronicles state that the library contained a Tripitaka which was inscribed on bronze plates (Saw Min New 1993–94, p. 51).

3. Moat-sate-taw Pitaka-taik is another library built by King Min Saw Mon. It is located on a hill near Moat-sate-taw Pagoda, about nine hundred feet to the northwest of Htont-kant-thein Temple. This stone library is decorated with floral arabesques (ဂြိုဟ်စီးဂြိုဟ်နက်) and finials (sul). It was built for use by monks of Sandar-Rama Monastery near the library. At present, the upper part of the library is badly damaged.

4. Lay-myat-nhar Pitaka-taik. This library near Lay-myat-nhar (Four-faced) temple was built of stone with a square brick base. The entrance to the library was located to the south. It would have been intended for use by monks from Guna-myit-zu monastery. The upper part was damaged.

5. San-gar-taung Pitaka-taik was a stone library located south of Mrauk-U and at the eastern foot of San-gar Hill. The building has fallen into ruins.

6. Mingalar Pitaka-taik was a stone and brick library located east of Mingalar Lake, about one mile from the Phaya-paw Pagoda west of Mrauk-U. The library has been damaged by treasure hunters. It had an entrance to the east.

Khain-Kaik Pitaka-taik

The only well-preserved example of the forty-eight Mrauk-U libraries that once existed is Khain-kaik Pitaka-taik which stands north of Htuparon Pagoda. King Min Phaloung built the library in 1591 to preserve the holy Tripitaka scriptures of the Buddhist cannon. The building was named after the Khain-kaik Wall, which in turn derived its name from the sluice gate which controlled the water flow from the nearby moat (Rakhine State People's Council 1988, p. 49).[2] The library would have been used by the monks and novices of Taung-nyo Monastery located west of it.

The library was constructed from stone and has a square base. It measures 4.3 metres from east to west, 3.05 metres from north to south, and 4.6 metres high from the ground to the roof (Forchhammer 1892, p. 31). The base of the building is square but the main body is concave in the shape of a blooming lotus so that the upper part is broader and wider than the foundation. The entrance to the library has an arched passageway

FIGURE 3.1
Source: John N. Miksic.

FIGURE 3.2
Source: John N. Miksic.

FIGURE 3.3
Source: John N. Miksic.

that opens towards the east. A *tuyin*, a vertical ornamental embellishment, decorates the top of the entrance.

The main body of the library has projecting corners at each side and is covered by five tiered roofs (Rakhine State People's Council 1988, p. 17). Its outer walls were ornamented with stone carving. Forchhammer remarked that the building is top-heavy. The base was constructed using thick heavy blocks of stone which gradually became thinner towards the upper levels (Forchhammer 1892, p. 31). The style of structure and ornamentation reflects the combined influences of east and west art styles as Rakhine was expanding to west and east during the Mrauk-U period.

The decorative motifs of the library are valuable evidence of the architectural skill and craftsmanship of the Mrauk-U period. The study of the structure and designs of the library can contribute to scholarly research on Rakhine's connections with other kingdoms in mainland Southeast Asia and other regions. Further comparative research is needed on this sole remaining library.

Conclusion

At present, Mrauk-U is one of the heritage cities of the Rakhine people. It features numerous ancient monuments dating to the 15th and 17th centuries CE. Stone sculpture and architectural styles of the Mrauk-U period can be distinguished from those of other time periods and regions of Myanmar. Few articles or surveys focus on repositories (libraries) established in the capital city, even though scholars and researchers have studied the religious monuments in Mrauk-U. Due to many causes, most of the ancient libraries have been damaged, and the lack of well-preserved remains makes it difficult to identify even the sites where they once stood. A fine example of an extant building is Khain-kaik Pitaka-taik of the 16th century CE, but the building has been little studied.

This study demonstrates that there is a need to conduct more in-depth research on the libraries of the Mrauk-U period in order to attain a more complete understanding of Mrauk-U's role in the history of Myanmar. Topics that require further research include the art style, architectural design, and craft production. Researchers, scholars and students alike should engage in further study of the art and architecture of ancient libraries in Mrauk-U, which can contribute to better understanding of Myanmar's global connections between the 15th and 17th centuries CE.

Appendix A

List of Remaining Monasteries of the Mrauk-U Period

1. Nan-tat (ascending throne) Monastery နန်းတက်ကျောင်း
2. Zi-na-mar-tha Monastery ဇိနမာသကျောင်း
3. Dok-kan Monastery ဒုက္ခံကျောင်း
4. Kaw Monastery ကောကျောင်း
5. Yey-lei Monastery ရေလယ်ကျောင်း
6. Sin-swe Monastery ဆင်စွယ်ကျောင်း
7. Anuk-Thiddi Monastery အနုသိဒ္ဓိကျောင်း
8. Mie Monastery မီးကျောင်း
9. Yaung Monastery ယောင်ကျောင်း
10. Pauk-kan Monastery ပေါက်ကံကျောင်း
11. Ma-htay-thein Monastery မထေရ်သိမ်ကျောင်း
12. Sae-maung Monastery စဲမောင်းကျောင်း
13. Ma-hein Monastery မယိန်ကျောင်း
14. Taung-myint Monastery တောင်မြင့်ကျောင်း
15. Dhamma Vilasa Monastery ဓမ္မဝိလာသကျောင်း
16. Ka-lar-myo Monastery ကုလားမြို့ကျောင်း
17. Mya-taung Monastery မြတောင်ကျောင်း
18. Pwe-shin Monastery ပွဲရှင်ကျောင်း
19. Maha-Vihara Taung-nyo Monastery မဟာဝိဟာရတောင်ညိုကျောင်း
20. Ratana-Beikman Monastery ရတနာဗိမာန်ကျောင်း
21. Ratana-Pya-that Monastery ရတနပြသာဒ်ကျောင်း
22. Ratana Shwe Kyaung Monastery ရတနရွှေကျောင်း
23. Zay-ta-wun Monastery ဇေတဝန်ကျောင်း
24. Mingalar-Oo Monastery မင်္ဂလာဦးကျောင်း
25. Mya-ta-saung Monastery မြတန်ဆောင်းကျောင်း
26. Sandar-Rama Monastery စန္ဒာရာမကျောင်း
27. Tayzar-Rama Monastery တေဇာရာမကျောင်း
28. Dhammika-Rama Monastery ဓမ္မိကရာမကျောင်း
29. Phaya-paw Monastery ဘုရားပေါ်ကျောင်း
30. Paramatta Monastery ပရမတ္တကျောင်း

Appendix B

List of Remaining Depositories (PItaka-taik) of the Mrauk-U Period

1. Pitaka-taik at hill stroke of Mahamuni Pagoda
2. Pitaka-taik at the southwest corner of lower terrace of Mahamuni Hill stroke
3. Pitaka-taik at hill of Mout-sate-taw Pagoda
4. Pitaka-taik at Dhammikarama Monastery
5. Pitaka-taik at Lay-myat-nhar Pagoda
6. Pitaka-taik at the foot of hill stroke to the east of San-kar Hill
7. Pitaka-taik in Kyauk-yit-ke village
8. Pitaka-taik near Di-wun-gyi Pagoda
9. Pitaka-taik near Mingalar Lake of Phaya-paw Pagoda
10. Pitaka-taik at the bank of Lat-sae Lake
11. Pitaka-taik near Yadana Manaung Pagoda
12. Pitaka-taik at Pyi-soe-gyi Pagoda near Amyint-taw fortress
13. Pitaka-taik at the hill of Princess Myang Pagoda
14. Pitaka-taik at the south of Yan-aung door
15. Pitaka-taik at Winmanar Kyitaw door
16. Pitaka-taik near Eainda Myitzu Pagoda
17. Pitaka-taik near Ngwe-taung Pagoda
18. Pitaka-taik near Ko-thaung Pagoda
19. Two pitaka-taiks to the west of Myint-mo Hill
20. Pitaka-taik to the west of Kyaung-lei-don fortress
21. Two pitaka-taik near Baung-dwet
22. Pitaka-taik at Thinbaw Sarkaing
23. Pitaka-taik at the foot of Shw gu-taun
24. Pitaka-taik to the north of Htu-pa-yon temple (Khain-kaik Pitaka-taik)

Notes

1. The coins can be used to trace the lineage of Rakhine kingship.
2. Local researchers note that the name of the library and city wall, "Khain-kaik", means "timing of the tides of the sluice gate".

References

Collis, Maurice. *The Land of the Great Image*. New York: Knopf, 1943.

Forchhammer, Emil. *Report on the Antiquities of Arakan*. Rangoon: Superintendent, Government Printing, 1892.

May Oung, Maung. "The Chronology of Burma". *Journal of the Burma Research Society* (1912).

Mrauk-U Tha. "ရခိုင်နိုင်ငံခြား:ဆက်ဆံရေး:" [Rakhine and its foreign relations]. *Rakhine Magazine*, no. 30 (2008): 95.

Rakhine State People's Council. မြောက်ဦး:လမ်:ညွှန် [Guide to Mrauk-U]. Sittwe, Rakhine: Rakhine State People Council, 1988.

San Tha Aung. ရှစ်ရာစုရခိုင်ဝေသာလီမင်: [Rakhine Vesali king of 8th century]. Yangon: Daw Saw Saw Sarpay, 1979.

San Tha Aung, U. ရခိုင်ဒင်္ဂါး:များ [Rakhine coins]. Yangon: Daw Saw Saw Sarpay, 1979.

Sandarmarlar Lingara, Taung Kyaung Sayataw. ရခိုင်ရာဝင်သစ်ကျမ်:ဒုတိယတွဲ [New Rakhine history], 2 vols. Yangon: Rakhinethagyi Sarpay, 1997.

Saw Win, Gawyamyay. ရခိုင်ပြည်နယ်နှင့်ဗုဒ္ဓသာသနာ [Buddhism and Rakhine State]. Yangon: Tetlan Sarpay, 1994.

Seik-kein-da, Ashin. "မြောက်ဦး:ခေတ်ထေရဝါဒသာသနာပြုခရီ:" [Buddhist missions of Mrauk-U period]. *Roma-Hlaing Magazine*, no. 3 (2000): 79.

Shwe Zan, U. "The Golden Mrauk-U: An Ancient Capital of Rakhine". Unpublished paper. 1995.

4

Religious Symbols as Decorations on the *Sikhara* of Ancient Monuments in the Late Bagan Period

Pyiet Phyo Kyaw

Bagan iconography displayed syncretic traits from the 10th to the 13th centuries. Southeast Asian classic art combined traits from India, China and indigenous sources, disseminated through maritime trade. The Bagan period can be divided into three phases: early (10–11th centuries), middle (12th century) and late (13th century). The late phase of the Bagan period can plausibly be dated from the end of the reign of King Narapatisithu or Cañsū II (1165–1211) to that of King Narasihapate or Tayokpyay Min (1256–87). The successors of King Narapatisithu were patrons of Buddhist cultural heritage, evident in many monuments of various sizes, big, medium and small.

Despite the short span of the late Bagan period, many monuments were constructed during this time. They can be dated by stone inscriptions and ink glosses concerning donations and Buddhist religious matters.

The significant features of the later Bagan monuments include:

1. The construction of pagoda complexes consisting of several structures;
2. The evolution of monastic complexes in the vertical dimension;
3. More complex stucco reliefs on the temple exteriors;
4. An increasing frequency of geometric items in the interior mural decorations;
5. Stone inscriptions providing factual information about donations (mostly written in Myanmar language);
6. Monumental complexes built at greater distances from the banks of the Ayeyarwady River;
7. An increasing tendency to build complexes consisting of a large number of smaller individual monuments rather than single massive structures.

In the late Bagan period, many small monuments were built in the form of complexes of stupas or monasteries. Important groups of small buildings built during this period include complexes at Winīdo, Sambūla, Sin Phyū Shin, Su ton Pyit monastery and Tāmani. Despite the large number of small buildings, some larger buildings, such as temples at Tayokpyay, Pyatthatgyī, Tha Htay Mote Gu and Thitsāwaddy, were also erected. Additionally, there are medium size buildings such as the temples of Thambūla, Phayāthons and Thetkyamuni. The large number of 13th-century buildings in Bagan suggests that the population grew more rapidly in late Bagan than in earlier periods.

The 13th-century buildings are characterized by informative stone inscriptions, ink glosses and rich decoration, but these decorative touches were not intended as static and massive sculptural forms and shapes; rather, they comprise many items or thematic objects related to the use of Buddhist Jataka and canonical motifs to decorate interior walls for didactic functions. Late Bagan monuments have more complicated ornamentation, such as anthropomorphic figures and foliage, than in earlier periods. Iconic symbols include gods and goddess (*deva* and *devi*), Bodhisattva, ogre faces or *kirttimukha*, Brahma, and other mythical creatures. The most beautiful and detailed achievements in the art of floral decoration appeared during the late Bagan period. Thus it can be stated that the 13th-century temples are smaller but decorative items became increasingly numerous. The designers wished to insert many items into restricted spaces in 13th-century architecture.

This study will concentrate on analysis of the upper portions of 13th-century temples called *sikhara*, or square tower, in the context of Mahayana

Buddhism. The three main motifs emphasized in this study are the sikhara, goddesses, and ogre heads.

Origin and Tradition of the Sikhara

Sikhara means "tower" or "spire" (Brown 1995, p. 62). Etymologically the word sikhara originates from the Sanskrit word śikra, meaning the "peak of the mountain". The sikhara is the tapering and pyramidal portion of temple-type buildings. Sikhara are important architectural features in all types of temple design in India. Several theories have been developed to account for the origin of the sikhara; the most acceptable is that the form originated from the Northern Indian or Indo-Aryan style (Brown 1995, p. 63). The Indo-Aryan sikhara may have originated from bamboo construction, but not directly from a primitive type: it is a later development, produced by the reduplication of vertically compressed storeys (Coomaraswamy 1927, p. 6).

The sikhara evolved from the peaked or domed huts of eastern and central India before the beginning of the Christian era (Brown 1995, p. 63). The sikhara is the spire tower of the Northern Indian type of temple that developed from the Buddhist stupa, gradually becoming elongated from the hemispherical mound, through the early centuries of the Christian era. In India, early sikhara-type temples appeared circa 500 CE (Brown 1995, plate 87). The first sikhara evolved as a feature of Gupta architecture (Coomaraswamy 1927, p. 75). The sikhara was combined with the Buddhist symbol of the *chaitya* or *ceti* (*zedi* in Myanmar pronunciation), which eventually merged with the ceremonial umbrella. Additionally, sikhara may have been derived from the tall covering of the processional vehicle (*ratha*) containing an image of the deity which was carried about on ceremonial occasions (Coomaraswamy 1927, p. 83). So sikhara symbolized both the vehicle and the monument.

Early evidence of sikhara-type temples can be found in the Pyu city of Sriksetra, such as Be Be Temple. The spire of Be Be Temple is, however, a circular tower, unlike those of Bagan. The early sikhara design can rarely be seen in the Pyu votive tablets. In Bagan votive tablets, sikhara were usually depicted with a branch of the Bodhi tree above the Buddha image. The sikhara motif in Myanmar developed in the Bagan period. Concerning the sikhara, Coomaraswamy said:

> the aspiring aspect of the mediaeval towers (sikhara) contrasts most markedly with the static character of the early low flat-roofed temples.

Just in the same way in Burma (Myanmar) and Siam (Thailand)
stupa, originally a hemispherical dome with one umbrella and clearly
differentiated division of parts, develops into soaring types like those
of the Shwe Dagon at Rangoon, with the continuous convex curve from
base to pinnacle. (Coomaraswamy 1927, p. 63)

In Bagan there were two types of sikhara of roughly equal significance.
One is the Mahābodi type with a pyramidal square tower; the other is
a curvilinear tower constituting the upper structure of the temple. The
Mahābodi-type sikhara is rare in the Bagan area; it is found in the temples
of Gūbyaukgyī (Wetkyī-In) (ca. 12th century), Mahābodi (ca. 12th century)
and Sīrī or Bochyomi Gūbyauk (ca. 13th century). The 13th-century
sikharas were almost identical in form and structure. In the sikhara of
Bochyomi Gūbyauk temple, it can be seen that the icons of Brahma in the
Anjali Mudra and the flying *vidyadhara* (pronounced *zawgyi* in Myanmar)
with festoons were composed in the circular niches on the projections of
sikharas. The flying *vidyadhara* had been carved profusely together with
kirttimukha in India since the 9th century CE. After the downfall of Bagan,
the sikhara gradually disappeared from Buddhist monuments in Myanmar,
although the sikhara was still used in India until the 19th century CE
(Coomaraswamy 1927, p. 63).

The Three Jewels of Buddhism and The Holy Triad of Mahayana Buddhism[1]

In Buddhism there are three jewels: Buddha; dhamma, the teachings
of Buddha; and *Saṁgha*, the sons of Buddha. In Esoteric Buddhism this
concept is called the Buddhist Triad and it is represented as three icons. For
instance, in Nepal, deification of the three jewels is illustrated as follows
(Bhattacharyya 1958, p. 32):

1. Buddha image for Gautama Buddha
2. Goddess image for dhamma[2]
3. God image for *Saṁgha*

In Mahayanism, Avalokitesvara symbolized great loving kindness, and
his Sakti (female aspect/consort) symbolized wisdom. The combination
of Avalokitesvara and his Sakti represented nirvana. Thus, the feminine
deities of Mahayanism represent wisdom and knowledge (Bhattacharyya

1958, p. 32). The goddesses merged with the icon to symbolize wisdom or dhamma. The Mahayanist school gradually evolved a wide range of deified concepts or beings (Chutiwongs 2002).

Early symbols of Buddhism included the wheel for dhamma and deer for the Deer Park; thus the first sermon, the Bodhi Tree for the Buddha, swastika or throne for the Buddha, et cetera. In the early phase of Buddhism, Theravada Buddhism did not depict the Buddha in human form, perhaps because they accepted that the Buddha is unrivaled. Likewise, the concept of the three jewels of Buddhism is also perceived as depicting the simplicity of Theravada Buddhism; Mahayanists transformed this concept into the holy triad of Buddhism represented by three iconic symbols.

Feminine Deities Depicted on the Upper Portions of Monuments

Feminine deities represent religious themes in Brahmanism. In primitive ritual practice, feminine statuettes fulfilled spiritual purposes. For example, the concept of the mother goddesses and the worship of maternity, for which figures of women with large wombs and robust bodies were

FIGURE 4.1
Source: Pyiet Phyo Kyaw.

FIGURE 4.2
Source: Pyiet Phyo Kyaw.

created. Feminine deities might have evolved in ancient society as mother goddesses.

Subsequently, this ancient concept was transformed into many icons representing the deification of women or female attributes as goddesses. In one example, the female reproductive organ, the *yoni*, was emphasized by devotees of Siva to symbolize fertility and strength. In Gupta-period temples of India, the pillars of the porch are decorated with figures of river goddesses; this characteristic feature persisted into the medieval period, circa 10th to 12th century CE (Coomaraswamy 1927, p. 79).

In the Esoteric Buddhist pantheon, the name *Tara* is applied to a large number of feminine deities. In Theravada Buddhism there is no pantheon to which worship was offered, but in Esoteric Buddhism a large number of deities are invoked (Bhattacharyya 1958, p. 220).

In Bagan monuments, the Indian influence is visible in the use of feminine deities to adorn the upper portions of religious buildings. The feminine deities can be identified as the goddess who symbolizes wisdom or fertility or auspiciousness. The icons of goddesses were mostly depicted on the upper portions of religious temples, such as the sikhara, spire or square tower, and as friezes, sometime on tympana. The feminine deities can be found together with ogres, Sīṁha the lion and other ornamental figures. Feminine deities were also placed at both sides of the entrances to buildings. After the decline of Bagan, no trace of feminine deities can be found on Buddhist monuments. No more goddesses or feminine deities can be found on the upper portions of Buddhist monuments in later styles of Buddhist art.

The style of feminine deities found on the sikhara of Bagan monuments display an affinity with that of Mahayana goddesses, for example, Tara. Sometimes they are depicted wearing royal clothing and flanked by attendants. Than Tun, however, concluded that the goddesses depicted on the sikharas of Bagan temples are directly related to the Hindu Sakti or feminine aspect of Siva and Visnu. The goddess is shown making one of two types of hand gestures, or mudra: Padumarhattha Mudra and Anjali Mudra. The goddess in Padumarhattha Mudra holds a lotus with both hands, while the goddess in Anjali Mudra is worshipping or paying homage. The goddess with Padumarhattha Mudra can be identified with Candi, the Sakti of Siva (Than Tun 2005, pp. 134–37, 140–43, 145–46, 150–52, 154, 156–58). The others ought to be identified as Sri Lakshmi, the Sakti of Visnu (Than Tun 2005, pp. 135, 148–49, 152).

The Head of the Ogre and Its Tradition

The head of an ogre is one of the most popular motifs in the decorative art of Bagan monuments. In the early Bagan period, most of the ogres consist only of a head, without forepaws or body. In the middle and late periods, the ogres are provided with various designs of forepaws. The ogre icon is known as *kirttimukha* or the Head of Glory; Sun-Face or Grotesque Mask (Brown 1995, p. 139; Panda 2005, p. 97); Grotesque *kirttimukha* (Coomaraswamy 1927, p. 202); or Monster Mask (Rawson 1993, p. 13). Than Tun opined that *kirttimukha* means "the famous mouth" (Than Tun 2005, p. 134, fig. 32).

This ogre motif probably symbolized time and fertility. The demon of time is well known in Indian mythology (Rawson 1993, p. 12): "each person's 'present-frame' is itself a mouth of that monster vomiting out his world of experience and knowledge. We will never be able to find the origin or causes of all things 'out there', among older projected things."

Kirttimukha, the Head of Glory, was carved profusely on the walls and upper portions of Indian temples from the 9th century (Panda 2005,

p. 97); however, on the doorjambs of temples from the 7th century, the *kirttimukha* motif was found with festoons of pearls coming out of its mouth. Whilst there are many legends relating to the *kirttimukha* in Indian mythology, the symbolic meaning of *kirttimukha* is immortality and fertility. The *kirttimukha* was associated with other popular motifs such as roaring lions and flying *vidyadharas*. In Europe (especially England and France), the *kirttimukha* is associated with the Green Man (Basford 1978; Harding, 1972; Lacoste 1998). Green Men are also characterized as having heads of humans, beasts, cats, et cetera, with the mouth made of foliage, the eyes and ears of leaves. The symbolic meaning of Green Men is almost the same as the *kirttimukha* symbol, as guarding, protecting and an emblem of glory.

In Bagan architecture, sikhara are sometimes decorated with *kirttimukha* carrying feminine deities on their shoulders, and sometimes foliage. Although the sikhara originated from the northern Indian or Indo-Aryan tradition, the Bagan sikhara were combined with indigenous motifs, indicating that early Indian influences were not that strong in early Bagan architecture.

Conclusion

The Sikhara is the holy part of the temple and symbolizes the peak of a mountain. It also symbolized the *ratha* or vehicle. In 13th-century Bagan, sikhara were constructed in large numbers.

The sikhara was related to the Indian architectural form named *Bhumija*, a tower tapering towards the top on all four faces. An example of a sikhara in Bagan is the Bochyomi Gubyauk Temple. The sikhara symbolized great power; strength and stability; the *ratha* or vehicle able to bear a burden forever; the pantheon of gods and goddesses. The sikhara was composed of a vertical dynamic concept and with horizontal rows all the way to the top. Symbolic decoration on the sikhara referred to feminine goddesses, *kirttimukha*, and others.

The temple roof is most important for the temple's dignity because this portion is not accessible to pilgrims, but exists only to represent the grandeur or impressiveness of the temple. Consequently, the arrangement of sikhara with goddesses or *kirttimukha* can symbolize the concept that the Buddhist missionary or Buddha dhamma will prosper for five thousand years from the time that Gautama Buddha passed. The Buddhist missionary was also popular in the stone inscriptions of Bagan. Sikhara symbolized the vehicle; the goddess symbolized wisdom or dhamma; the *kirttimukha* symbolized time or eternity. Probably these three symbols were intended to represent the concept that the Buddhist religion would prosper until five thousand years had passed.

Notes

1. The term *Mahayana* (Greater Vehicle) is often used to refer to those versions of Buddhism which incorporate worship of many deities. Skilling (2003) has demonstrated that this term, while very commonly used, is misleading, because it implies a firm distinction between Buddhists, which does not exist in practice. The term "esoteric Buddhism" is one way of referring to the difference in approach without implying a schism.
2. In Theravada Buddhism, the symbol of the dhamma is a wheel with spokes representing the teachings of Dhammacakara in *Migadavon*, the Deer Park at Sarnath.

References

Bhattacharyya, Benoytosh. *The Indian Buddhist Iconography.* Calcutta: Mukhopadhyay, 1958.

Brown, Percy. *Indian Architecture (Buddhist and Hindu).* Bombay: Taraporavala, 1995.

Coomaraswamy, Ananda K. *History of Indian and Indonesian Art.* New York: Weyhe, 1927.

Harding, Mike. *A Little Book of the Green Man.* London: Aurum, 1972.

Jacques, Lacoste, ed. *La Sculptor Romane en Saintonge.* Saint-Cyr-sur-Loire: Christian Pirot, 1998.

Kathleen, Basford. *The Green Man.* London: Brawer, 1978.

Panda, S.S. "Kirtimukha, a Roaring Lion and Flying Vidyadharas in the Temple Art". *Orissa Review* (April 2005): 97–104.

Pichard, Pierre. *Inventory of Monuments at Bagan,* vols. 2–3. Paris: UNESCO, 1994.

Rawson, Philip. *Tantra the Indian Cult of Ecstasy.* London: Thames and Hudson, 1993.

Skilling, Peter. "Dvāravatī: Recent Revelations and Research". In *Dedications to HRH Princess Galyani Vadhana Krom Luang Naradhiwas Rajanagarindra,* edited by Chris Baker, pp. 87–112. Bangkok: The Siam Society, 2003.

Than Tun. သၡိင်းထဲကာဒၢိင်း (Myanma Design). Yangon: Plastic Rainbow Book, 2005.

5

The Viṣṇu on Garuḍa from the Nat Hlaung Kyaung Temple, Bagan

Olga Deshpande and Pamela Gutman[†]

From Bagan to St Petersburg

For nearly seventy years, four Burmese stone sculptures dating to the 11th–12th centuries have been in storage at the Hermitage Museum, St Petersburg. They arrived in Russia after World War II, part of a large group of Asian art objects (from India to Japan and Indonesia) from two institutions in Berlin, the Museum für Volkerkunde and the Museum für Ostasiatische Kunst. It was only after the radical political changes in the Soviet Union in the early 1990s that, after a long period of obfuscation regarding their background, Russia and Germany were able to begin to work together, and with other specialists, on these collections.

The Burmese sculptures comprise three images depicting events from the life of the Buddha: the cutting of the hair in preparation for his life as an ascetic; the Naga King Mucalinda sheltering him from a storm in the sixth week after the Enlightenment; and the taming of the raging elephant Nālāgiri. We discussed these images at the EURASEAA 14 Conference in Dublin in September 2012 and our findings will be published in the conference proceedings. The fourth image, examined here, represents Viṣṇu on Garuḍa, Viṣṇu Garuḍāsana.

These sculptures were sent to the Museum für Volkerkunde between 1894 and 1896 by a German geologist and palaeontologist, Friedrich (Fritz) Wilhelm Nötling (1857–1928), who at the time was employed by the Geological Survey of India and was working at the Yenangyaung oil fields near Bagan. Nötling studied geology and related subjects before graduating in 1885, after which he worked as a private docent (tutor) at the University of Königsberg. In the same year, he was assigned by the Berlin Academy of Sciences to go on a mission to Palestine, and he subsequently published his first paper for the *Geological Survey of Prussia* in 1886.[1] Until the University Reforms of the late 1900s, palaeontology was not taught at English universities, and the Geological Survey of India from time to time found it necessary to resort to Germany to find suitable people to fill palaeontological posts. In January 1887 Nötling sailed to Calcutta and served in the Geological Survey until 1903. He became a prolific researcher on geological, paleontological, prehistoric and ethnological subjects and published over forty papers and three books (Struwe 2006, p. 33). In 1892 he wrote his *Report on the Petroleum Industry in Upper Burma from the End of the Last Century up to the Beginning of 1891*[2] and in 1900 *The Miocene of Burma*.[3] He was also a committed careerist, taking advantage of the places in which he worked to make collections that he either sold or donated to various institutions in the expectation of social advancement. By 1907 he had acquired the honorary aristocratic title of *Hofrat* as a consequence. He spent nearly eight months in Northern Baluchistan, then part of British India, in 1898 and his reports were published in the *Zeitschrift für Ethnologie*.[4] His ambition soon overtook him. It was discovered that he had transferred an official collection of six hundred Cretaceous-period fossils from Northern Baluchistan to Tübingen University, and had subsequently been awarded the Cross of the First Class of the Order of Frederick by the King of Württemberg. He was forced to resign from the Geological Survey in 1903, and some thousands of items were repatriated to the Indian Museum in Calcutta.

Although he later vehemently denied it, he sent another fossil collection from Baluchistan to the eminent Russian geologist Feodosji Tchernyshev of the Russian Geological Society[5] (figure 5.1) in St Petersburg in 1901. Thanks to the help of A.P. Solokov, the director of the All-Russian Research Geological Karpinsky Institute, the Society's successor, we have discovered

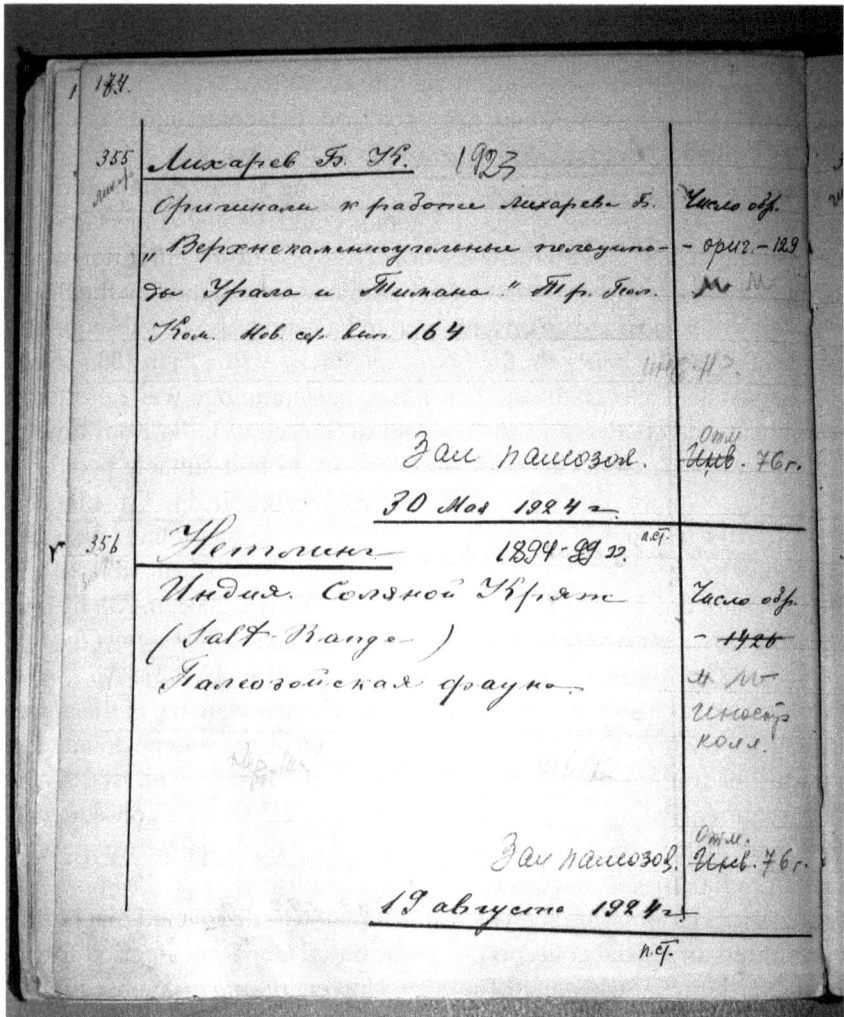

FIGURE 5.1
Source: A.R. Sokolov/Central Scientific-Research Geological-Prospecting Museum (CNIGR Museum).

receipts from 1894–98 for about 1,500 fossils, five hundred of which remain today. Today, collections made by him can also be found at the Berlin Ethnological Museum (Museum für Volkerkunde), the Leipzig Ethnological Museum (Museum für Volkerkunde), the Museum of Prehistory (Landes Museum für Vorgeschichte) in Halle and the Museum of Pre- and Proto-History in Weimar (Museum für Ur und Frühgeschichte).

Nötling had married an Australian, Marian Seal (whom he had persuaded not to marry Lord Baden-Powell), in 1899 and it was to her state of Tasmania that they retreated from the scandal. He became a naturalized Australian citizen and sought to regain his former social status. He pursued his interest in human evolution through the study of Australian aboriginal artefacts, and his research methods led him to conclusions with distinctly racist overtones. He became a member of the exclusive Tasmanian Club as well as the Royal Society of Tasmania and a trustee of the Tasmanian Museum. In 1914 he was appointed Acting German Consul in Tasmania (Struwe 2006, p. 33). This was not an auspicious time for a nationalistic German in the British Empire. The Tasmanian newspapers at the beginning of World War I were questioning the allegiances of Germans settled there, more so after the Austro–German drive into Galacia.[6] He was accused of being a spy in the Tasmanian Club (Brown 1997), and the authorities, censoring his mail, discovered that he was "communicating information to Germany" by writing, through his sister in Switzerland, to General von Mackensen on the Eastern Front about the situation in Australia and making "disloyal statements". He was interned for the duration of the war, after which he was denaturalized and returned to Germany.

This, in short, is what we know about Nötling. We have little information about his unofficial pursuits in Burma, other than that he managed to transport ten boxes of glazed tiles depicting Jatakas from the Mingalazedi and the Dhammayazika (Luce 1969–70, vol. 1, pp. 220n105, 230, 278n88), some fragments of wall paintings and some other, smaller sculptures, as well as those noted above. Many of the plaques and two of the sculptures, including the Viṣṇu under discussion, were published by Albert Grünwedel in 1897. The colonial authorities did not hear of Nötling's theft until well after the event, and soon after, in 1899, were not able to prevent Gilles Thomann from taking some important frescoes and selling them to the Ethnographische Museum in Berlin, although he and his party were eventually deported.[7]

The Nat Hlaung Kyaung

The Nat Hlaung Kyaung (monument 1600) is the single Brahmanic shrine remaining at Bagan. The translation of its name today, "Shrine confining the Devas", suggests the containment of the power of its Brahmanic images within its boundaries. Less common is the older name, Nat Daw

Kyaung, "Shrine of the Sacred Devas", found in U Kala's *Mahayazawingyi*, which acknowledges its Brahmanical function. Another, perhaps much older name, Nat Hlé Kyaung, "Shrine of the Reclining Deva", recalls the now-lost and excruciatingly restored Viṣṇu *Anantasayin* image, once the cult image of the temple.

The shrine has often been described in the literature (Crawfurd 1829, pp. 53–54; Grünwedel 1897, pp. 128–30; Thomann 1923, pp. 48–51; Duroiselle 1912–13, pp. 136–39; Ray 2001, pp. 33–44; Luce 1969–70, vol. 1, pp. 219–22, vol. 2, plates 143–49; Strachan 1989, pp. 39–41; Pierre Pichard 1995, pp. 236–39; Stadtner 2005, pp. 142–45). Luce (1969–70, vol. 1, p. 284) pointed out that the Nat Hlaung Kyaung was "honourably sited, little more than a stone's throw from the palace ... within the city, near its south wall", implying its importance to the rulers of early Bagan. Duroiselle called attention to a tradition which dated the building to the early part of the 10th century, ascribing its foundation to King Taung Thugyi (931–64 CE), a date not supported by other evidence. He also mentioned a late Burmese manuscript, "Record of the Pagodas of Bagan" (*Bagan Myo Hpaya Thamaing*), which ascribes its construction to King Aniruddha after his return from conquering Thaton.

Architecture

There is general scholarly agreement, on architectural grounds, that the building dates to the early Bagan period, around the 11th century. Briefly, it is a medium-sized, single-storey temple with a solid square core. The main shrine on the east face of the core, two metres deep, is flanked by two narrow, round arched shallow niches, above which are "strong recessed and swelling capitals" on which rest two round-topped niches joined by an arch pediment (*clec*) of an archaic type found at Sriksetra (Luce 1969–70, vol. 1, p. 219n103). There are shallow niches in the centre of each of the other faces (figure 5.2). It was designed with two concentric inner corridors, the outer now missing. Stadtner[8] suggests that the original plan was square, and may have been, like the Ananda, a square concentric temple with two sets of corridors. An entrance hall would have extended beyond the (modern) platform. Its original function may have been no longer relevant by the time of the Mongol invasion of 1284–87, when, according to a local tradition, its outer wall and possibly outer corridor were demolished to use their bricks to strengthen the nearby city wall (Pichard 1995, vol. 6, p. 50).

1600 f - Core, east face and main niche, from east

FIGURE 5.2
Source: Deshpande.

Sculpture and Painting

The original temple sculptures were made of both brick and plaster and grey sandstone. The main image, almost totally lost and now so badly restored, was placed in the central niche of the east face of the core, some 2.6 metres wide. It represented Viṣṇu in the Anantaśayin mode, depicting the moment of creation of the universe at the beginning of each world era when the god in human form sleeps on the *naga* Ananta. This was a favoured form of Viṣṇu in the art of mainland Southeast Asia, where it resonated with earlier *naga* cults and creation myths. It was particularly powerful in Khmer art of the 11th century. Whereas in India and Cambodia it is Brahma who emerges from a lotus stem protruding from Viṣṇu's navel, in Burma three deities — Brahma, Viṣṇu and Śiva — appear, apparently a local development of the cult. At the Nat Hlaung Kyaung, only traces of these deities remain. The few depictions of Viṣṇu Anantaśayin from Bagan, Sriksetra and the Kaw-gun caves near the Mon capital of Thaton show Viṣṇu with a mitred headdress in the Pala style of the 11th century, as do the Viṣṇu avataras at the Nat Hlaung Kyaung. It is interesting that the Kaw-gun Viṣṇu not only shows a strong connection with Khmer art in the garments and the *naga* heads but also illustrates a strong tendency to syncretism, as it includes a Buddhist stupa, a Gaṇeśa, favoured by Indian traders, and a man on a horse reminiscent of an old Nanzhao tradition (Gutman 2013, pp. 134–39).

Many of the remaining Nat Hlaung Kyaung sculptures are now "restored" in concrete to fanciful forms unknown to Vaiṣṇavite iconography: for instance, the image on the west wall of the sanctum now has two extra arms. But from photographs taken before the restoration it can be seen that the craftsmanship was of exceptional quality. Luce (1969–70, vol. 1, p. 220) remarked that the images of Viṣṇu on the three sides of the sanctum "were once, I expect, the most beautiful brick images at Pagán; but they are now, alas, so damaged that we can only guess at the beauty of the whole from the delicacy of a few parts". The figures, depicted standing frontally, are static, but the curves of the body are graceful and the treatment of the waistband is delicate, although not enough remains for comparative purposes. The walls of the inner corridor were once covered with paintings, which, according to U Mya (1934–35, p. 193), represented seated figures of Viṣṇu, both two and four armed, and his devotees, bearded ascetics with their hair done up in two knots, arms raised in *namaskāra mudrā* towards the fire before him on a salver.

Viṣṇu and Śiva

Two unattached images were noticed by Crawfurd in 1826 and Yule in 1855, and one by Thomann in 1899. One was the Viṣṇu seated on Garuḍa now in the Hermitage, taken by Nötling around 1895, the other a Śiva now in the Bagan Museum. Both are made of grey sandstone.

Viṣṇu Garuḍāsana

As a preserver and saviour of the universe, Viṣṇu often travels on his mount, Garuḍa, who is described as faster than the mind (Bautze-Picron 2002, pp. 3–13; Pal 2003, p. 215). This theme was popular in Nepal, North India, Cambodia, Champa and Java, but not usual in South India in the 11th century.

While the Hermitage Viṣṇu (figure 5.3) (H. 114 cm; B. 47 cm; D. 33 cm) has no immediate counterparts in the art of Burma, Viṣṇu Garuḍāsana

FIGURE 5.3
Source: The State Hermitage Museum, St Petersburg.

images, with Viṣṇu standing on his mount, have been found at Sriksetra and Vesali and occur seated *in situ* at the Nat Hlaung Kyaung. But this image, executed in bold, sharp relief, is stylistically different from other images of Viṣṇu at the Nat Hlaung Kyaung. It has a prominent *jaṭamākuṭa*-like headdress (figure 5.4) with a narrow three-pointed crown at the base and locks arranged in three symmetrical tiers, a feature typical of Śiva and Brahma images but rarely found on Viṣṇu, although a similar treatment is found at Angkor. Indeed, the same headdress, without the crown section, is found on the Brahmas of the Nanpaya, which are similarly surmounted by a knob shape on a rosette, probably a lotus bud, here depicted in a manner more akin to Choḷa than Pala sculpture (figure 5.5). An unprovenanced head, probably of a Bodhisattva, in the Bagan Museum has a similar headdress with the crown (figure 5.6). An interesting comparison can be made with the headdresses of the portrait often identified as the Chola king

FIGURE 5.4
Source: The State Hermitage Museum, St Petersburg.

FIGURE 5.5
Source: Bob Hudson.

Rajaraja and his guru in a mural at the Great Temple at Tanjore, dated to circa 1010 (Dehejia 1990, p. 50). This headdress does not appear on any of the other Viṣṇu images at the Nat Hlaung Kyaung, which wear the more usual *kiritamākuṭa*[9] in the shape of the five-pointed crown typical of the Pala style. On either side of the crown are rosettes from which ribbons fly upwards, and tassels fall over the shoulders, features typical of Choḷa and Pala art of the 11th century. The body ornaments, too, can be compared to both Choḷa and Pala art, and also to Khmer art of the same period.

The most unusual features of this image are the facts that Viṣṇu sits in *padmāsana* on a lotus throne, identical to Buddha images, and that the portion of his lower garment emerging from under his ankles is also found in seated Buddha images. The solid treatment of the face and body, too, recalls the image of the Buddha, and we can assume that the sculptor was more familiar with Buddhist than Brahmanical art. This configuration of

FIGURE 5.6
Source: Bob Hudson.

Garuḍāsana is not found in Chola art, but occurs, in various forms, in the
Pala art of Bihar and Bengal, where Viṣṇu often sits, albeit with one leg
pendant, on a throne over Garuḍa's shoulders.[10] Viṣṇu carries the usual
attributes, *cakra* and conch, in the upper hands. The missing attribute
carried in the lower right hand was most likely a *mahi* or earth symbol,
more common in Southeast Asia than India. Interestingly, neither he nor
his mount wears the usual sacred cord.

His vehicle Garuḍa (figure 5.7) has more in common with Khmer than
Indian models, and is closest to those found on lintels from 10th and 11th
century Khmer sites, sharing their power and strength. The winged figure
is represented with a human face and chest, and with a bird-like lower

FIGURE 5.7
Source: The State Hermitage Museum, St Petersburg.

body. His clawed feet grasp the *naga* while his hands are raised in front. He wears a narrow crown surmounted with a smooth *mākuṭa* topped again with a protuberance on a lotus base, as do the deity he bears and the Nanpaya Brahma bas-reliefs.

The sculptor appears to have adapted identifying motifs from a range of sources — Pala, Choḷa and Khmer — in his effort to depict Viṣṇu Garuḍāsana. It is worth noting that at this time Anantaśayin images (the Nat Hlaung Kyaung central image) are almost unknown in North India, but they are favoured in the South, while Viṣṇu Garuḍāsana is practically unknown in the South at this time,[11] but both are found at the Nat Hlaung Kyaung, indicating contact with both regions.

Śiva

The Śiva image (figure 5.8), its face and part of its headdress inexpertly repaired, also appears to be closer in style to the Hermitage Viṣṇu (and the Nanpaya Brahmas); the *mākuṭa*, jewellery and the manner in which the hands hold the weapons being so similar as to appear that they came from the same atelier. Ray, however, was of the opinion that it was a century later than the Viṣṇu, and, following Duroiselle, considered that it had been brought to the Nat Hlaung Kyaung from a ruined Śaiva shrine (Ray 2001, pp. 59–60). The image stands rigidly with the trident and what may be an unusual *vajra* (or a mallet?) in the upper right and left hands, sword and mace in the lower, and is crowned with a high and ornate *jaṭamukuṭa*. Luce noted that the broken animal at the feet was probably a bull. The style of the ornaments and garment recalls the early Choḷa, possibly late 11th/ early 12th century, although the disposition and depiction of the god's attributes is unusual: the *gada* is rarely associated with Śiva.

Provenance

The question here is the original placement of the standing Śiva and the Hermitage Viṣṇu, given that the central image of the Nat Hlaung Kyaung represented Viṣṇu Anantasayin. Ba Shin suggested that the Śiva (H. 178cm) might have come from one of the shallow, narrow round-arched lower lateral niches on either side of the main east niche, each of which is about 183 centimetres high; probably the niche to the northeast. It is unlikely, however, that these lower niches would have held stone rather than brick and plaster images.

Luce (1969–70, vol. 1, p. 220) suggested that the Hermitage Viṣṇu (H. 114 cm) could have been originally placed in the north upper lateral niche. The corresponding niche on the south side has a brick-and-plaster Viṣṇu on Garuḍa, stylistically somewhat dissimilar to ours, with its lotus throne rounded at the base, and a different Garuḍa (Pichard 1995, pp. 1600–1601, fig. 2). It is unlikely that its counterpart would have been made of stone. Moreover, the Hermitage Viṣṇu is shorter than is appropriate for the niche and wider than the niche allows. The remaining images around the core — standing Viṣṇus at the centre of the north, west and south sides, now unfortunately destroyed — were also made of brick and plaster. Only the images of the Viṣṇu Avataras in the niches of the present outer wall were made of stone.

FIGURE 5.8
Source: Bob Hudson.

The problem we have here is whether the Hermitage Viṣṇu and the Bagan Museum Śiva originated at the Nat Hlaung Kyaung or were brought there from elsewhere, as the name "Shrine confining Devas" implies a containment of the powers of these Brahmanic deities. It is possible that they may have originally belonged to a part of the Nat Hlaung Kyaung which has long since been destroyed, possibly the entrance hall, as was the case with the Nagayon. It is unlikely that they originated at the Nanpaya, where (despite Luce's contention that this was a Buddhist shrine) there is no evidence of Buddhist worship. One of the two niches on the east wall could indeed have held the Viṣṇu, although stylistically it differs from the extant Brahmas there, and the Śiva is too tall to fit.

Viṣṇu and Kingship in Southeast Asia

Even if our Viṣṇu on Garuḍa did not originate from the Nat Hlaung Kyaung, it is useful to explore its position in relation to similar sculptures in India and elsewhere in Southeast Asia, and their role in the religion of the 11th to 12th centuries. Vaiṣṇavism had been known in Southeast Asia from the early centuries of the first millennium and had become associated with royal power and the foundation of urban centres (Gutman 1999, pp. 29–36; Manguin and Dalsheimer 1998, pp. 87–123; Dofflemeyer 1999, pp. 34–48). Gutman and Hudson (2012–13) have recently shown that a proto-Vaiṣṇavite Bhāgavata ("devotees of the Blessed", also known as Pāñcarātra) cult existed, in tandem with Buddhism, in Sriksetra as early as the 1st century CE at the beginning of urbanization of Southeast Asia.

In early Indian Vaiṣṇavism, Viṣṇu was considered to enter the king at the time of his consecration. By identifying himself with Viṣṇu, the king would be able to conquer the three worlds. All *cakravartins* or paramount sovereigns were regarded as bearing a portion of Viṣṇu's personality. The role of the king was to guarantee stability and to ensure the fertility of the land. It was the king's duty to make rain and to cause the crops to thrive, and the same functions are attributed to Viṣṇu, who is always concerned with stability, regeneration and fertility. Viṣṇu was associated with the foundation of urban centres in Thailand and in Burma. The name of one of the oldest Pyu sites in Burma, Beikthano-myo, translates as "Viṣṇu city", and local tradition claims that it was founded by Viṣṇu, although no Vaiṣṇavite remains have been found there. Later inscriptions and chronicles make reference to the roles of both Buddhism and Brahmanism in the founding of Sriksetra and Bagan. King Kyanzittha's (fl. 1084–1113 CE) "prophetic" inscriptions from Pyay (1093), Bagan and near Thaton (1098) — directed towards the unification of the Pyu, Mon and Burmese peoples under his rule, in particular — recount that the Buddha, while in the Jetavana monastery, prophesized that in the year when he entered Parinirvana, Kyanzittha, here an incarnation of the ascetic Viṣṇu, would found first the city of Sriksetra and later reign in its successor city, Bagan. Moreover, it is forecast that the people of Bagan (Arimaddanapura) will be disciples of the Buddha, the Law and the Sangha, the rain will fall and great prosperity will be enjoyed. Kyanzittha is described as a mighty *cakravartin* king and a Bodhisattva who will become a Buddha. Here, Vaiṣṇavism is acknowledged but made subservient to Buddhism, a syncretic process which may have derived from Lower Burma, as illustrated by the Kaw-gun images.

Similarly, the *Jinakamali* and the *Camadevivamsa* (Coedès 1925) relate that the *rṣi* Vasudeva (an epithet of Viṣṇu) was associated with the foundation of the Mon city of Haripunjaya. Images of Viṣṇu do not appear in India before the 4th or 5th century, and in Burma, and elsewhere in Southeast Asia, soon after that, often at sites like Sriksetra, and Dhannyawadi and Vesali in Arakan, where there is also extensive evidence of Buddhism. There was no dichotomy between Brahmanism and Buddhism in ancient India or in the countries culturally influenced by India. While members of the lay community followed the precepts and doctrines of the sangha in their search for salvation, their daily lives continued to be governed by Brahmanical rituals (Ray 2003, pp. 129–33). Buddhism was unable to resolve the problem of providing ritual identity for its lay followers. In contrast to the detailed rules laid down for the monastic order, the laity were left to adopt the Brahmanical rites and rituals for their day-to-day functioning, and it was the ruler who dictated the nature of the ritual.

Vaiṣṇavism became a favoured cult in various courts throughout Southeast Asia in the 11th and 12th centuries, temporarily gaining supremacy over Śaivism, particularly in the Khmer-controlled lands and in Champa and East Java. One reason it did so may be the contemporaneous revival of Vaiṣṇavism in India (Klokke 2003, p. 22; Basham 1961, pp. 332–33; Eliot 1968, pp. 233–36). The great Dravidian theologian, the Brahman Ramanuja in the first half of the 11th century, following the Pāñcarātra tradition, taught devotion to Viṣṇu as a means to salvation. Through *bhakti-yoga* the worshipper realized that he was but a fragment of the god, and totally dependent on him. An inanimate object (i.e., image of Viṣṇu), if duly consecrated according to the Pāñcarātra rites, acquires a miraculous power, and the Sakti of Viṣṇu descends into it.

The inanimate image acquires a new meaning, becomes the object of love, of heart's desire and of the eye's rest. It was therefore attractive to rulers claiming an affinity with Viṣṇu. It is interesting that in Kyanzittha's palace inscriptions, the Brahmans involved in the building were clearly Vaiṣṇava, always beginning proceedings by worshipping *Nār*, i.e., Narayana, Viṣṇu (Blagden 1923, A2tr), the name also used by Ramanuja. And it is likely that some of these Brahmans came from the Mon country (Blagden 1923, H12).

Cambodia and Thailand

We have already mentioned the importance of Viṣṇu Anantasayin images in the pre- and early Bagan periods. This was the cult image of the Nat Hlaung Kyaung, on the eastern face of the core. Eleventh century equivalents are found at Angkor, at Kbal Spean (Boulbet and Dagens 1973) near the source of one of the tributaries of the Siem Reap River, and at Phnom Kulen, the sacred mountain which is a major source of Angkor's water supply. There, the riverbeds have been engraved with a great number of images of the sleeping Viṣṇu, together with clusters of *lingas* and *yonis*. The carvings are associated with the reigns of Suryavarman I and his successor Udayadityavarman II, who was consecrated in 1050. The sites appear to symbolize a royal connection with the act of creation and the sanctifying of the waters needed for the crops, which would guarantee the fertility of the land. A similar symbolism is seen in the massive bronze from the Western Mebon temple, which may, according to the Chinese envoy Zhou Daguan, originally have had a fountain of water flowing through his navel. Similarly, the Nat Hlaung Kyaung Anantaśayin could have identified the ruler with Viṣṇu in the act of creation.

East Java

In 11th century East Java, Airlangga described himself as an avatar of Viṣṇu descended to earth to recreate order and prosperity in the phenomenal world, and the kings of Kadiri similarly identified with Viṣṇu (Weatherbee 1968, pp. 278–82). The best-known Viṣṇu Garuḍāsana is the so-called portrait statue of King Airlangga, previously thought to have been made after his death in 1049 but now considered to be later.[12] This image is closely connected to the Pala Viṣṇu Garuḍāsana model: the four-armed Viṣṇu sits on Garuḍa's shoulders in a relaxed attitude, the bird kneels, left leg bent, and appears to be about to fly. Garuḍa is largely human with added wings and a bird's beak in place of a nose. He is taller than Viṣṇu, unlike the Pala examples, reflecting his growing importance in the Javanese context.

Champa

In Champa, where Śaivism was also the dominant cult, Jayarudravarman was regarded as an incarnation of Viṣṇu in the mid-12th century, while his sons each had portions of Viṣṇu's essence (Golzio 2006, p. 63). Cham Viṣṇu Garuḍāsana images, while conforming to a strong Cham aesthetic, appear to be iconographically connected to the Pala/Khmer/Javanese examples, most particularly adopting the beak of the hornbill, which in Indonesian culture was believed to transport the souls of the dead to the abode of the ancestors (Bernet-Kempers 1959, plates 17–19).

The Historical Background

These Viṣṇu Garuḍāsana representations reflect close relations between North and South India and Southeast Asia and intra-regional connections around the 11th century. This was the time of Muslim raids on North India from the west and the Chedi invasion of Bihar in 1039. It was also the time of the expansion of Chola influence in the first half of the 11th century. The Cholas gained control over all of South India, the Maldives and much of Sri Lanka and clashed with Srivijaya over its hold on the Malacca Straits, exerting control over much of the Malay Peninsula. Simultaneously with their expansion, the kingdom of Angkor extended its powers beyond its homeland into Laos, central Thailand and the Malay Peninsula (Kulke 2009, pp. 3–6). Bagan under Aniruddha had unified central and coastal Burma with parts of the northwestern coast of the Malay Peninsula. Kyanzittha, as Aniruddha's successful general, had succeeded in repelling the Khmer from Lower Burma (Gutman 2013), and both rulers had connections with the Cholas. Bagan was playing a significant role in regional affairs in the 11th century, and it is not surprising to find Chola, as well as Pala, influence in a temple as significantly sited as the Nat Hlaung Kyaung.

Significance

The jury remains out on the question of whether the Viṣṇu from the hermitage was originally situated at the Nat Hlaung Kyaung, but it is definitely contemporaneous with it. The architecture and iconography of the Nat Hlaung Kyaung indicate an 11th-century date, contemporary with the erection of the city walls (Grave and Barbetti 2001). We would like to propose that the Nat Hlaung Kyaung was built before Kyanzittha came to the throne, at a time when the royal consecration and other associated rituals were performed by Brahman priests of Pāñcarātra affiliation. This carried on a long tradition of rulers, whether Pyu, Mon or Arakanese, acquiring aspects of Viṣṇu through the abhiṣeka; aspects which were then shared by his people. Kyanzittha's inscriptions reflect, in Tambiah's words, "the Buddhist transformation of *rajadharma* (in which the brahman sanctifies kingship) to the larger conception of the *dharmaraja* (wherein the king is the wielder of the worldly dharma and the maintainer of society, in which brahmans serve as subordinate functionaries, and wherein he has the duty of protecting and tending the members of the sangha as the seekers of higher truth)" (Tambiah 1976, p. 83). This transformation would have required a different edifice for the royal ceremonial, one which could incorporate the sangha. The builder may well have been Aniruddha, whose regional connections with the Pala, Choḷa and Khmer kingdoms are reflected in the Viṣṇu Garuḍāsana made at the same time as the Nat Hlaung Kyaung.

Acknowledgements

The authors would like to thank Pierre Pichard, Don Stadtner, Claudine Bautze-Picron and Marilyn Longmuir for their suggestions in the preparation of this chapter.

Notes

1. British Library India Office Records IOR L/E/&/137-S&C 1717, Letter from W.T. Blandford, London, 19 August 1886 to the Under Secretary for State for India and IOR L/E/7/137, Minute Paper – S&C No. 1717, 20 August 1896, signed Horace Walpole. We thank Marilyn Longmuir for bringing these to our attention.
2. Rangoon, 1892.
3. In the series *Verhandelingen der Koninklijke Nederlandsche Akademie van Wettenschappen, Afdeeling Natuurkunde*, Amsterdam.

4. "Über prehistorische Niederlassugen in Baluchistan", *Zeitschrift für Ethnology. Organ des Berliner Gesellschaft für Anthropologie, Ethnologie und UrGeschichte,* 1899, pp. 100–107.

5. The Russian Geological Society became the Geological Committee of Russia in 1903, and its successor today is the All-Russian Karpinsky Institute of Geological Research.

6. Australian War Memorial Archive File 2DRL/0693.

7. *Proceedings of the Department of Revenue and Agriculture,* August 1900, pro. no. 1, "Spoliation of Sacred Edifices at Bagan by German Archaeologists", pp. 75ff. Thanks to Andrew Huxley for bringing this to our attention.

8. Personal communication, 19 December 2011.

9. As do later Bodhisattva and Brahmanical images. Luce 1969–70, vol. 3, plate 219. Abeyadana Tondoes, Brahmanic (?) deities, 280 a, b, c Nanda, Life of Gotama.

10. E.g., the Garuḍāsanas at the Cleveland Museum and at LACMA.

11. Thanks to Michael Rabe for this information.

12. For a definitive refutation of this theory, see Pauline Lunsingh Scheurleer 2009.

References

Basham, A.L. *The Wonder That Was India.* London: Sidgwick and Jackson, 1951.

Bautze-Picron, Claudine. "Flying from Heaven to Earth". *Aziatische Kunst* 32, no. 2 (2002): 2–12.

Bernet Kempers, A.J. *Ancient Indonesian Art.* Amsterdam: C.P.J. van der Peet, 1959.

Blagden, Charles Otto. "An Inscription Found Near the Tharaba Gate, Pagan". *Mon Inscriptions Nos. IX–XI, Epigraphia Birmanica,* vol. 3, pt. 1, no. 9 (1923).

Boulbet, J., and B. Dagens. "Les sites archéologiques de la région du Bhnaṃ Gūlen (Phnom Kulen)". Special issue, *Arts Asiatiques* 27 (1973).

Brown, G.D. "1915 — A German Spy in the Club". *Tasmanian Club Newsletter* (April 1997).

Coedès, George. "Documents sur l'histoire politique et religieuse du Laos Occidental". *Bulletin de l'Ecole française d'Extrême-Orient* 25, nos. 1–2 (1925): 1–201.

Crawfurd, John. *Journal of an Embassy from the Governor-General of India to the Court of Ava, in the Year 1827.* London: Henry Colbourn, 1829.

Dehejia, Vidya. *Art of the Imperial Cholas.* New York: Columbia University Press, 1990.

Dofflemeyer, Virginia. "Visnu Images from Ancient Thailand and the Concept of Kingship". In *Art from Thailand,* edited by Robert L. Brown, pp. 34–48. Mumbai: Marg, 1999.

Duroiselle, Charles. "The Nat-Hlaung-Kyaung, Pagan". *Archaeological Survey of India* (1912–13): 136–39.

Eliot, Charles. *Hinduism and Buddhism*. London: Routledge and Kegan Paul, 1968.

Golzio, Karl-Heinz. "L'Hindouisme au Champa après les sources épigraphiques". In *Trésors d'art du Vietnam- la sculpture du Champa, v–xv siècles*, edited by Pierre Baptiste and Thierry Zephir. Paris: Musée Guimet, 2006.

Grave, Peter, and Mike Barbetti. "Dating the City Wall, Fortification and the Palace Site at Pagan". *Asian Perspectives* 40, no. 1 (2001): 75–87.

Grünwedel, Albert. *Veröffentlichungen aus dem Königlichen Museum für Völkerkunde, V Band, 4. Skulpturen aus Pagan*. Berlin, Dietrich Reimer, 1897.

Gutman, P., and Bob Hudson. "A First Century Stele from Śrīkṣetra". *Bulletin de l'École française d'Extrême-Orient* 99 (2012–13): 17–46.

Gutman, Pamela. "Visnu in Burma". In *The Art of Burma*, edited by Donald Stadtner, pp. 29–36. Mumbai: Marg, 1999.

———. "Religious Syncretism in 11th-century Thaton: A Southeast Asian Transformation of Viṣṇu". In *Materializing Southeast Asia's Past: Selected Papers from the 12th International Conference of the European Association of Southeast Asian Archaeologists*, vol. 2, edited by Marijke J. Klokke and Véronique Degroot, pp. 134–39. Singapore: NUS Press, 2013.

Klokke, Marijke. "Hinduism and Buddhism in Indonesia". In *Worshipping Siva and Buddha*, edited by Ann R. Kinney, pp. 17–27. Honolulu: University of Hawai'i Press, 2003.

Kulke, Hermann. "The Naval Expeditions of the Cholas in the Context of Asian History. In *Nagapattinam to Suvarnadwipa: Reflections on the Chola Naval Expeditions to Southeast Asia*, edited by H. Kulke et al., pp. 1–19. Singapore: Institute of Southeast Asian Studies, 2009.

Luce, Gordon Hannington. *Old Burma–Early Pagan*, 3 vols. Ascona and New York: Artibus Asiae Supplementum, 1969–70.

Manguin, Pierre-Yves, and Nadine Dalsheimer. "Visnu mitrés et réseaux marchands en Asie du Sud-Est: nouvelles données archéologiques sur le Ier millénaire apr. J.-C." *Bulletin de l'École française d'Extrême-Orient* 85 (1998): 87–123.

Mya, U. "Note on the Nanpaya Temple and Images of Brahmā Carved on the Pillars inside It, Myinpagan, Burma". *ASI 1934–35* (1934–35): 101–6.

Pal, Pratapaditya. *Art from Sri Lanka & Southeast Asia, Asian Art at the Norton Simon Museum*, vol. 3. New Haven: Yale, 2003.

Phayre, Arthur Purves. "Memorandum on the Pagoda at Pagán with Hindoo Images". In *A Narrative of the Mission to the Court of Ava in 1855*, edited by Henry Yule. London: Oxford University Press, 1968.

Pierre Pichard. *Inventory of Monuments at Pagan*, vol. 6. Paris: UNESCO, 1995.

Ray, Himanshu Prabha. *The Archaeology of Seafaring in Ancient South Asia*. Cambridge: Cambridge University Press, 2003.

Ray, N.-R. *Brahmanical Gods in Burma*. Calcutta: 1932; repr., Bangkok: White Orchid, 2001.

Scheurleer, Pauline Lunsingh. "The Javanese Statue of Garuḍa Carrying Wiṣṇu and Candi Kidal". *Artibus Asiae* 69, no. 1 (2009): 180–218.

Stadtner, Don. *Ancient Pagan — Buddhist Plain of Merit*. Bangkok: River Books, 2005.

Strachan, Paul. *Pagan-Art and Architecture of Old Burma*. Arran: Kiscadale, 1989.

Struwe, Ruth. "An Ambitious German in Early Twentieth Century Tasmania: The Collections Made by Fritz Nötling". *Australian Archaeology*, no. 62 (2006).

Tambiah, S.J. *World Conqueror and World Renouncer — A Study of Buddhism and Polity in Thailand against a Historical Background*. Cambridge: Cambridge University Press, 1976.

Thomann Th. H. *Pagan- ein Jahrtausend Buddhistischer Tempelkunst*. Stuttgart/ Heilbronn: Verlag Walter Seifert, 1923.

Weatherbee, D. "Aspects of Ancient Javanese Politics". PhD dissertation, Johns Hopkins University, 1968.

6

A Thousand Years before Bagan: Radiocarbon Dates and Myanmar's Ancient Pyu Cities

Bob Hudson

There are now sufficient radiocarbon dates for the walled cities of Halin, Beikthano and Sriksetra to suggest that they were all functioning by the early centuries CE. In the light of the new data, approaches to the periodization and interpretation of Myanmar's early urban system may need to be modified.

If you want to know the exact date of an ancient object or structure, find an inscription. In the 11th–13th century Bagan period, stone inscriptions give the founding year of dozens of pagodas. Some inscriptions, motivated by an urge to commence building at an auspicious moment, go so far as to nominate the day, hour or even minute when construction began (see, for example, Luce 1932). From Bagan onward, these absolute dates have provided a vital chronological framework for historical and archaeological analysis. When monks and scholars sat down in King Bagyidaw's "Glass Palace" in 1829 to try to bring together the often contradictory narratives of earlier chronicles, pagoda histories and religious commentaries, they recognized the value of inscriptions for their dates as well as for their dedicatory content (Pe Maung Tin and Luce 1923).

A "scientific" date, generally from carbon, can also provide an accurate time for a past event, but the time is within a range of centuries, not a specific year. However, radiocarbon dates can also go back many thousands of years before inscriptions. So far there have been relatively few samples from Myanmar tested to provide carbon dates, but the results of carbon dating so far show, among other things, that construction and other economic and cultural activity was taking place between the 1st and 3rd centuries CE at Sriksetra, Halin and Beikthano (figure 6.1). These date ranges help provide a framework within which we can view changes in art styles, palaeography, architecture and expressions of religious ideas in text or sculpture during the early urban period, before inscriptions appear.

Radiocarbon Dating

Radiocarbon dates tell us when the material being tested was alive. The material is usually wood which, before it rotted away in the ground, was converted to charcoal by burning and was thus preserved. During its lifetime the wood took in an isotope, Carbon-14 (written as ^{14}C). When the tree or other carbon-based organism died, it stopped absorbing atmospheric carbon. Over time the proportion of ^{14}C in the dead organism decreased as the ^{14}C decayed into ^{12}C, a stable isotope. By measuring the proportion of ^{14}C to ^{12}C that remains, the elapsed time since death of the organism can be estimated. This is done by several different laboratory methods (Scott, Aitchison et al. 1990; Bayliss, McCormac et al. 2004), but the result is that we end up with a radiocarbon date, stated in years BP, Before Present (radiocarbon "present" is arbitrarily chosen as 1950), with a possible degree of error. These data can be converted to a range of historical years allowing for the error, and calibrated more finely according to variations in the past of the amount of ^{14}C in the atmosphere. The dates in this chapter are calibrated at 95.4 per cent (also called 2 σ) probability using computer programs such as Oxcal and the most recent calibration data available (Bronk Ramsey 2002; Reimer, Baillie et al. 2009).

Beikthano

A number of archaeological reports on this site have been published (Aung Thaw 1968; Bronson 1969; Aung Thaw 1972; Stargardt 1990; Thaw Kaung 1998; Myo Theingyi Cho 2003; Hudson 2004, pp. 129–32; San Shwe 2004),

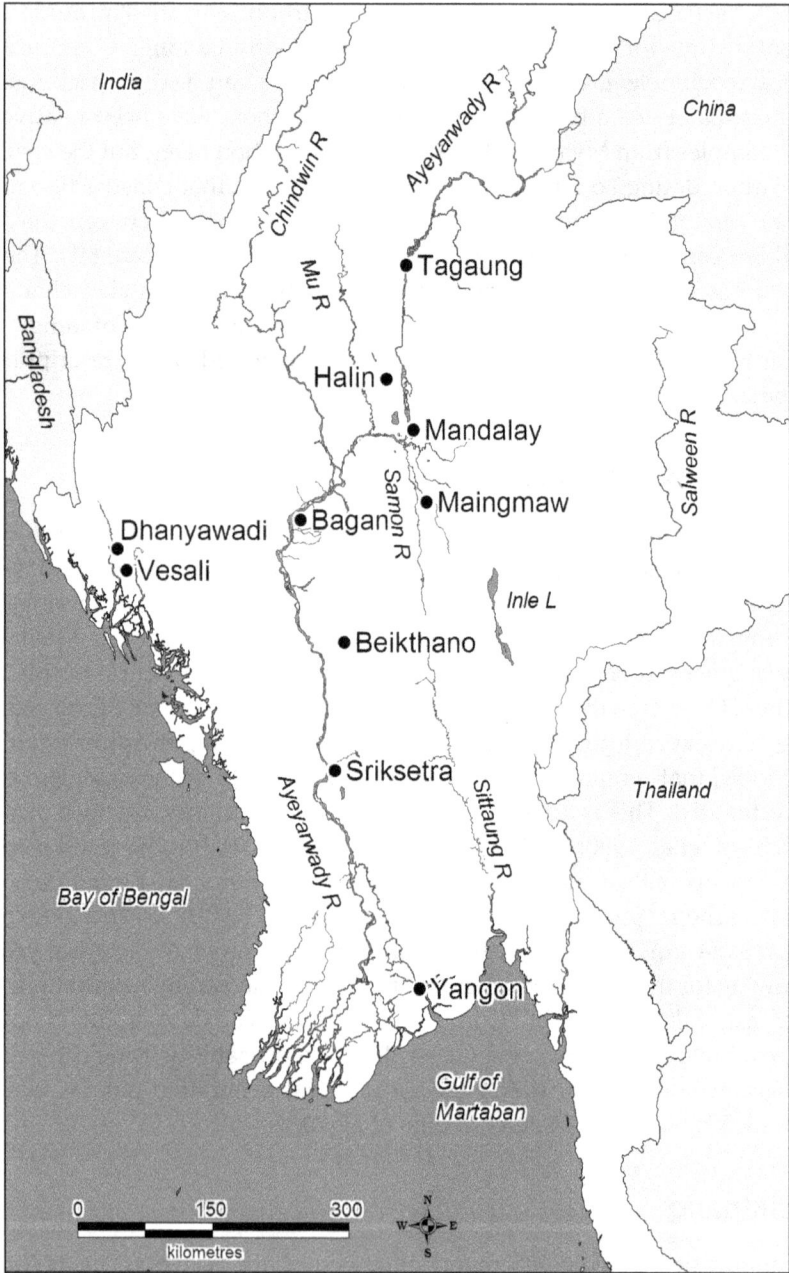

FIGURE 6.1
Source: Bob Hudson.

including a vigorous discussion about the degree of imported versus local influence on the site, between Janice Stargardt, who favours indigenous development, and Peter Bellwood, who suggests that Indian influence is paramount (Bellwood 1992, 1993; Stargardt 1993, 1994). Four radiocarbon dates, covering two sites within the city walls, were acquired in the 1960s. Three more radiocarbon results, for site BTO 32, a brick complex outside the south wall of the city, and for timber found below the destruction layer of two of the gates, were obtained recently (figures 6.2 and 6.3).

The radiocarbon date range for KKG 9, a rectangular brick structure, came with a relatively large margin of error. Sample I434, 1950 ± 90 BP, calibrates to a range from 190 BCE to 260 CE. It is reasonable to claim that the structure dates to this *period*, but we must not be tempted to take a median date as "true". Nor should we get too excited over the 190 BCE end of the range. The carbon date tells us that there was construction activity

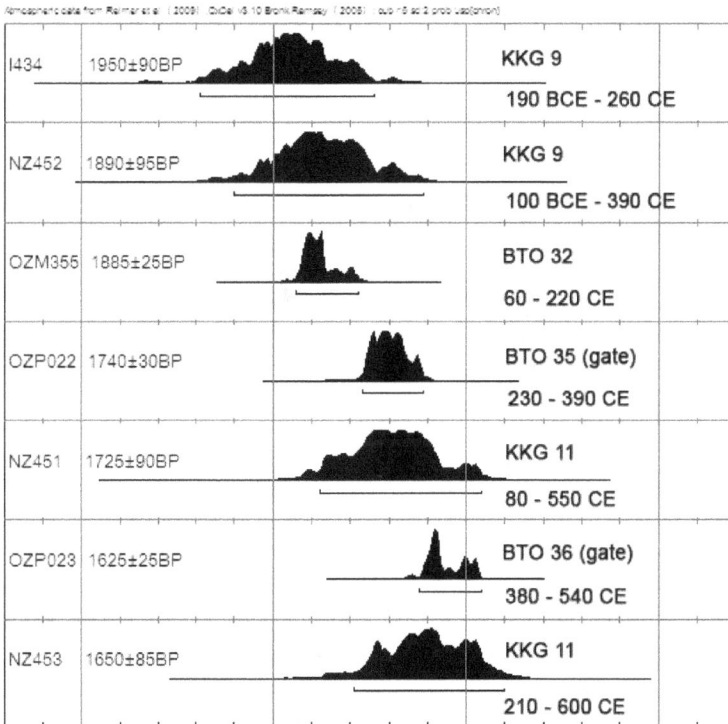

FIGURE 6.2
Source: Bob Hudson.

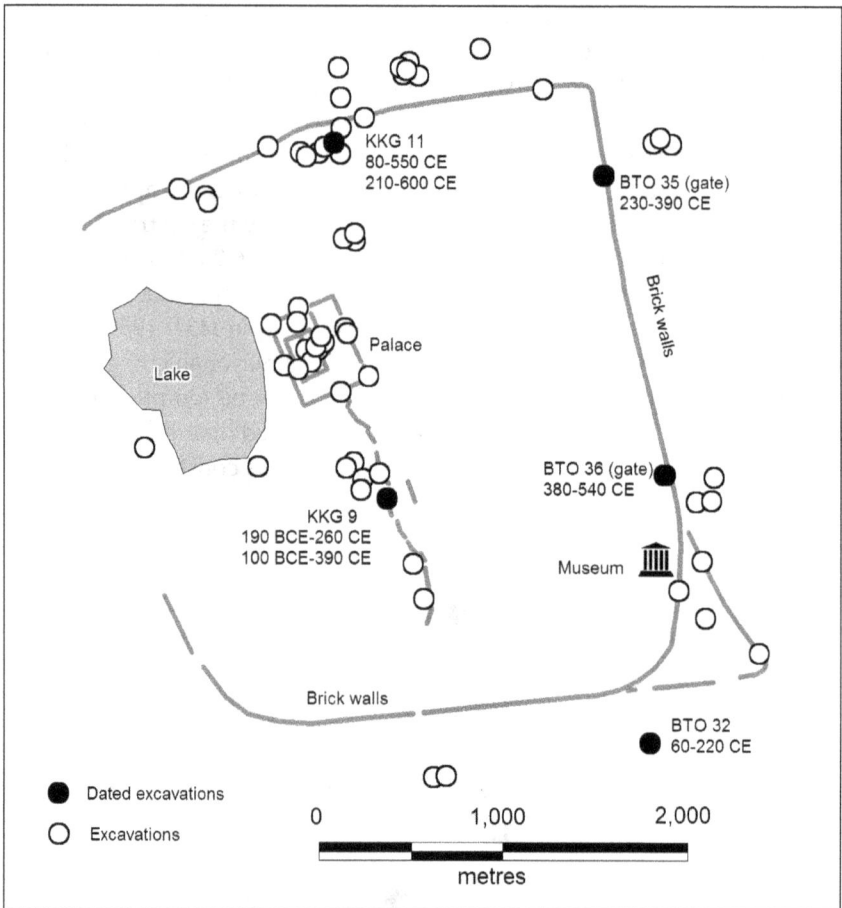

FIGURE 6.3
Source: Bob Hudson.

at KKG 9 *sometime* between 190 BCE and 390 CE. Similarly, construction at KKG 11 was between 80 CE and 600.

The new dates have a narrower margin of error because they were acquired using accelerator mass spectrometry, or AMS, which provides a more accurate count of the decay of the ^{14}C isotope (Fink, Hotchkis et al. 2004; Hua, Zoppi et al. 2004). Sample OZM355 came from a layer of ash and charcoal sitting on a brick floor in BTO 32. This means that the building must have been constructed in or before the 60–220 CE period. It is not certain whether the charcoal was from a cremation or from something as simple as a cooking fire. The ash lens was an isolated feature, and there is no indication that the entire structure had been destroyed by fire. The building consists of a square central structure surrounded by a platform (figure 6.4). In places, there are several layers of brick floor.

This structure is outside the city walls. We might suggest that by the 60 CE to 220 period, construction had spilled beyond the walls, assuming that the original plan had been for the walls to contain the settlement fully. At least eleven buildings have so far been excavated outside the walls. However, it could also be argued that it was appropriate for some buildings to be constructed *outside* a walled town, just as Buddha's Jetavana monastery, according to textual records, was 1,200 paces outside the south gate of Sravasti (Legge 1886, p. 56).

The burial urns at BTO 32 are varied. A tubular shape, wider at the base, is common (figure 6.5), as is a domed handle on the lid (figure 6.6). There is often castellation around the rims (figure 6.7). Urns are decorated with moulded birds, horses or flowers (figures 6.7 and 6.8), or with incised or punctated patterns (figure 6.9). One urn (figure 6.10) was painted with a

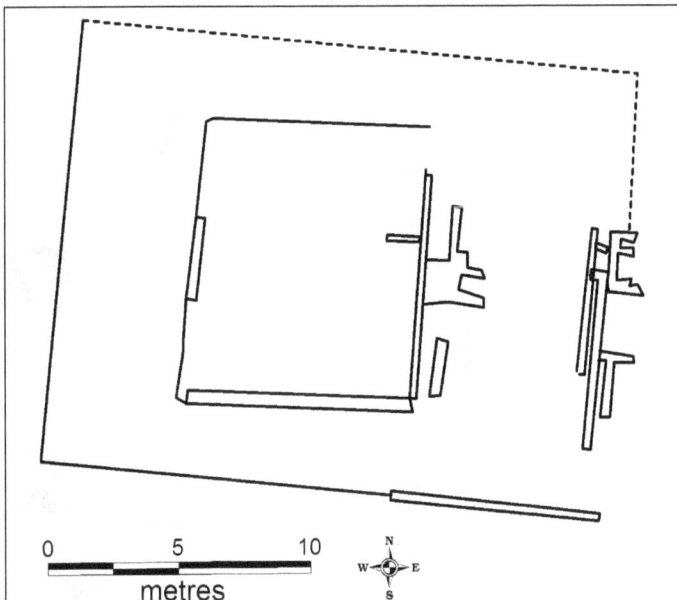

FIGURE 6.4
Source: Bob Hudson.

FIGURE 6.5
Source: Bob Hudson.

FIGURE 6.6
Source: Bob Hudson.

FIGURE 6.7
Source: Bob Hudson.

FIGURE 6.8
Source: Bob Hudson.

FIGURE 6.9
Source: Bob Hudson.

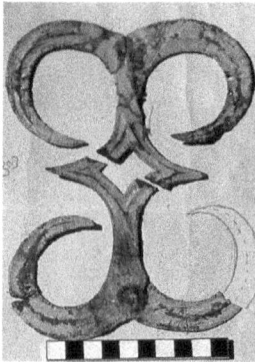

FIGURE 6.10
Source: Bob Hudson.

pattern reminiscent of that found in metal on Iron Age coffin decorations in the Samon Valley (see Hudson 2004, pp. 82, 107). There is no evidence of the use of stamps, and no sign of the Indic auspicious symbols that we usually identify with the inhabitants of Myanmar's early urban system.

Michael and Maitrii Aung-Thwin have made a convincing argument that the inhabitants of the first millennium CE settlements should not be identified with a "Pyu" ethno-linguistic group (Aung-Thwin and Aung-Thwin 2012, pp. 63–65). However, since the term is so common, we will continue here to use "Pyu", with the caveat that we are referring to a population which has left behind a particular set of cultural remains. Among these remains is the varied design programme at BTO 32, which suggests that in the 60–200 CE period there were no strict rules about how burial urns should be made.

The newly acquired dates from the gate material at Beikthano need to be considered with caution. In both cases the charcoal samples came from within the gateways, below a layer of brick rubble that marks the abandonment and deterioration of the gate structures. However, the radiocarbon ranges for BTO 35 (230–390 CE) and BTO 36 (380–540 CE) cannot be confirmed as representing the construction phase of the gates, because neither sample came from wood that was connected to any structure. They may, of course, have been part of original structures, repaired structures, or extensions of the original, but their context gives no strong support for any of these possibilities. We can at least suggest on the basis of the location and position in the stratigraphy of the samples that the gates fell into disrepair, on the reasonable assumption that they were abandoned at the same time, after the period 380–540 CE during which the charcoal at BTO 36 was deposited.

While it would always be good to have more supporting radiocarbon dates, and, in the case of the gates, dates from a better defined context, OZM355 suggests that BTO 32, a ritual site with brick walls and floors, containing burial urns, was functioning outside the city walls some time before 380–450 CE. Brick construction, ritual deposits and the manufacture of complex earthenware suggest that the city was operational by 60–220 CE. If we take walls and gates as a defining, integral feature of an early Pyu city, then they should have existed at this time, but in the case of Beikthano our radiocarbon dates for the gates give no firm indication.

Pre-urban Halin

An earthenware firing site southwest of the old city walls and salt fields at Halin (figures 6.11 and 6.12) is one of a group of mounds of potsherds and ash (Hudson and Nyein Lwin 2012). This site can be convincingly placed by radiocarbon dates in the range 2890 to 2470 BCE (figure 6.11). While these dates precede the urban period that is the focus of the present discussion, they are significant in that among incised wares that can be seen as diagnostic of the spread of agriculture in the Neolithic period (Bellwood 2005), there are several examples of forms that appear much later, during the early urban phase.

Thin-walled three-millimetre-thick sherds, made from a fine whitish paste and burnished grey/black (figure 6.13), resemble the form and fabric of the rounded black bowls known from the first millennium CE as monks' bowls. A spout (figure 6.14) suggests that spouted vessels have a long history in Myanmar before they appear in the first millennium CE debris of religious complexes (see, for example, Aung Thaw 1968). A sherd with some elementary castellation (figure 6.15) may leave us unsurprised that 2,500 or more years later, this form had been elegantly developed at locations such as BTO 32 (figures 6.7 and 6.10).

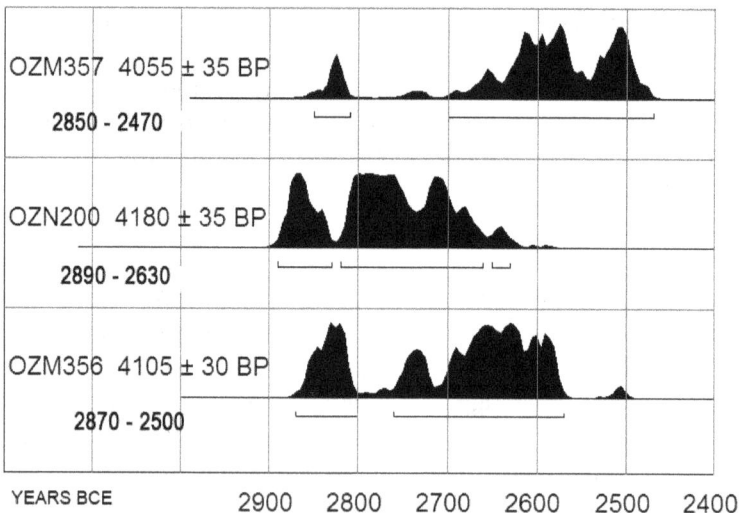

FIGURE 6.11
Source: Bob Hudson.

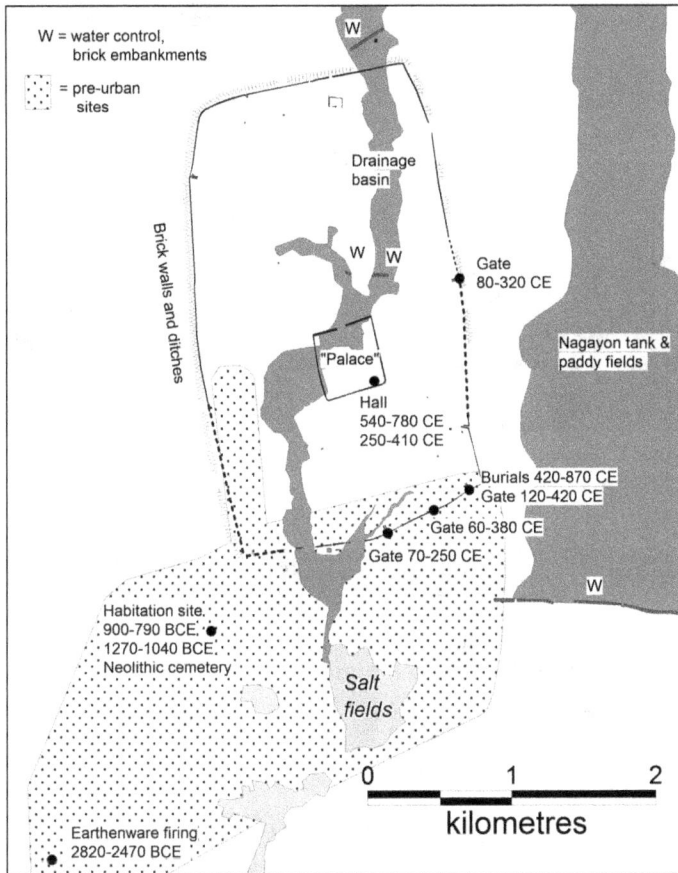

FIGURE 6.12
Source: Bob Hudson.

Early Urban Halin

The radiocarbon dates for the earthenware firing mound confirm that Halin was settled by at least 4,500 years ago, with its salt resources, still exploited today, probably a key attraction. Continuity of occupation has been demonstrated by excavations of Neolithic, Bronze Age and Iron Age burials (Hudson 2009, 2010) and by the construction of gates, walls and ritual buildings in the Pyu period (Myint Aung 1970). Radiocarbon dates from Myint Aung and from more recent excavations (HL 31 and 32) by

FIGURE 6.13
Source: Bob Hudson.

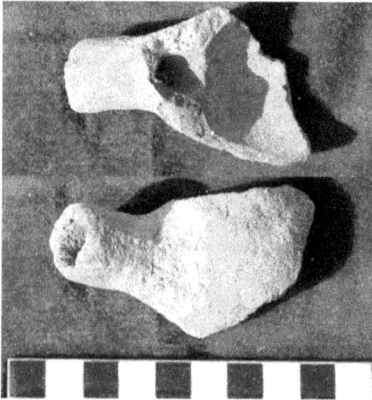

FIGURE 6.14
Source: Bob Hudson.

FIGURE 6.15
Source: Bob Hudson.

Nyein Lwin can now be combined to point to a specific period in which the city walls and gates were built (figures 6.12 and 6.16). Four separate gates have been radiocarbon dated. The ranges for all four overlap in the period 120 CE to 250. The timber from HL 31 and 32, at least, appears to be palm, not a long-growing hardwood such as teak. Wood sampled from the core

IntCal13 atmospheric curve (Reimer et al 2013)OxCal v3.10 Bronk Ramsey (2005); cub r:5 sd:12 prob usp[chron]

NZ895 1818 ± 65 BP		Gate HL 10 60-380 CE
OZN912 1845 ± 35 BP		Gate HL 31 Gatepost, final phase 70-250 CE
OZN914 1825 ± 30 BP		Gate HL 32 80-320 CE
NZ896 1750 ± 65 BP		Gate HL 17 120-420 CE
OZS480 1695 ± 25 BP		HL 9, outside edge of 25 cm pillar 250-410 CE
NZ894 1369 ± 64 BP	HL 9 Wooden pillar 540-780 CE	
NZ898 1403 ± 98 BP	HL 17 Bone from inhumation 420-870 CE	

BCE/CE   Calibrated date   500 CE   1000 CE

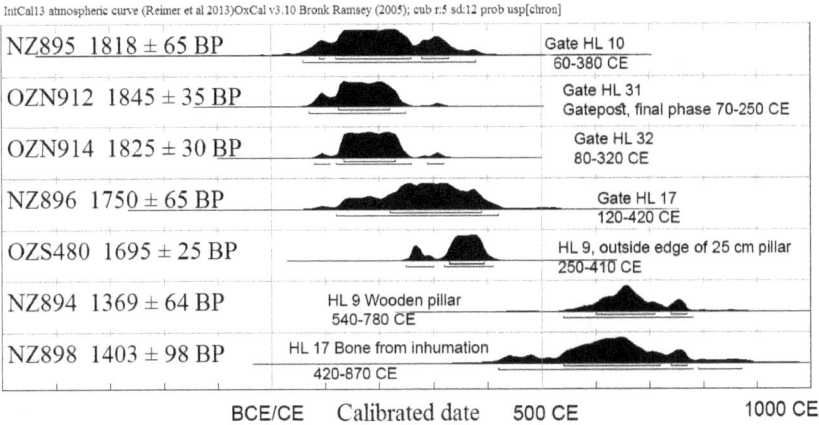

FIGURE 6.16
Source: Bob Hudson.

of a two-hundred-year-old tree will yield a carbon date two hundred years earlier than wood from the outside. Palms mature in under twenty years, and the "old wood" factor need not come into consideration, although it could also be argued that older, non-productive palm trees might have been used for their timber. We can suggest that the gates were controlling entry into the city by the early 2nd to mid-3rd century CE, or a little later if we give old palm trees the benefit of the doubt.

The sample from HL 31 was from the remains of one of fourteen pillars that may have supported a gatehouse, or a ceremonial entranceway, over the corridor that entered the city (figure 6.17). Excavation showed that this corridor was at times closed by a wooden gate which swung on iron pivots. There was a layer of fire debris at road level. In the corridor entering HL 32 (figure 6.18) there was also fire debris, including a lamp, potsherds and burnt palm logs, one of which provided radiocarbon date OZN914. The two gates excavated by Myint Aung (1970) had also been burnt. Four gates, all burnt, is more than coincidental. It looks like someone deliberately set fire to each of the gatehouses. Sections of the wall at HL 31 and 32 were removed down to the level of the natural soil (figures 6.17D and 6.18D). The fire debris was not cleared, the gates were not rebuilt, and the gaps in the walls were not repaired. The layers of ash, and the deliberately created gaps, became covered by brick debris from the deterioration of the walls.

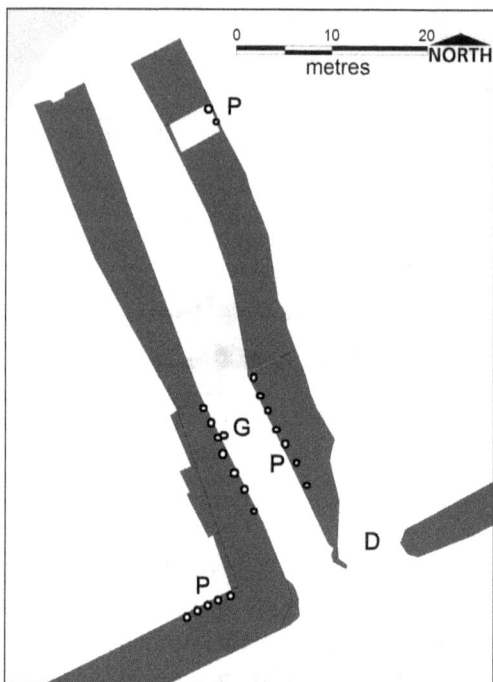

FIGURE 6.17
Source: Bob Hudson.

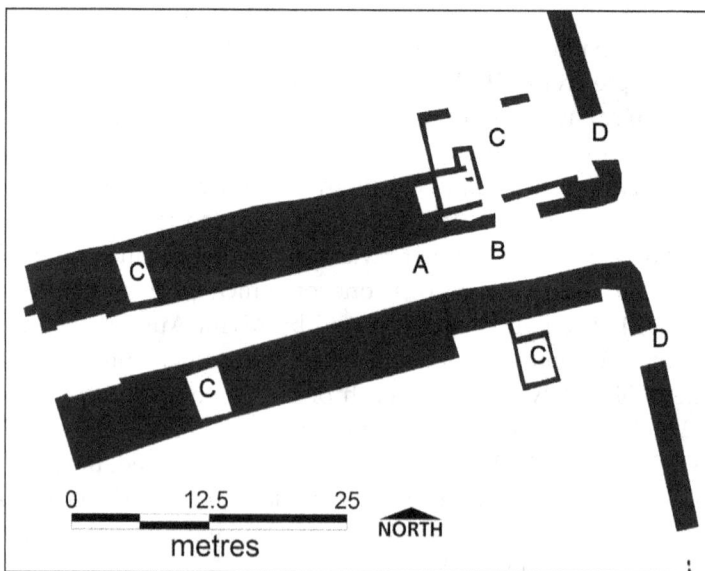

FIGURE 6.18
Source: Bob Hudson.

It is not clear when this happened. Within a walled complex in the centre of Halin, a hall (HL 9, excavated by Myint Aung) with a pillar dated 540–780 CE was also burnt (figures 6.12 and 6.16). A traditional story tells of a rebellion against a king of Halin by his subjects which resulted in a fire destroying the city (Myint Aung 1970, p. 56), though there is no date. Burning of the gates after 780 CE might fit the Chinese record of "the Pyu kingdom" being attacked by "Man rebels" in 832 CE (Luce 1961, p. 91), though this brief mention is not specific to any city. The evidence against either the rebel subjects or the Man rebels would be unlikely to produce a conviction in court, but the facts seem clear. A deliberate attack resulted in the permanent destruction of Halin's gates and gatehouses. Gaps created in the wall beside the gates were either the result of some precise military engineering either during or immediately after the attack to reduce the functionality of the wall, or action taken some time after the event to make the city accessible from outside without actually repairing the original entrances.

The excavation of gate HL 32 has also provided evidence that in the 120–250 CE period, Halin was matching world standards in some important aspects of engineering and transport. During the excavation, a trench was cut across the gateway, down to natural soil (figure 6.19). A vertical section

FIGURE 6.19
Source: Bob Hudson.

of this trench revealed a forty-centimetre bedding of stones topped with a compressed layer of fine gravel, sand and lime. It can be compared to the industrial-era McAdam method of building a road with courses of unbound angular stone (Lay 2009, pp. 19–22). This single lane passed through the corridor gate. It seems to be limited to the corridor. There was no trace of the same road material projecting further inside or outside the city.

The roadbed may have been laid in response to damage by cart traffic. Several large stones were situated on either side of the brick corridor entering the city, perhaps to keep carts from straying and damaging the wall. Below the layered stone road there was further evidence of the culprits who had provoked the gate administrators, who seem to have occupied a series of rooms (figure 6.19C) as well as the timber gatehouse perched above the corridor, to pave the entry way. Below the road there are two deep ruts, most likely formed by the wheels of bullock carts. The ruts are 142 centimetres, or four feet eight inches apart: the ancient world standard, giving a couple of centimetres either way, from Pompeii to Yunnan (Ogata, Tsutsumi et al. 2006). Measurement of the wheelbase of a passing bullock cart showed that these dimensions are the same in Myanmar today.

From between 120 CE and 250, then, Halin had walls, gates that were manned day and night to the extent of needing lamps, traffic management, and enough goods going in and out of the city to require an engineering solution to road wear. Some of this traffic may have been local, from the paddy fields situated on lower ground east of the city, in the Nagayon tank. More widespread economic activity at Halin is reflected in its coinage. More than ten thousand surviving examples of Halin's silver rising sun/ *srivatsa* coin, which Mahlo (2012, pp. 33–45) dates to the 5th and 6th century period, are known.

Sriksetra

Current archaeological evidence suggests that Sriksetra was constructed in several phases. First, the existing east wall and the "inner rampart" excavated in the 1960s (ASB 1964), which is still visible at ground level on both sides of the railway line that crosses the old city, encircled what is now the city centre (figure 6.21). But annual inundation from the southwest to the northeast became overwhelming. The rampart and its drainage channel were replaced five hundred metres further up the western slope by a physically larger wall and an eight-kilometre drain, which remain prominent today. The southern end of the drain was diverted in part to a canal which passed back through the city wall and distributed a controllable supply of water through the centre of the city.

This system also succumbed to siltation during the Pyu period. Two gates, Yahanda and Lulin-kyaw, filled with silt that overflowed from the drains to the extent that smaller brick gates, now uncovered by archaeological excavations, were built across the originals, on top of the silt. The Hmot-she causeway/bridge, which crossed the drainage channel on the western side, filled on its upstream side with silt, and water began to flow out of the drain and around the causeway. The central canal became so silted that a rectangular walled complex, known today as the palace, could be built right over it, using the vestigial flow from the canal to fill its moat (Hudson and Lustig 2008). By this stage, corridor gates (Aung Myint 1998) seem to have gone out of style. The palace complex was entered by passageways with ninety-degree turns (figure 6.22). A thermoluminescence (TL) date of 710 CE (for a discussion of Myanmar TL dates, see Hudson 2004) for a piece of pottery found within the palace area hints that all this happened before the fragment was made and discarded, although the TL date does not tell us how long before.

The earliest radiocarbon date range for Sriksetra, OZN909, can be calibrated to 50–200 CE (figure 6.20). The sample came from the lower layers of Tabet-ywa, a mound of iron slag which is more than two metres deep and covers an area of fourteen thousand square metres (figures 6.21 and 6.22). It is 120 metres north of the northwest corner of the palace. Four hundred metres to the northeast, extensive brick ruins three metres below the surface were briefly exposed by treasure hunters in 2006. This digging was recorded at the time by the author and Archaeology Field School staff. The holes have since been refilled. It seems to have been a significant structure, perhaps a ritual or administrative centre preceding the palace. Excavation of this complex would be a difficult task as it is below the water table. Just to the east are two groups of stone Buddhist triads (Luce 1985, vol. 2, plate 12) preserved in modern buildings that are used as archaeology stores.

Of key significance in this area is a two-sided stele (figure 6.23) that was found in the old bed of the central canal (figure 6.22). This stone, with a warrior and his followers on one side and a throne guarded by two female figures on the other, may date to the period during which

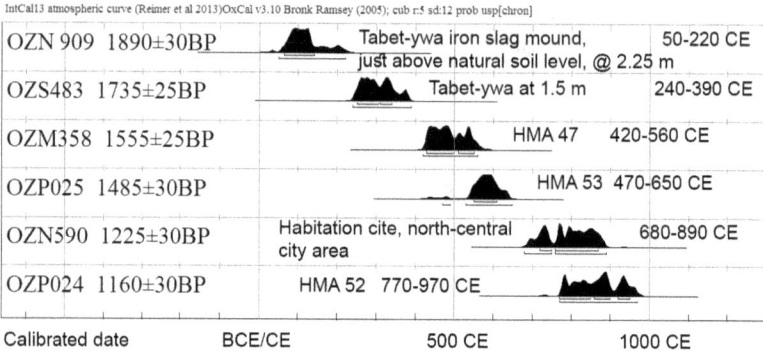

IntCal13 atmospheric curve (Reimer et al 2013)OxCal v3.10 Bronk Ramsey (2005); cub r.5 sd:12 prob usp[chron]

OZN 909	1890±30BP	Tabet-ywa iron slag mound, just above natural soil level, @ 2.25 m	50-220 CE
OZS483	1735±25BP	Tabet-ywa at 1.5 m	240-390 CE
OZM358	1555±25BP	HMA 47	420-560 CE
OZP025	1485±30BP	HMA 53	470-650 CE
OZN590	1225±30BP	Habitation cite, north-central city area	680-890 CE
OZP024	1160±30BP	HMA 52 770-970 CE	

| Calibrated date | BCE/CE | 500 CE | 1000 CE |

FIGURE 6.20
Source: Bob Hudson.

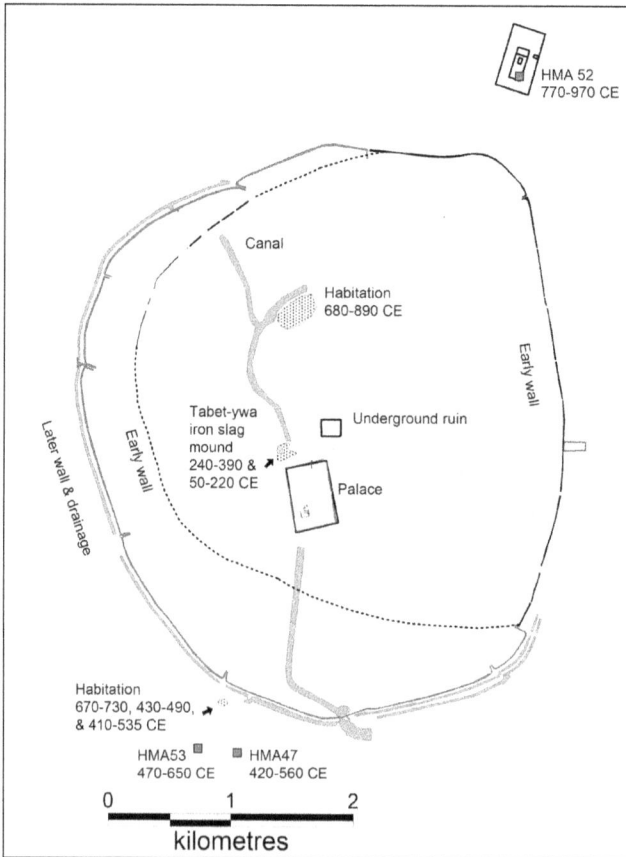

FIGURE 6.21
Source: Bob Hudson.

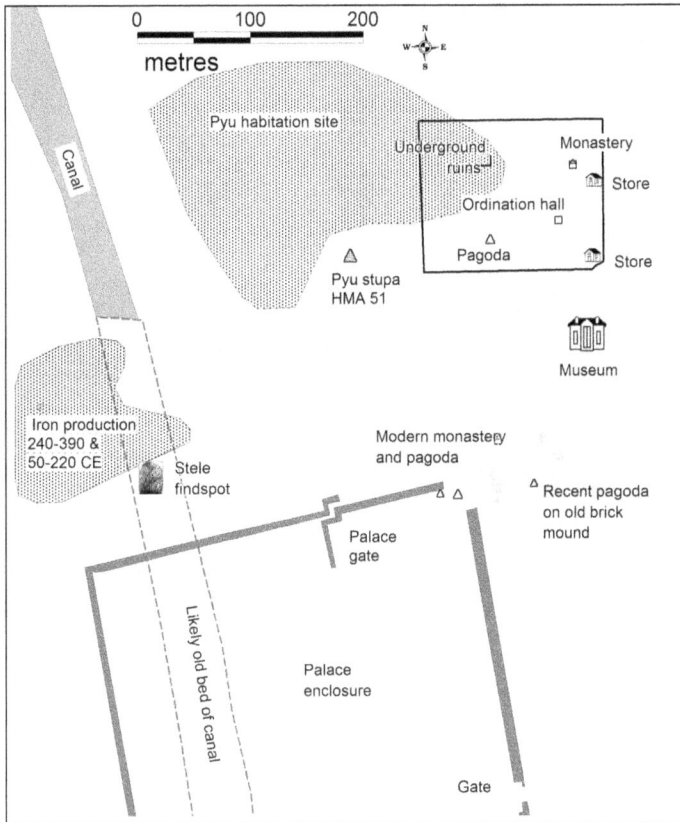

FIGURE 6.22
Source: Bob Hudson.

iron production was taking place (Hudson and Lustig 2008; Gutman and Hudson 2012–13).

More than half the resources put into the construction of buildings at Sriksetra were used outside the enclosure walls (Hudson and Lustig 2008). By 420–570 CE, a radiocarbon date (figure 6.20) for HMA 47, a brick complex outside the south wall (figures 6.21 and 6.24), shows that construction activity was well established. Finds here include earthenware votaries showing Buddha in the posture of meditation (figure 6.25) and fragments of a plaque (figure 6.26) similar to fragments found at Kyaukkat-gon, four hundred metres to the east (Thiripyanchi U Mya 1961, fig. 69; Luce 1985, vol. 2, plates 38–39).

FIGURE 6.23
Source: Bob Hudson.

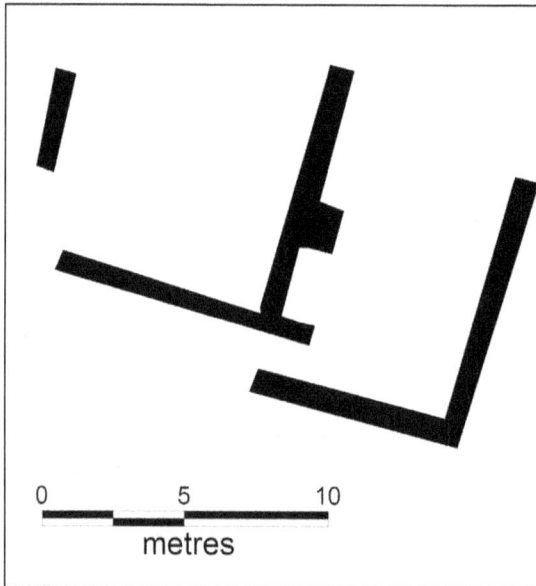

FIGURE 6.24
Source: Bob Hudson.

FIGURE 6.25
Source: Bob Hudson.

FIGURE 6.26
Source: Bob Hudson.

With more than 260 urn burials, HMA 53 (figure 6.21) is clearly a site with specialist funerary functions. Excavation has revealed a series of platforms, with steps from the north approaching the higher, central platform (figure 6.27). A radiocarbon date range of 530–650 CE was obtained from an ash lens in the middle of the upper platform. This dates activity at the building, not its construction period. The ash is contained in a discrete area (figure 6.28), not spread over the building as it would be if the structure had burnt down. Many of the urns are drum-shaped, with castellation and domed lids (figure 6.29). The bone in the pots is fragmented. The discovery of a stone pestle in the debris (figure 6.30) suggests that skeletal material may have been reduced by pounding to fit into the pots. HMA 53 is maintained under a roof as a site museum.

A somewhat predictable result comes from OZN590, charcoal recovered from material dug up by treasure hunters who were looking for beads,

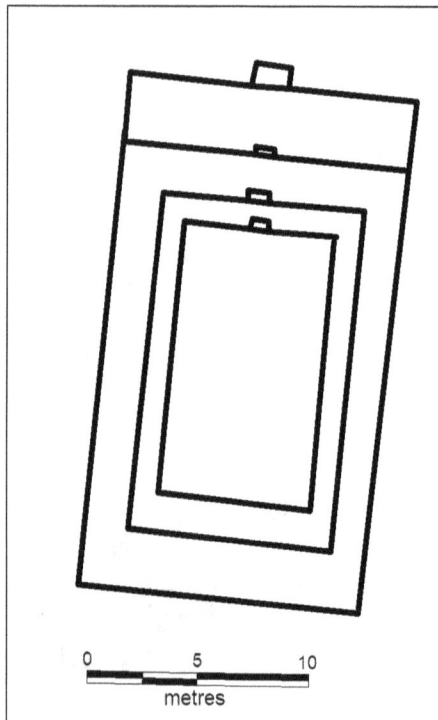

FIGURE 6.27   HMA 53.
Source: Bob Hudson.

FIGURE 6.28 HMA 53.
Source: Bob Hudson.

FIGURE 6.29 HMA 53.
Source: Bob Hudson.

FIGURE 6.30   HMA 53.
Source: Bob Hudson.

gold and spindle whorls in an old habitation site (figure 6.21). The sample covers the range 680–890 CE. This is in keeping with the currently accepted chronology of the Vikrama dynasty that is named on a series of stone burial urns; provided, of course, that the dates on the urns are Myanmar era, and not based on earlier calendars, an issue on which there is still room for debate (San Win 2003; Tun Aung Chain 2003).

A later funerary site, HMA 52, is located within the north Pyu-taik, a walled compound northeast of the city (figures 6.21 and 6.31). At least ninety-seven cremation burials in relatively simple round pots with paddle-impressed decoration (figure 6.32) were associated with the date range 770–970 CE.

The most significant radiocarbon date for the early functioning of Sriksetra, though, is the Tabet-ywa iron site. It suggests that iron was being produced, by burning a mixture of charcoal and haematite in furnaces, between the latter half of the first and the very early third centuries CE. Iron blooms from the production site would have been available to be forged into nails, both functional and symbolic (such as the nails more than a metre long in the Hmawza museum), and other hardware. By the

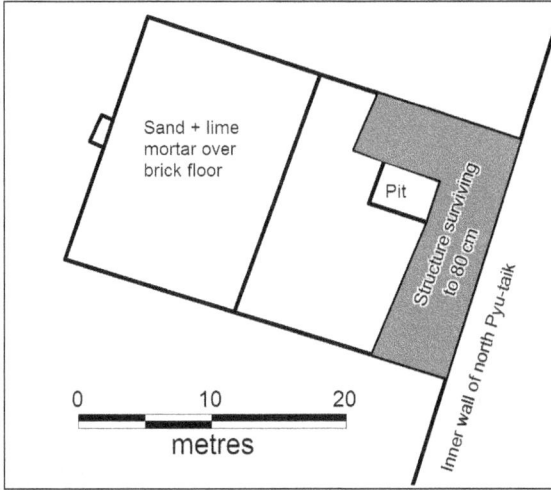

FIGURE 6.31   HMA 52.
Source: Bob Hudson.

FIGURE 6.32   HMA 52. Cremation burial.
Source: Bob Hudson.

period 50–220 CE, then, this important economic activity was taking place in the heart of the city.

Discussion

The radiocarbon dates we have so far suggest that Beikthano was functioning by the period 60–220 CE, Halin by 120–250 CE and Sriksetra by 50–220 CE. These date ranges are consistent between the three centres. They suggest that we are looking at the independent and effectively simultaneous development (Hudson 2014) of a number of walled cities, all with characteristic corridor gates. Such gates are common in 2nd century BCE India, though, curiously, the Indian examples project outward from the walls (see, for example, Yule 2008), while the Myanmar examples project inward. Corridor gates are also seen in the Rakhine walled cities of Dhanyawadi and Vesali (Thin Kyi 1970; Hudson 2005a), and one was recently excavated by Kyaw Myo Win at the central plains Pyu city of Pinle/ Maingmaw. As we see at Halin, the gates controlled human movement, although finds of Buddhist scriptural extracts and "magical" iron artefacts buried within the gates of Sriksetra (Sein Maung Oo 1993) suggest that there may also have been concern to keep out intruders from the spirit world, or at least to provide a kind of magico-religious backup for the authority of the gatekeepers.

Who were these urban folk we call (*pace* Aung-Thwin) the Pyu? The pottery excavation at Halin suggests that there is no need to propose an immigration around 100 CE of city-building Tibeto-Burman speakers, because that group may have been present since at least 2500 BCE as part of the expansion of Sino-Tibetan-speaking agriculturalists west and southwest from China (this model is discussed in Bellwood 2005).

An alternative hypothesis is that they were a population formed from the admixture of those incoming Neolithic agriculturalists and people descended from the first modern *Homo sapiens* expansion between seventy thousand and fifty-five thousand years ago, who are known in Myanmar by their stone tools (Movius 1943) and more broadly in the region by DNA studies (Oppenheimer 2004; Soares, Ermini et al. 2009). An expansion of population around the late first millennium BCE and the early first millennium CE from the economically booming Iron Age settlements of the Samon valley (Hudson 2005b; Moore 2007; Pautreau 2007; Pautreau, Coupey et al. 2010) coincided with the selective adoption of Indic ritual, religion, imagery, architecture and notions of kingship. Indic information had been available in transferable form since the late centuries BCE when the *Arthasastra* (Shamasastry 1915), effectively a management handbook for urbanized leadership, was compiled in India. But, as we have seen at Beikthano, where early burial urns suggest that while bricks and cremation had been adopted by the second century CE there was as yet no interest in Indic auspicious symbols or stamped pottery technology, it did not all come at once.

The specific mechanism of transfer of ideas and technologies in the "Indianization" process is beyond the scope of this chapter, and not directly relevant to the topic of radiocarbon dating. For the present purposes, the selective adoption and adaptation of Indic notions by the occupants of early Myanmar is taken as a given. The motivation for enclosing clusters of settlements within brick walls may have been because that was how a book, or a returned traveller, or a Brahmin, or discussion over campfires along trade routes, or popular wisdom, said a royal leader should live. We could reasonably use the term "cosmological" for basing this kind of settlement on an Indic ideal, though, as will be suggested below, the physical form of the walled cities seems to have owed more to engineering decisions that to cosmological directives. This is not to say that there would have been no magico-religious content. In the early Bagan period we have a description of extensive rituals associated with construction of a palace (Blagden 1923). We might imagine, perhaps, similar rituals at Sriksetra as scriptural extracts were buried within the gates (Sein Maung Oo 1993) or as pairs of protective iron ogres and ogresses (Hudson and Lustig 2008, p. 293), like those now held in the National Museum, were enshrined.

The existence of Beikthano, Halin and Sriksetra around the second century CE is relevant to ongoing discussion about the shape of Myanmar's ancient cities. Scholars have at times proposed that if a ruined wall is oval, it is likely to be early, while later cities are square or rectangular. This generalization is contradicted by Halin, which despite having rounded corners is essentially rectangular, given the undulating landscape. I would suggest instead that an eccentric shape suggests that the wall was enclosing existing sites, while a more rectangular shape was built to contain future structures. There are recent examples of oddly shaped enclosures in the Kabaw valley on the Myanmar–India border. Earthworks at Yazagyo, Myothit and Khampat were pointed out to me, Pamela Gutman and

Tampawaddy Win Maung when we visited the area in 2008 as being "ancient" city walls. However, their age and purpose is apparent from the historical records of the region. Existing villages were enclosed in the 19th century by ditches and stockades to keep out the marauding Chin (Carey and Tuck 1895; Grant Brown 1911).

At Halin, Iron Age burials have been found under and within the walls, but the bulk of pre-urban occupation seems to have been around the salt fields (figure 6.12) south of the walls (Hudson 2009, 2010). So, hypothetically, construction preceded occupation. At Sriksetra, by contrast, we can suggest that the oval walls were built around existing structures or villages, perhaps including the iron production site, although the sloping landscape may also have had an influence. The two square, moated sites at Sriksetra, the central palace and the structure known as Beikthano-myo, outside the south wall (Hudson 2007) would have been purpose-built to be occupied after construction.

Defence seems an unlikely reason for wall construction. Apart from swordsmen riding mythical beasts on terracotta plaques at Kinmungyon (ASI 1925) and Mathigyagon-Gwebindet (ASI 1928) at Sriksetra and at building PL20 at Pinle/Maingmaw (figures 6.1 and 6.33), excavated in 2010, there is nothing that compares, say, with the triumphant war reliefs on the walls of Angkor which testify to battles with the neighbouring Cham. Iron excavated at Beikthano is architectural, not military (Aung Thaw 1968). A few iron caltrops were found at Halin, but on the best evidence available the city was attacked just once, put out of action and never repaired. There is no repository of weapons known so far. The famous Chinese description of the idyllic life of the inhabitants of a Pyu city (Luce 1961) suggests that, in their relatively isolated location, the Pyu may have been too peaceful for their own good (the external and internal stresses that may have contributed to the decline of the Pyu system are discussed in Hudson 2004, pp. 148–53).

Conclusion

This chapter has looked at the available radiocarbon dates in their best light. While the science that provided the results is uncontroversial, there is always room for critical analysis of the context of the samples, just as there is always room for more radiocarbon dates to support other archaeological and historical evidence. The data has the potential to help periodize sites on

FIGURE 6.33 Pinle/Maingmaw.
Source: Bob Hudson.

the basis of their structure and assemblage, as example the variation over time in architecture and pottery styles at BTO 32, HMA 53 and HMA 52, and the relationship between objects such as the putatively dated HMA 47 plaque and similar plaques at other sites.

More immediately, we can suggest that on the available evidence from the radiocarbon dates, Myanmar's three biggest early urban period or "Pyu" cities — Beikthano, Halin and Sriksetra — were operational in the period between the late 1st and early 3rd century CE. When Bagan expanded, these sites had been functioning for many centuries, agriculturally if not administratively, as indeed they continue to do today (Stargardt, Amable et al. 2012). Their landholdings and irrigation works would have provided a useful economic base for the 11th–13th century Bagan Empire. Exactly how this transition occurred, the fading away of the Pyu cities and the incorporation of their territories into Bagan, remains one of the key questions facing researchers of early Myanmar.

Acknowledgements and Technical Notes

In 2014, Halin, Beikthano and Sriksetra received UNESCO World Heritage status.

This paper was first presented at the "Early Myanmar and its Global Connections" conference, Bagan, February 2012. Radiocarbon dates in the OZ series were provided by a grant from AINSE, the Australian Institute of Nuclear Science and Engineering. The carbon samples were processed by Dr Geraldine Jacobsen and her team on the ANTARES nuclear accelerator at ANSTO, the Australian Nuclear Science and Technology Organisation. My thanks as always go to the Myanmar Department of Archaeology, National Museum and Library for access to archaeological sites, and to Nyein Lwin, Thein Lwin, Win Kyaing, Kyaw Myo Win, Win Maung (Tampawaddy) and Pamela Gutman.

Archaeological sites are referred to by their Archaeology Department identification letters and numbers. Myanmar language references used in this paper have been read in English translation, thanks to the efforts of several professional translators and academic colleagues. Maps and photographs are by the author unless otherwise indicated.

References

ASB. *Report of the Superintendent, Archaeological Survey of Burma*. Rangoon: Office of the Superintendent, Government Printing, 1906–65.

ASI. *Annual Report of the Archaeological Survey of India*. Delhi: Manager of Publications, 1902–36.

Aung Myint. "Site Characteristics of Pyu and Pagan Ruins. A Comparative Study of the Dry Areas in Southeast Asia". International Seminar, Kyoto, Japan, 1998.

Aung Thaw. *Report on the Excavations at Beikthano*. Rangoon: Revolutionary Government of the Union of Burma, Ministry of Union Culture, 1968.

———. *Historical Sites in Burma*. Rangoon: Ministry of Union Culture, 1972.

Aung-Thwin, Michael, and Maitrii Aung-Thwin. *A History of Myanmar since Ancient Times*. London: Reaktion, 2012.

Bayliss, A., G. McCormac, and H. Plicht. "An Illustrated Guide to Measuring Radiocarbon from Archaeological Samples". *Physics Education* 39, no. 2 (2004): 137–44.

Bellwood, Peter. "Early Burmese Urbanisation: Inspired Independence or External Stimulus? (Review of Stargardt, Janice 1990 *The Ancient Pyu of Burma*)". *Review of Archaeology* 13, no. 2 (1992): 1–7.

————. "Smokescreens?" *Review of Archaeology* 14, no. 2 (1993): 33–35.

————. *First Farmers: The Origins of Agricultural Societies*. Oxford: Blackwell, 2005.

Blagden, C.O., ed. *Epigraphia Birmanica*, vol. 3, pt. 1. Rangoon: Superintendent of Government Printing. Union of Burma, 1923.

Bronk Ramsey, Christopher. *OxCal 3.9*. Oxford: Oxford Radiocarbon Accelerator Unit, 2002.

Bronson, Bennet. "(Review of) *Report on the Excavations at Beikthano*. Aung Thaw". *Asian Perspectives* 12 (1969): 142–43.

Carey, Bertram S., and H.N. Tuck. *The Chin Hills: A History of the People, Our Dealings with Them, Their Customs and Manners, and a Gazetteer of Their Country*. Rangoon: Superintendent, Government Printing, Burma, 1895.

Fink, D., M. Hotchkis, Q. Hua, G. Jaconsen, A.M. Smith, U. Zoppi, D. Child, C. Mifsud, H. van der Gaast, A. Williams and M. Williams. The ANTARES AMS facility at ANSTO. *Nuclear Instruments & Methods in Physics Research Section B, Beam Interactions with Materials and Atoms*, B223–B224 (2004): 109–15.

Grant Brown, G.E.R. *Burma Gazetteer, Upper Chindwin District, Volume A*. Rangoon, Superintendent, Government Printing and Stationery, Union of Burma, 1911.

Gutman, Pamela, and Bob Hudson. "A First-century Stele from Sri Ksetra". *Bulletin de l'École Française d'Extrême-Orient* 99 (2012/13): 17–46.

Hua, Q., U. Zoppi, A.A. Williams, and A.M. Smith. "Small-Mass AMS Radiocarbon Analysis at ANTARES". *Nuclear Instruments and Methods in Physics Research*, B223–224 (2004): 284–92.

Hudson, Bob. *The Origins of Bagan*. PhD dissertation, University of Sydney, 2004 <http://hdl.handle.net/2123/638>.

————. "Ancient Geography and Recent Archaeology: Dhanyawadi, Vesali and Mrauk-u". *The Forgotten History of Arakan Conference*. Chulalongkorn University, Bangkok, 2005a.

————. "A Pyu Homeland in the Samon Valley: A New Theory of the Origins of Myanmar's Early Urban System". *Myanmar Historical Commission Conference Proceedings*, vol. 2, pp. 59–79. Yangon, Ministry of Education, Union of Myanmar, 2005b.

————. "Sriksetra Survey Map 2005–2007". *SOAS Bulletin of Burma Research* 5 (2007): 1–2.

————. "Recent Excavations, Conservation and Presentation of Inhumation Burials at Halin, Myanmar (Burma)". *Bioarchaeology in Southeast Asia and the Pacific: Newsletter* 5 (2009): 3–7.

————. "Completing the Sequence: Excavations in 2009 Confirm Neolithic, Bronze and Iron Age Burials at Halin, Myanmar (Burma)". *Bioarchaeology in Southeast Asia and the Pacific: Newsletter* 6 (2010): 18–23.

————. "A Mobile Phone? Yes, I Want One! A Royal City? Yes, I Want One! How International Technology Met Local Demand in the Construction of Myanmar's First Cities, 1800 Years Ago". *Suvannabhumi* 6, no. 1 (2014): 2–25.

Hudson, Bob, and Terry Lustig. "Communities of the Past: A New View of the Old Walls and Hydraulic System at Sriksetra, Myanmar (Burma)". *Journal of Southeast Asian Studies* 39, no. 2 (2008): 269–96.

Hudson, Bob, and Nyein Lwin. "Earthenware from a Firing Site in Myanmar (Burma) Dates to More Than 4,500 Years Ago". *Bulletin of the Indo-Pacific Prehistory Association* 32 (2012): 19–22.

Lay, Maxwell G. *Handbok of Road Technology*. New York: Spon Press, 2009.

Legge, James. *A Record of Buddhistic Kingdoms: Being an Account by the Chinese Monk Fa-Hien of his Travels in India and Ceylon (A.D. 399–414) in Search of the Buddhist Books of Discipline*. Oxford: Clarendon Press, 1886.

Luce, G.H. "Burma's Debt to Pagan". *Journal of the Burma Research Society* 22, no. 3 (1932): 120–27.

————., ed. *Man Shu (Book of the Southern Barbarians)*. Data paper 44. Southeast Asia Program, Cornell University, 1961.

————. *Phases of Pre-Pagan Burma*. Oxford: Oxford University Press, 1985.

Mahlo, Dietrich. *The Early Coins of Myanmar (Burma)*. Bangkok: White Lotus, 2012.

Moore, Elizabeth. *Early Landscapes of Myanmar*. Bangkok: River Books, 2007.

Movius, Hallam L. "The Stone Age in Burma". *Transactions of the American Philosophical Society* 32, no. 3 (1943): 341–94.

Myint Aung. "The Excavations at Halin". *Journal of the Burma Research Society* 53, no. 2 (1970): 55–62.

Myo Theingyi Cho. "Beikthano Find Resolves an Historical Mystery". *Myanmar Times*, 2003.

Ogata, Masanori, Ichiro Tsutsumi, Yorikazu Shimotsuma, and Nobuko Shiotsu. "Origin of the World's Standard Gauge of Railway is in the Interval of Wheel Ruts of Ancient Carriages". *The 3rd International Conference on Business & Technology Transfer, Japan Society of Mechanical Engineers* 3 (2006): 98–103.

Oppenheimer, Stephen. *Out of Eden: The Peopling of the World*. London: Robinson, 2004.

Pautreau, Jean-Pierre. *Ywa Htin: Iron Age burials in the Samon Valley, Upper Burma*. Chiang Mai: Mission Archéologique française au Myanmar, 2007.

Pautreau, Jean-Pierre, Anne-Sophie Coupey, and Aung Aung Kyaw. *Excavations in the Samon Valley: Iron Age Burials in Myanmar*. Chiang Mai: Mission Archéologique francaise au Myanmar, 2010.

Pe Maung Tin and G.H. Luce. *The Glass Palace Chronicle of the Kings of Burma*. Rangoon: Rangoon University Press, 1923.

Reimer, P.J., M.G.L. Baillie, E. Bard, A. Bayliss, J.W. Beck, P.G. Blackwell, C. Bronk

Ramsey et al. *INTCAL 09 and MARINE09 Radiocarbon Age Calibration Curves, 0–50,000 Years Cal BP*. Tucson: University of Arizona, 2009.

San Shwe. "The Culture of Vishnu City (Beikthano), Upper Myanmar". Paper presented at the European Association of Southeast Asian Archaeologists conference, London, 2004.

San Win. "Dating the Hpayahtaung Pyu Stone Urn Inscription". *Myanmar Historical Research Journal* 11 (2003): 15–22.

Scott, E.M., T.C. Aitchison, D.D. Harkness, and M.S. Bazter. "An Overview of All Three Stages of the International Radiocarbon Intercomparison". *Radiocarbon* 32, no. 3 (1990): 309–19.

Sein Maung Oo. "Ancient Sriksetra". *Myanmar Ancient Cities (in Burmese)*, pp. 111–69. Yangon: Ministry of Information, News and Periodicals Enterprise, 1993.

Shamasastry, R., trans. *Kautilya's Arthashastra*. Bangalore: Government Press, 1915.

Soares, Pedro, Luca Ermini, Noel Thomson, Maru Mormina, Teresa Rito, Arne Rohl, Antonio Salas, Stephen Oppenheimer, Vincent Macaulay, and Martin B. Richards. "Correcting for Purifying Selection: An Improved Human Mitochondrial Molecular Clock". *American Journal of Human Genetics* 84 (2009): 1–20.

Stargardt, Janice. *The Ancient Pyu of Burma: Early Pyu Cities in a Man-Made Landscape*. Cambridge: PACSEA, 1990.

———. "The Battle of Beikthano". *Review of Archaeology* 14, no. 2 (1993): 26–32.

———. Urbanization before Indianization at Beikthano, Central Burma, c. 1st Century BC – 3rd Century AD?" In *Proceedings of the 5th International Conference of the European Association of Southeast Asian Archaeologists, Paris*, edited by P.-Y. Manguin, vol. 1, pp. 125–38. Hull: Centre for Southeast Asian Studies, University of Hull, 1994.

Stargardt, Janice, G. Amable, and B. Devereux. "Irrigation is Forever: A Study of the Post-destruction Movement of Water across the Ancient Site of Sri Ksetra, Central Burma". In *Satellite Remote Sensing: A New Tool for Archaeology*, edited by R. Lasaponara and N. Masini, pp. 247–68. Dordrecht: Springer, 2012.

Thaw Kaung. "Beikthano, Vishnu City: An Ancient Pyu Centre". *Myanmar Perspectives* 2, no. 6 (1998): 97.

Thin Kyi. "Arakanese Capitals: A Preliminary Survey of Their Geographical Siting". *Journal of the Burma Research Society* 53, no. 2 (1970): 1–13.

Thiripyanchi U Mya. *Votive Tablets of Burma (in Burmese)*. Rangoon: Ministry of Union Culture, 1961.

Tun Aung Chain. "The Kings of the Hpayahtaung Urn Inscription". *Myanmar Historical Research Journal* 11 (2003): 1–14.

Yule, Paul. "Early Forts in Eastern India". *Antiquity* 82, no. 316 (2008) <http://antiquity.ac.uk/projgall/yule/> (accessed 6 September 2016).

7

Ta Mok Shwe-Gu-Gyi Temple Kyaukse and Bagan[1]

Elizabeth Howard Moore and
Win Maung (Tampawaddy)[2]

The processes by which Buddhism was introduced and mediated in the culturally specific context of Kyaukse are exemplified by the Ta Mok Shwe-gu-gyi temple complex. While to some degree its development was stimulated through its relation to Bagan, Ta Mok's principal identity is local. In this context, it deepens our understanding of the complex interrelationships and definitions that constituted Bagan and questions normative concepts of centre and periphery. The archaeology of Ta Mok authenticates national traditions of the founding of the eleven *khayaing* of Kyaukse by King Anawrahta (1044–77 CE) (Than Swe 1994, p. 19). Pyu (2nd to 9th century CE) pottery, burnished wares, and bones possibly dating to 3000 BCE from Ta Mok highlight earlier connections to other regions. Thus, in both its prehistoric and historic dimensions, the Ta Mok evidence demonstrates the nuanced manner in which global ideas and styles were used to address issues of active local concern.

Chronology of the Site

The Shwe-gu-gyi temple complex, 9.65 kilometres west of Kyaukse, is located inside the Ta Mok fort, the only one of the nine Pan Laung Shwe-gu ("golden cave") located within the *khayaing* fort wall. Based on the plan, brickwork and iconography, five features of the complex are dated here to the reign of Anawrahta: the central temple, two *gu* or small caves on the southwest of the complex, the *thein* or ordination hall, the innermost of the encased images of the Buddha in the southwest *gu*, and a row of three images of the Buddha in the *thein* and the *palin* or thrones of these images.

Based again on stylistic grounds, we argue that Myit-taw Narapatisithu (1174–1211 CE) enlarged the central temple and added an upper storey.[3] The interior and upper storey of the main temple and other buildings such as the ordination hall and images of the Buddha were repeatedly encased and redecorated from the 11th to 14th century CE. However, as described below, the many unique aspects of the temple set out new parameters for the art, patronage and chronology of wider Bagan.

The earliest structure that has been unearthed is located on the northeast of the two-storey temple: a square building provisionally dated to the 8th to 10th century CE late Pyu period, with burial urns at the foundation level. There are additional ash and bone deposits without urns extending south along the east side of the temple complex that date to the same period or earlier. There has not previously been any Pyu settlement documented in the Kyaukse area or along the Pan Laung River. However, the Ta Mok Pyu were certainly cognizant of and probably trading with the Pyu tribes of the sizeable walled site of Pinle (Maingmaw), located forty kilometres to the southwest on the Zawgyi River. In addition to the Pyu burial urns and structure, evidence of earlier habitation at Ta Mok was excavated in June 2011 on the north edge of the temple complex. This consisted of a cache of bone, ash and hard thin burnished black ware similar to sherds found in Bronze Age levels at Halin, dated to the late first millennium BCE and possibly earlier. We discuss this further below.

The Ta Mok chronology has been explored by U Win Maung (Tampawaddy) following discussions on the *shwe-gu* tradition with U Maung Maung Tin (Mahaweiza) in the late 1980s, with closer documentation since

2008 when permission was received from the Department of Archaeology, Ministry of Culture, to remove a 14th-century stupa encasing the two-storey temple and part of the *thein*. We summarize here the architecture, stucco decoration, sculpture, traces of painting, pottery and other finds from the temple complex. This is preceded by a short account of the traditional history of the region and the relationship of the *shwe-gu* and *khayaing*, as it is from this regional context that much of the unique architectural and seemingly ritual character of the temple and site are best understood.

Tradition and Prehistory of Kyaukse

The Ta Mok Shwe-gu-gyi ("large golden cave") temple is said to have been founded by King Thiri-dhamma (Asoka) when he spread Buddhism throughout the nine divisions and places (ko-taing-ko-htana) at the time of solar "escape" following a lunar eclipse.[4] The original name of the temple, Mu-taw, has been retained in the present wording of *ta-mok*, a measure of approximately eighteen inches from the thumb to the elbow.

FIGURE 7.1   Ta Mok northwest compound seen from the upper level showing the *thein* (ordination hall) during excavation in 2010. Photo: Tan and Bagan Min Min Oo.

The temple was one of nine *shwe-gu* temples said to have been repaired by Anawrahta, although it is the instigation of the Kyaukse canal system which is the most well-known work of this ruler. Traditional chronicles note that, upon returning from a military expedition, he slept on the summit of Pyetkaywe Hill (Kayut-taung), overlooking the Kyaukse Plain. The king dreamt of three snakes that he cut into parts. In the morning, when he saw the same layout of rivers on the plains, his dream was interpreted for him by soothsayers to mean the Pan Laung, Zawgyi and Myit Ngeh Rivers. As a result, he built four weirs on the Pan Laung (Kinta, Nganaingzthin, Pyaungbya, Kume) and five on the Zawgyi, but none on the Myit Ngeh, which by the early 20th century still had not been structurally controlled (*Burma Gazetteer* 1925, pp. 66–67; Harvey 1967, p. 25; Pe Maung Tin and Luce 1960, p. 96).

Damming of the streams flowing southeast to north across the Kyaukse plain began in the earlier first millennium CE, but the date is debated. Luce noted that the original system was probably not developed by the Burmans, but possibly by recent Mon migrants from the north coming via Nanzhao (Luce 1960, pp. 326–27). Setting up an ethnic dichotomy to explain the local water management may not be relevant, however, as small-scale weirs and exploitation of seasonal water bodies were an intrinsic part of the augmentation of rice cultivation and origins of massive Pyu walled sites such as Pinle and satellite forts such as Ta Mok (Moore 2007, pp. 247–48). The suitability of these systems to the local ecology is demonstrated by their continued use, with the old canals augmenting the scarce rainfall (784 mm) of this region (*Burma Gazetteer* 1925, pp. 5, 13).

Anawrahta's canal system was expanded by Alaungsithu (r. 1113–67 CE) and codified by Narapatisithu within three years of his ascending to the throne (Yin Myo Thu 2011, p. 6). Narapatisithu is also said to have constructed the stone weir that joined the Ta Mok canal to the Samon River (*Burma Gazetteer* 1925, p. 15). The Bagan administration appointed a *thu-gyi* at each *khayaing* to oversee and report to the head administrative officer for all the villages (11-ywa thu-gyi).[5] As seen in Table 7.1, the *khayaing* administration, with a fort wall for rice storage and distribution, subsumed at least one or two *shwe-gu* temples.[6] Located along the Pan Laung, Zawgyi and Myit Ngeh Rivers, the *shwe-gu* and subsequently the *khayaing* were not only rich rice-producing areas, but strategically bridged lowland centres such as Bagan and Inwa to the upland resources of the Shan Plateau and beyond to Yunnan.

TABLE 7.1
Pan Laung Shwe-gu and Estimated Khayaing Fort Size

Khayaing	Present village	Township, River	Shwe-gu	Fort (ha)
Pin le	Myo twin	Myit tha, Samon/Pan Laung	none[a]	31
Pyi mana	Near Kume	Myit tha, Pan Laung	Shwe ku me	11
Myit tha	Myit tha	Myit tha, Pan Laung	Kyun hla	11
Ywa mon	Near Saba daw	Kyaukse, Pan Laung	Shwe inn	34
Myin gon daing	Myin kyeh daing	Kyaukse, Pan Laung	Kyet ma	59
Pa nan	Near Pan kwa	Kyaukse, Pan Laung	Panan; Ma gyi daw	4
Ta Mok	Near Nyaung bin zauk	Kyaukse, Pan Laung	Ta Mok	10
Thin daung	East of Thin daung	Kyaukse, Zawgyi	Zaw gyi River	4
Met kaya	Ay bya	Hsint kaing, Myit Ngeh	Zaw Gyi and Myit ngeh Rivers	17
Ta bet kar[b]	Hsint kaing	Hsint kaing, Myit Ngeh	Myit ngeh River	8
Kan lu	Kan myuu	Hsint kaing, Pan Laung	Wun pate; Saw ye	4.2

Notes:
[a] There is no Shwe-gu in the Pin le khayaing, as it lies midway between the Samon and Pan Laung Rivers.
[b] Win Maung (Tampawaddy) locates this site along the Myit ngeh, in contrast with Berliet's location on the Zaw Gyi River (2008, p. 197).

FIGURE 7.2   West facade showing areas of reconstruction, original stucco and preservation of portion of later encasing stupa in 2014. Photo: E. Moore.

FIGURE 7.2a   West facade showing ordination hall, main temple and preservation of portion of later encasing stupa in 2010. Photo: Tan and Bagan Min Min Oo.

FIGURE 7.3   The present junction of the Pan Laung and Samon Rivers, west of Ta Mok.
Photo: E. Moore 2010.

Ta Mok Location

Ta Mok is in the midst of fields (eighty metres above sea level), 1.34 kilometres from the juncture of the Pan Laung and Samon Rivers, ten kilometres northwest of Kyaukse. There is no Ta Mok village today, but surface finds of Bagan-period pottery are common in the western half of the area enclosed by the Ta Mok fort wall. Although much of the wall has eroded, excavations undertaken in 1999–2000 by Win Maung (Tampawaddy) of one section on the northwest of the wall (21°38′633″N, 96°03′289″E) exposed a brick wall two to three metres in height.

There is a monastery today at Ta Mok, and additional monasteries in the three surrounding villages: Nyaung bin zauk Tha-bye bin, Nyaung bin zauk kyaung and Kyaung pan kon Taw Ya kyaung. As there is at present no village at Ta Mok, the surrounding villages contribute to supporting the Ta Mok temple and monastery, as well as annual ceremonies to bless the rice fields around Ta Mok (Moore and Win Maung 2016, pp. 177–78).

To the south, at the village of Ngeh-to, is the Ngwe Twin Tu: Taw Ya, "silver well forest-monastery". A damaged stone slab donated by the three "Shan" brothers while they were *myosa* or governors and a broken *andagu* or small stone carved votary have been documented at this monastery. The inscription bears a date of 1300 CE (662 ME), noting that after Mekkhaya was destroyed, donations were made to renovate the old garden at the Ta Mok *khayaing*.[7] While Naung bin zauk and Ngeh-to villages trace their origins to Anawrahta's era, the villagers of Naung bin zauk rank their village as the chief contributor of rice to Ta Mok. Kyaung pan kon villagers date the village founding to the Inwa period, but also have a tradition that the blacksmith Maung Tin Deh, fleeing King Anawrahta at Bagan, was captured at Kyaung pan kon.[8] We postulate that the old Ta Mok village was either destroyed or its population dispersed after the Pinya period, when the last major donation was made to the Ta Mok complex. The discovery of the pre-Anawrahta artefacts at Ta Mok mentioned above has stimulated a new iteration of local history to include habitation during the first millennium CE Pyu era. As this suggests, the local village communities are closely involved in the archaeological and restoration work at Ta Mok that has turned it into a local centre of pilgrimage and donation.

Ta Mok Discovery and Dating

In 684 ME (1322 CE), Pyinba King Ussana enclosed the earlier Ta Mok *gu* and *thein* within a 27.89-metre high (61 taung) stupa, which we postulate was similar in shape to the Shwe-zi-gon stupa at Bagan. A large number of Bagan-period bricks (e.g., 40 × 21 × 6 cm) were used to construct the Pinya-era stupa, documented during its disassembly in 2008, as described below. Several small constructions identified as stucco-mixing tanks on the east and west of the central structure date to the 14th century CE Pinya period. Ussana's stupa was completed in the reign of Hsin-Phyu-thakin Kyaw-swa-min-gyi (1355–62 CE) and commemorated with a 1356 CE inscription. Ussana, together with his chief queen, made a royal pilgrimage from Inwa to Ta Mok Shwe-gu gyi in a Pyi-gyi-kyet-thwa barge modelled after an auspicious animal.[9] In an offering made to sustain the Sāsana for five thousand years, the king donated five fields and two male and two female slaves. Further donations to the temple are seen in a radiocarbon date of 1440–1640 CE from a burnt layer above a set of foundations on the southeast side of the main building.[10]

Over time, the stupa slowly fell into disrepair, and although there were periodic donations and refurbishments, bushes and vegetation gradually turned the stupa into a hill. In 1277 ME (1905 CE), donations were made by U San Htwa from Kyaung-pan-kon village, who had the face of the hill cleared of vegetation and raised a *hti* with a diamond bud on the summit. The height of the small stupa (*nyan*) plus the diamond bud was 6.1 metres.

In 1993, Amarapura Maha-ganda-yon-taik Ashin Sandawbatha, native to Ngeh-to village, came to settle at Ta Mok. While meditating inside an opening on the north side of the stupa, he noticed layers of brick in the small cell. Word reached U Win Maung (Tampawaddy), who as noted above was carrying out research to document the Pan Laung Shwe-gu. He visited the site in 1993 and in collaboration with Ashin Sandawbatha began work on the temple. In 1994 CE the broken bricks and debris were removed to reveal a brick structure on the south containing an image of the Buddha. In 2008, when permission to unearth the stupa was received from the Ministry of Culture, volunteers from local villages began to clear away the broken bricks. By 2009 (1371 ME, Taw-ta-lin Full Moon Day), the inner structure was fully revealed to expose the stucco work covering the surface; a base of circa 1.2 metres on all sides and a 3.65 metre wall on the southwest corner were left to show the plan and sectional view of the Pyinna stupa. By August 2011, a number of additional structures had been unearthed in the compound. The temple continues to be a focal point of local veneration and assistance, with volunteers from a factory at In-kon south of Kyaukse coming to the site every weekend and more than twelve thousand pilgrims arriving every month.[11] As of 2012, the site veneration, excavation and donation, combined community and archaeology in the ongoing work to document the principal structures is described below.[12]

Double *Gu* with Three Encased Images

Two back-to-back *gu* or cells located southwest of the two-storey building are dated here to the late 11th or early 12th century based on the style of the encased images of the Buddha and *palin* or thrones in each cell. The *gu* are 8.95 metres east to west and 3.2 metres wide, with the floor being 1.52 metres below ground level. We propose that, at the time of Anawrahta, the *gu* were located outside the temple wall; then, at the

TABLE 7.2
Buildings Unearthed in the Ta Mok Temple Complex as of 2012

No	Building	Location in complex	Stylistic date, CE	Length (m)	Width (m)	Notes
1	Double *gu*	SW	11–13th C	8.95	3.2	Total length, both *gu*
2	*Thein*	W	11–14th C	21.75	9.3	Total length with additions
3	Two-storey temple	C	11–13th C	18	12	Width at widest point
4	*Zayat* foundation	SW	Uncertain	7.4	7.4	Inner structure offset 1.26 (W); 1.18 (S); 1.0 (N); 0.54 (E)
5	*Ta-wa-gu* temple	SE	11–13th C	10	7	Width at widest point
6	Stucco-mixing tank	E	13–14th C	2.9	3.6	Among additional walls on the east
7	Naung-taw-gyi temple	NE	11–14th C	14.7	10	Foundation 1.95 m below ground level
8	Square structure with urns	NE	9–10th C	10.5	11.2	Measured on west and north; 2.26 m below ground level

FIGURE 7.4 Encased images of the Buddha in double *gu*. Photo: E. Moore 2010.

time of Narapatisithu's expansion, within the wall. With the building of the stupa by Ussana, the *gu* and the images in the *thein* described below appear to have been encased.

There are three encased images of the Buddha in both the east- and west-facing *gu*. On the west outer image, the nose and mouth can be attributed to the 12th century, but the smooth head without curls or *usnisa* indicates early 13th-century remodelling. Three thrones have been unearthed, widening from 40.3 to 56 centimetres from the inner to outermost throne, although the height (10.3 centimetres) remained consistent. Post holes have also been excavated between the *gu*, indicating a wooden superstructure.

The three encased images on the east are each on a higher and wider throne. The inner image dated stylistically to the 11th century CE has been partially excavated and repaired, leaving the face of this image visible at chest level of the taller encasing 12th century CE one. The increasing height of the encased images can be seen in the measurement from the forehead to the waist: the inner image is 86 centimetres, while the second image from forehead to waist measures 126 centimetres. The height increases from 120 to 180 centimetres for the outermost image, datable to the 13th century late Bagan period (measurements courtesy U Kyaw, retired from the Department of Archaeology). Terracotta snail-shell shaped hair curls were recovered from all three images, each moulded and attached to a slightly hardened layer of stucco on the head.[13]

One of the most indicative stylistic traits to identify the chronology of the encased images of the Buddha is the style of the throne or *palin* on which the image is seated. Fully appreciating the design changes which took place, it is necessary to detail the layering of the throne and the proportions of the seven layers and "waist" which make up the throne, and the use of these for modelling of the profile. The throne of the 11th century displays a distinct redented proportionality and stepped profile weighted towards the upper half of the throne. The upper section of four layers, for example, are 1/25th of the width of the lowest layer, with the waist indentation being 1/9th the lowest layer width. Thus, a throne with a lowermost width of 100 would have an upper-section of 98 and a waist of 96. In contrast, Pyu thrones of the 1–7th century CE have only two layers above and below, giving a much more rounded profile, with 1/30th and 1/10th for upper section and waist indentation. Konbaung thrones of the 19th century are once again different; elaborately layered but with all layers equal, achieving a less-stepped effect of indentation with a further diminishing of the waist, with ratios of 1/12 and 1/7 for upper section and waist indentation (Win Maung 2005, p. 2).

The thrones of the Ta Mok double *gu* encased images follow the typical pattern of 11th-century Bagan in the lotus throne of the innermost image.

This has a cup-like shape with upturned and downturned lotus petals, also seen at Taw-pon-lawka-nanda (IMP 315) and two structures at Kyauk Saga (IMP 1026 and 1029) (Pichard 1992–96, vols. 1 and 4). However, most thrones at Bagan are carved from bricks rather than stucco modelled on a brick core as seen at Ta Mok.

Thein or Ordination Hall

Northwest of the main two-storey temple is a rectangular west-facing *thein* (21.75 × 9.3 m) with three seated east-facing images of the Buddha along the west wall. The original building was repeatedly extended to the west. The last extension, based on the brick size and masonry, can provisionally be dated to the 15th century. A flat black stone *sima* (1.2 metres high) was found outside the *thein* wall of the easternmost section. The *sima* flares outward from a 40-centimetre-wide base with small "wings" to a width of 60 centimetres at the base of a triangular apex. Two additional *sima* stones have been unearthed under extensions to the west. One is an eroded round *sima* (50 cm) of marble and dated to the Pinya period. A second (70 cm long, with each face 10 cm) is a hexagonal grey sandstone inscribed with 13th-century late Bagan floral design.

The large seated images of the Buddha fill the back or eastern wall of the *thein*, their thrones showing repeated rebuilding that extended the thrones upward but not outward. The *palin* of the innermost image, stylistically datable to the late 11th or early 12th century, is similar in style to the *palin* in the double *gu* described above. Additional support for the dating comes from the right side of a 40-centimetre stucco face found at the base of the images. The face has a thin flaring nose, downturned eyes and a small V-shaped slightly smiling mouth, all characteristic of the late 11th to early 12th century era of Anawrahta and Kyanzittha (1084–1113 CE). Following the wish of the Sayadaw, the three images are being reconstructed, the central one circa 5 metres high.[14] When the Ussana-period stupa was built, the central image of the *thein* appears to have been encased but left visible via doors on the north and west. Based on the excavated layers, the sequence for the *thein* indicates a wooden superstructure with three images against a backdrop in Anawrahta's era, followed by the same plan made of brick, and then the exposure in an opening on the northwest of the Ussana-period stupa.

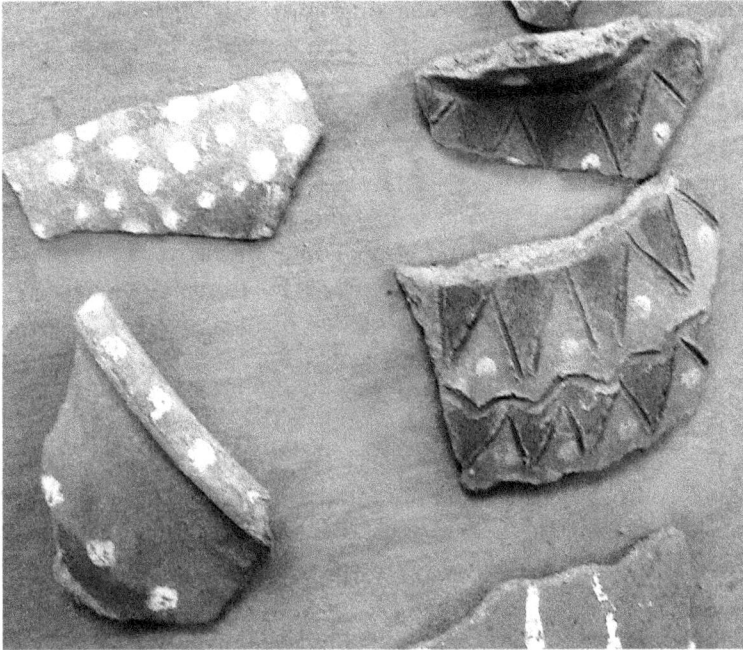

FIGURE 7.5   Painted sherds excavated from *thein* foundations. Photo: E. Moore 2011.

Comparisons with Bagan

Initial construction of the *thein* during the era of Anawrahta is supported by finds of flared jars and red and white painted pot sherds, recalling ones from the excavations of the Bagan palace attributed to Anawrahta and also Tagaung excavations.[15] There are in addition temples at Bagan with a row of three images (Pichard 1992–96, vols. 2, 5 and 6):[16]

1. Temple IMP 320 south of Wetkyi-in on the north side of the Sule Group, estimated date of 13th century CE;
2. Temple IMP 480 northeast of Le-myet-hna monastery complex, dated by epigraphy to 1223 CE;
3. Pahto-hta-mya (IMP 1605), estimated date of late 11th century CE;
4. Kya-hsin south Minnanthu (IMP 1219) with the central image in

bhūmisparśa mudra and the flanking images of Maitreya on the right and Avalokiteśvara on the left in *pralambasana* or European style, estimated date of 13 century CE;

5.   Kubyauk Nge (IMP 1391), dated from epigraphy to 1198 CE.

All of these temples, of which IMP 320 in the Sule group is one of the clearest examples, have a large central image flanked by smaller images. The Kubyauk Nge (IMP 1391) is of note both for the row of three images and other iconographic similarities, such as the frontal depiction of a lion akin to the fallen pediment at Ta Mok described below and the reclining image of the Buddha (Pichard 1992–96, vol. 5, p. 332, figs. 1391k, 1391s).[17]

Votive Tablets

Four types of tablet have been found under the central image of the *thein* on the west and the temple surrounds. Four tablets (14–15 cm high, 10 cm wide and 2 cm thick), provisionally dated to the 11–13th century CE, depict a single image of the Buddha in *bhūmisparśa mudra* surrounded by the eight scenes of the life of the Buddha. The central image is surmounted by a *takeh* or surround, with tall flame-like projections, a unique decorative device not seen at Bagan (Moore, Win Maung, and Htwe Htwe Win 2013). Two tablets show the Buddha in a standing posture on a lotus under a trefoil arch surrounded by eight stupas. The left hand is pendant in *varada mudra* and the right at breast level in *mahākārunika mudra*. Two other tablets depict the Buddha in *bhūmisparśa mudra* with the left leg above the right (Paryankasana) on a double lotus throne with traces of a two-line Pali inscription below the throne. Parallel examples from Bagan bear an inscription on the reverse noting they were donated by a higher village official or *Ka-lan-than-byin-min* (Mya 1961, vol. 1, figs. 78–80). As these details indicate, the tablets are largely similar to examples elsewhere, indicating donations to the temple by a range of patrons.

Main Two-Storey Temple Structure

The main two-storey temple, on the basis of the plan, arches and stucco decoration, is dated here to the late 11th to early 12th century. However, we propose that the original structure did not have a central pillar faced with four images of the Buddha; analogies for the Anawrahta-period structure are the Pahto-hta-mya (IMP1605), the 1113 CE Myinkaba Gūbyaukgyī (IMP 1327) and the Ngwe Hpaya Gu (IMP 1209?) (Pichard 1992–96, vol. 5). The plan of the central temple is similar to the Gu-ni (north, IMP 766), the Sein-nyet-ama (IMP 1085) and the Gu-taw-thit-hpaya (IMP 1486) at Bagan (Pichard 1992–95, vol. 5). While these, particularly the 13th-century Gu-taw-thit-hpaya (IMP 1486) south of Shwe-hsan-daw, give comparisons to Bagan, the parallels focus on details; none provides a model for the Ta Mok Shwe-gu-gyi temple complex. The parallels thus establish a relationship between Ta Mok and Bagan but they do not explain the dynamic. For example, innovations from Ta Mok could have moved from Kyaukse to Bagan rather than from Bagan outwards, the generally presumed centre-to-periphery paradigm.

As in some of the Bagan examples, the temple may have originally been one storey with a single north entry, main chamber and image on the south that was then enlarged with an antechamber on the north and a second storey in the reign of Narapatisithu. The antechamber can be entered from east and west as well as the north, with the side doors surmounted by a single pediment in contrast to the double pediments over the four principal entries. The *saing-paung* or ox-haunches are set at an angle of circa 15 degrees rather than the more usual 30-degree cant of *saing* at Bagan. Analogies for the overall profile of the temple are seen at the 1183 CE Sulamani (IMP 748) (Pichard 1992–96, vol. 4).

The central chamber is notable for the sixteen niches containing seated images of the Buddha, each 30 centimetres in height. Most images are in *bhūmisparśa mudra*, although five in side niches on the east side display the *dhyani mudra*. The central core is flanked by four images with traces of late Bagan painting remaining on the arch over the east-facing image, and an area of multiple or Thamboddha Buddha images remaining on the east entry arch.[18] As with the upper storey, the south-facing image is reclining; a painted inscription dated to 1322 CE (684 ME) remains on the upper part of a door arch on this side. The larger north-facing image of the Buddha (2.13 m) in *bhūmisparśa mudra* would have been built at this time, although encased with a second image in the late Bagan period. Two staircases in the antechamber lead to the upper storey.[19] The pointed arches of the upper level contrast with the rounded early Bagan images of the ground level, supporting our premise that the upper storey was added to the original temple. As with the ground level, images of the Buddha are seen flanking the central core: Birth on the west, Enlightenment on the north (the orientation of the temple), First Sermon on the east and Demise of the Buddha on the south.[20]

Orientation and Pre- and Proto-historic Significance of Ta Mok

The focus on the north fits with the orientation of the site, which from its prehistoric occupation appears to have faced this direction. The orientation, popularly related to Htwet-yat-lan or Htwet-pauk method and practice, is commonly linked to veneration of Maitreya, the future Buddha, also *weikza* and "going out" from rebirth through supernatural means, including lead and iron alchemy, graphic diagrams (*in*) and medicinal practices (Myanmar Language Commission 1993, p. 207; Rozenberg 2010, pp. 51, 162n7; Than Swe 2004, pp. 20–21).[21] The degree to which this type of veneration typifies the Ta Mok Shwe-gu-gyi temple is suggested by the orientation and popular belief; determining its ancient dimensions of course remains open to discussion. The significance of the temple, however, is also indicated by its central position within the *shwe-gu* and the *khayaing*, being the only

FIGURE 7.6 Upper level reclining image on the south depicting the Demise of the Buddha. Photo: Tan and Bagan Min Min Oo 2010.

shwe-gu located within a *khayaing* fort wall. Its earlier significance, from at least the first millennium CE, is seen in the prehistoric and Pyu mortuary finds from the north and northeast of the site. Auspiciousness following this orientation is indicated for over two thousand years at Ta Mok, a chronology itself giving grounds for a locally innovative and context-sensitive meaning for the Bagan-period structure. This premise is further supported by the unique stucco work which covers the surface, including a unique set of inscribed stucco *Jataka* depictions on the different tiers of the temple and a patterning of the lateral walls with a *marabein* design derived from palace screens and composed of multiple roundels.

Temple Encasement and Stucco Preservation

There are no examples of stucco *Jataka* depictions found at Bagan or elsewhere, with examples of surviving stucco roundels restricted at present to Bochomi Gubyauk (IMP 995) dated to the 13th century CE (Pichard 1992–96, vol. 4, pp. 219–23). There are similar paintings on the interior of caves at Shwe-gu-Oo-min (21°35′N, 96°12′E) east of Kyaukse, but no other contemporary examples of stucco work. In addition, although there are numerous examples of encased images of the Buddha and encased stupas and images of the Buddha at Bagan, the encasement of the temple within the Pinya-period stupa of King Ussana is unique. Excavation of additional structures in the compound has yielded post holes, indicating earlier wooden superstructures with foundations composed of brick of varying sizes (e.g., 40 × 21 × 6 cm; 43 × 23 × 6 cm; 44 × 21 × 7 cm; 48 × 23 × 7 cm). Stone such as mica schist is found at many of the door thresholds, a traditional guard against the "ground ogre", Mye-bok-bilu Ta-hseh-thuu-yeh (မြေဘုတ်ဘီလူး:တစေ့သူရဲ).[22]

As we noted above, much of the *khayaing* fort wall was dismantled by Ussana, who used the bricks to build the new stupa. However, stucco *Jatakas* on the earlier temple were protected at the time of encasement with a 2.5-centimetre layer of mud, with over seventy votive tablets (5 cm high, 3 cm wide) embedded into the mud layer. The tablets were all probably stamped from the same mould, showing the Buddha seated in *bhūmisparśa mudra* on a double lotus throne under a trefoil arch topped by an umbrella. Their use and treatment here indicates encasement of the temple more in the sense of *htarpanar* or sacred deposit than a simple augmentation.

Approximately eighty per cent of the exterior of the Ta Mok two-storey temple remains covered with stucco, also used to complete brick sculptures on the outside of the temple. The stucco work is detailed, filling the surface with zoomorphic, anthropomorphic and floral motifs. Sculptures include crowned *lokapala* or *Nat-min-gyi* on the upper storeys, four on each side of the temple, with two on the middle terrace and two on the uppermost. Similar figures, repaired in recent years and painted red, are seen at the Dhammayazika (1196 CE, no. 937, IMP 947), although these no longer have heads or the ornamental details seen at Ta Mok (Pichard 1985, plates 27–28).

The upper-storey corners are decorated with double-bodied mythical lions (*chinthe*) and *biluor* ogre heads below. Similar *chinthe* are seen on the corners of Nga-myet-hna temple near Mingalazedi (IMP 1410), although there the head is missing, with comparable *bilu* at the Sulamani temple (IMP 748). Alms bowls (*thabeik-myauk*) with a cup-shaped bell (*khaung-laung*) are seen on sixteen of the upper corners, having rings (*phaung-yit*), upper tiers (*Hsat-ta-wa-li* [*chattravali*]) and a lotus-bud finial. The bowls are decorated with a row of pearls and a bottom edge of upturned lotus petals, but not a more common "belt" around the mid-section. Each is set on a square pedestal decorated with eight upturned rounded diamond shapes (*sein-htaung-waing*), floral details and *bilu*.

The detailed stucco work is well seen on the pediments and tympanums over the doors of Ta Mok Shwe-gu-gyi. On the south, the tympanum bears a *galon* standing on a crowned *naga-min*, having two further *naga* draped around him. Below is a seated figure of the fertility goddess Sri, hands grasping floral strands curling up from two *nget-hsin* or elephant birds. On the east tympanum, Sri is seen again, raised on a lotus pedestal above the doorway arch with a large *kirttimukha*. The north upper pediment, recently recovered, bears a large frontally seated male lion. We postulate that the pediment was removed when the outer wall of the 14th-century stupa cut through the north face of the earlier temple. This was found facedown and carefully covered with hardened mud in front of the Naung-taw-gyi temple northeast of the two-storey temple during excavation in 2011. The pediment has now been cleaned and placed near the two-storey temple's north entry. The lion sits on the heads of three elephants, with a seated crowned figure above, possibly a *kinnari*, deva or *galon*.

Stucco covers the broad surface of the long, side walls of the main temple, with different patterning used on the upper (*taing-htaung*),

FIGURE 7.7 North seated lion pediment shortly after discovery. Photo: E. Moore 2011.

FIGURE 7.7a Detail of North lion pediment shortly after discovery.
Photo: E. Moore 2011.

FIGURE 7.8 Stucco detail of *nget-hsin* or *hti-hlaing-ka* elephant bird on *marabein* on west facade. Photo: Tan and Bagan Min Min Oo.

middle (*taik-ma-nan-yan*) and lower (*nyaung ywet*) sections. While this is common at Bagan, the detailed *marabein* or screen design such as seen in mural paintings at Bagan is unique. The *marabein* have multiple roundels arranged in rows, with an irregular number of circles varying from nine to seventeen in relation to the size of the area to be filled. The roundels contain figures of deva, animals and mythical creatures and, sometimes, floral patterns (*kanote-pan*). One panel of fifteen on the east side depicts a seated deva at the centre, with lions above and below, deer to the right and left, and the other ten roundels with various birds. However, in other panels there is no central figure, so while each roundel may be narrative, the overall scheme, if present, is not clear, as has been decoded for example in the "tapestry" roundels of the corner pavilions at Angkor Wat. Twelve types of mythical birds are seen, many in pairs, a feature also seen at Angkor (Roveda 2002, pp. 224–38). They include the mythical *lun-kyin*, intensely devoted to its mate, and the *nget-hsin* or elephant bird, a roc-like creature with a proboscis, also known as the *hti-hlaing-ka* (Pali: *hati-lain-ga*, *hatilinka*). There are also elephants, horses, *hintha* (*hangsa*, Brahminy duck), peacocks, egrets, owls, doves, hens, monkeys, human and *nat* figures, flower blossoms and buds.

On the upper and lower storey, upturned *sein-htaung* depict intertwined birds and lotus buds, two deer and a wheel of law (*dhamma-cakra*), *chinthe*, and human and *nat* figures. There is a *galon* on top of a triple *naga* on a side arch, recalling stucco work at Kusinara (IMP 1266) and a pentagonal stupa (IMP 1410) east of Mingalazedi at Bagan. Varied figures fill diamond-shaped triangles (*Sein-htaung-kyun*), roundels on the main walls and sides of the doorway (*thekkadan-pan*) and the moat-pan or main arch. While there are some stucco roundels at Bagan — for example, on *sikhara* of the Bochyomi Gubyauk (IMP 995) — most parallels at Bagan and in the Pinya period, such as at Shwe-gu-Oo-min caves (21°35′N, 96°12′E) east of Kyaukse, are paintings in the interior of temples.

On the upper and lower levels of the temple are stucco reliefs (circa 10 × 15 cm) of the 550 *Jatakas*, the previous lives of the Buddha. Identifying inscriptions in Myanmar are seen below some of the scenes, although the names of the Bodhisattvas are in Pali. The arrangement is shown in Table 7.3.

Writing in stucco has not been documented at Bagan or elsewhere from this era, so the reliefs are unique. In this and the other storeys, the style is unique to Ta Mok, but the interpretation of the elements recalls examples at Bagan.[23] Thus, in the Kaṭṭhahāri-Jātaka (no. 7), the bodhisattva is the son of a king and a slave woman. Upon taking the child to court

TABLE 7.3
Arrangement of Stucco Reliefs by Terrace

Level	Location	Total Niches	Existing	
			No. of Reliefs	No. of Captions
A	Upper storey, Third Terrace	24	24	24
B	Upper storey, Second Terrace	24	24	12
C	Upper storey, Shrine Hall	11	6	0
D	Upper storey, Main Hall	50	50	29
E	Lower storey, Shrine Hall	18	7	0
F	Lower storey, Main Hall	55	0	0
	Total	182	111	65

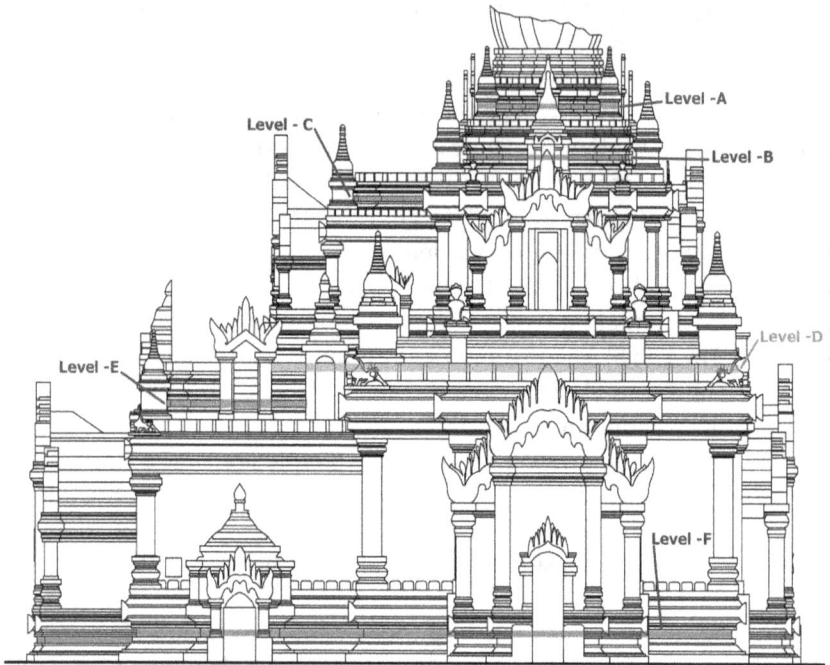

FIGURE 7.9 Profile of temple showing location of stucco reliefs.
Photo after a drawing by U Win Maung (Tampawaddy).

FIGURE 7.10 Jataka No. 7 Kaṭṭhahāri-Jātaka. Photo: Si Thu, Ta Mok Project 2011.

to present to the king, the mother throws the bodhisattva into the air and appeals to the truth in vowing that if she speaks the truth the child will remain suspended. The bodhisattva does this, is received by the king and, upon his father's death, rules the realm.

Other Structures of the Ta Mok Temple Complex

A number of other structures have been excavated in the Ta Mok compound, each further underlining the continued patronage of the site.

Zayat

South of the *thein* on the west side of the compound is a square brick foundation with an inner square enclosure (7.4 m^2). Post holes in the foundation layer and a number of flat roof tiles (16 cm long with a 4 cm angled overhang) suggest a wooden superstructure and tiled roof, possibly a *zayat* or rest house. The foundation has two enclosures, with the inner wall irregularly offset from the outer one at a distance of 1.26 metres on the west but only 0.54 on the east, where it butts up against the two-storey temple. Provisionally, we suggest initial construction early in the site's chronology, with the outer enclosure dating to perhaps Ussana's stupa construction in the 14th century CE.

Ta-wa-gu with *Andagu*

To the southeast of the main temple is a single-entrance or *ta-wa* structure (16 × 5 m), with two foundations provisionally dated to the 11–13th century CE. A finely carved *andagu* (15 cm) has been recovered within a carefully prepared stone-lined cavity on the south side of this structure (Moore et al. 2012, p. 156). As with other structures in the compound, the *ta-wa-gu* shows repeated additions, sitting adjacent to a series of walls running north to south underneath the 11th century temple. One of the ash and bone burial deposits described below was unearthed on the north edge of the *ta-wa-gu* wall.

There are also burial urns of later periods on the east side of the compound, one a Pinya-period piece found east of the two-storey temple at a depth of 1.9 metres below ground level. The pot (43 cm high, 31 cm at the rim and 27 cm at the widest part) is tall with an everted rim and curved bottom, its surface marked with a comb pattern, possibly impressed on the surface. The neck is smooth apart from two sets of multiple incised rings. The vessel was capped by a shallow red-slipped bowl (28 cm wide, 3 cm deep). Other red-slipped bowls were found nearby, one 13.5 centimetres in width and 5 centimetres in depth. A polished sandstone grinding stone (9 cm long, 4.5 cm diameter) was found nearby. Survey of the Pan Laung has yielded a range of pots, including wide bowls, globular jars with everted rims and cylindrical vessels with knobbed lids (Win Maung [Tampawaddy], 2000, 2010).

Stucco-Mixing Tank

North of the *ta-wa-gu* stupa is a north–south rectangular structure with a single opening on the north, provisionally identified as a stucco-mixing tank dated to the construction of Ussana's stupa.

Naung-taw-gyi

North of the stucco-mixing tank is the four-entry Naung-taw-gyi (24 × 15 m), in front of which the main temple's dislodged pediment described below was unearthed. The structure is oriented to the west, with two upraised floors dated to the 11th to 13th century CE. However, ash and bone deposits have been documented on the basal level, with additions to the structure dating provisionally to early and later Bagan, with a colonial-period structure at the top. Images of the Buddha of the second Bagan phase have been found in niches facing the four directions.

Square Structure with Urns

North of the Naung-taw-gyi stupa is a square structure with two enclosures with a staircase on the west and entry to the inner structure. Around the exterior wall, three urns have been found on the southeast, northeast and northwest. From the style of the urns and the condition of the bones, U Win Maung (Tampawaddy) provisionally dates the burials to the Late Pyu period, circa 8–10th century CE. We suggest that the building was rebuilt in the later Bagan period on a foundation similar to 2nd–9th century CE Pyu sites such as Beikthano's KKG-4, where a number of urns have been recovered. A large quantity of pottery typical of the Bagan and Pyu periods has been recorded around the square structure. Other burials of ash and bones without containers and deposits of bone and tuff-like slag have been found in the basal level of Naung-taw-gyi and along the east side of the temple compound. Under the north entrance at a depth of 190 centimetres, a bone deposit (80 cm in length) of a mammal has been excavated. Along the same north line of the temple complex a cache of thin (2 mm) hard glossy burnished black ware was found, tentatively identified as a begging bow. Similar black wares have been identified at the Bronze Age Nyaung-gan cemetery and in three-millimetre-thick sherds from burial contexts at Halin dated to 2890–2470 BCE.[24] As mentioned above, these deposits substantially widen the chronology of the site and the region.

Conclusion

The Ta Mok temple complex is the first and, at present, only intact example of Bagan-period architecture documented outside Bagan. Its location, artefacts, form and iconography provide new perspectives on the complex interconnections between Bagan and the rice fields of Kyaukse. The Kyaukse temple elicited royal patronage and provided cultural as well as economic outputs to the court. Ta Mok is not provincial art of greater Bagan but a cultural region in its own right, with a history spanning the prehistoric to Pinya period — and continuing to change today.

The long habitation of the Ta Mok site, the unique stucco decorative scheme and the preservation of the two-storey temple when it was encased within a stupa in the 14th century, all point to a particular ritual significance attributed to the site. The most salient reason for this is its proximity to the Pan Laung, a closeness embedded in "Ta Mok". It was by name, for instance, that the site's garden was mentioned in the inscription at the Ngwe Twin Tu: Taw Ya, "silver well forest-monastery", noted earlier. The "silver" in this case was not a natural resource but money said to be placed within the well to protect it from treasure hunters of the time.

It is this, the often-ignored social dimension, that underpins the continuity of Ta Mok. More specifically, it is the way that "religion, economic and politics cluster together" that is articulated (Reynolds 1995, pp. 429–30). With the eleven *khayaing*, the Pan Laung Shwe-gu temples were subsumed in a new administrative network. Ta Mok, sited within the *khayaing* fort, unusually amalgamated both traditions. In its prehistoric and Pyu phases, the site charts the animistic precedents, arrival and local flowering of

Buddhism. There is a potency achieved through this repetition, events being both additive and cumulative to unambiguously relay the message of transfer (Tambiah 1970, p. 207). The reception is unambiguously and strikingly distinct. It is not one of a provincial "residual culture" untouched by the outside world, but a particular context within which the global was not just mediated but redefined by its specific role in Kyaukse (Clarke 2002, pp. 239–40). Much remains to be done at Ta Mok, but the information to date allows us to begin to define a new Bagan landscape.

Notes

1. This chapter is based on a paper delivered at the conference "Early Myanmar and its Global Connections" at the Bagan Archaeological Museum on 13 February 2012. Portions have been published in *Connecting Empires and States: Selected Papers from the 13th International Conference of the European Association of Southeast Asian Archaeology* (Singapore: National University of Singapore Press, 2012, vol. 2, pp. 144–60) and the *Journal of Burma Studies* 20, no. 1 (2016): 149–98.

   We have used John Okell's system of Romanization (2000) for place names, proper names and terms in this article.

2. Elizabeth Howard Moore is Professor of the Art and Archaeology of South East Asia, SOAS, London and Visiting Researcher at the Nalanda-Sriwijaya Centre, ISEAS – Yusof Ishak Institute, Singapore; U Win Maung (Tampawaddy) is an independent scholar and traditional architect based in the Tampawaddy Quarter of Mandalay and Sagaing.

3. Myit-taw here refers to Narapatisithu's lineage as the great grandson (Myit-taw) of Anawrahta.

4. Strong cites completion of the 84,000 stupas on the same day at the time of the eclipse in the Sanskrit *Asokavadana* and the Pali *Maha vaṁsa*, although, in the latter, Strong notes letters arriving from all 84,000 cities rather than an eclipse (Strong 2004, pp. 137–38).

5. The king made numerous additional donations to temples, monasteries and ordination halls and founded forty-three fortresses along the eastern border of the empire (Berliet 2008*b*, p. 203, 2011; Brac de la Perrière 1989, pp. 47, 338–41).

6. The fort walls were documented by one of the authors, Win Maung (Tampawaddy), although Berliet noted fortified areas only at Met kaya, Myin gon daing, Pyi ma na and Pinle (2008, p. 196).

7. My thanks to Aung Mon, Tin Myet Lat, Than Than Aye and Nweh Nweh Moe for discussion on this inscription, 14 August 2011.

8. ချောင်းဖမ်းကုန်း rather than ကျောင်ပန်းကုံးဝ "monastery of a flower garland", an astrologically derived name, as the numerical equivalents for the first consonant of the three syllables are 2 + 5 + 2, which when added together equals the auspicious number 9. Personal communication, Ta Mok trustees, 10 July 2011.

9. Royal barges were generally made in the shape of auspicious animals such as the mythical *karaweik* bird or a double-bodied *naga* and standing *galon* (Garuḍa) (Htun Yi 1984).

10. OZO290 375 ± 35 BP. Australian Institute for Nuclear Science and Engineering (AINSE) Cal 1440–1640 CE, courtesy Bob Hudson, University of Sydney, Australia and Australian Institute for Nuclear Science and Engineering, October 2011.

11. Personal observation, June–July 2011.

12. The documentation, excavation and restoration work of U Win Maung (Tampawaddy) from 2008 to 2014 was followed by the 2015 designation of Ta Mok as a Notified Zone by the Department of Archaeology, Ministry of Culture in 2015 (Moore and Win Maung [Tampawaddy] 2016, p. 183).

13. At the Shwe-zi-gon pagoda at Tagaung, dated to Anawrahta's period, numerous images of the Buddha with similar snail-shell-shaped hair curls were documented by U Win Maung (Tampawaddy).

14. The proportions are taken from the stucco face recovered from excavation and the proportions of the throne, based on a model for seated images with the width from knee to knee equalling the combined height of (1) the bottom of the image to the navel; (2) the navel to breast nipples; (3) breast to neck; and (4) chin to top of forehead.

15. U Win Maung (Tampawaddy), personal communication.

16. Three images are also seen at IMP 1081, 1148 and 1237 (Shin-ota-ma-hpaya).

17. The Ta Mok reclining image, however, is not flanked by the detailed figural sculpture surrounding the Kubyauk Nge image.

18. There are numerous examples of such paintings at Bagan, with a close parallel seen in the paintings at Gu-taw-thit-hpaya (IMP 1486) (Pichard 1992–96, vol. 6).

19. Similar examples found at Bagan are especially seen in the 13th century, including Tayoke Pyay, Tha-htay Mote Gu and Thitsāwaddy temples. Pyiet Phyo Kyaw, personal communication, April 2011.

20. The more common form is to depict the Birth on the north, Enlightenment on the east, First Sermon on the south, and reclining Buddha on the west.

21. This recalls early accounts that the Ari moved east from Bagan to the "Shan" areas around Kyaukse where Mahayana practices were well established, although Mahayana, Buddhist tantra, Brahmanical and animist practices were commonly mixed at Bagan in all periods (Bode 1965, pp. 16–18; *Burma*

Gazetteer 1925, pp. 10–11, Phayre [1883] 1998, pp. 22, 33; Pranke 2004, p. 18n57; Than Tun 1988, p. 43).

22. U Win Maung (Tampawaddy), personal communication, 8 July 2011.
23. Lilian Handlin, personal communication, 14 September 2011.
24. The HL29 pieces from Halin, Shwebo Township, Sagaing, were a bowl associated with an inhumation burial, animal bones, shells, beads, stone rings and bronze artefacts likened to those from Nyaunggan cemetery, Budalin. The HL29 strata, located two kilometres southwest of the modern village of Halingyi, exposed twelve layers of circa 2.74 metres (9 feet). Traces of a wooden coffin were found in the transitional layers (personal communication, Pyiet Phyo Kyaw, 7 September 2011). Other sherds from a pottery mound at Halin yielded dates of 2850–2470 BCE, 2890–2630 BCE and 2870–2500 BCE (95.4 per cent probability, Bob Hudson, personal communication, 25 September 2011; Hudson and Nyein Lwin 2011).

References

Aung-Thwin, Michael. Pagan: *The Origins of Modern Burma*. Honolulu: University of Hawai'i Press, 1985.
———. "The Myth of the 'Three Shan Brothers' and the Ava Period in Burmese History". *Journal of Asian Studies* 55, no. 4 (1996): 881–901.
Berliet, Ernelle. "The Eleven Khayaing of Kyaukse: An Example of Territorial Pattern and Resources Management in Central Burma (Myanmar) during the Pagan Period (1044–1287)". In *From Homo Erectus to the Living Traditions, Choice of Papers from the 11th International Conference of the European Association of Southeast Asian Archaeologists, Bougon 25–30 September 2006*, edited by Jean-Pierre Pautreau, A. Coupey et al., pp. 195–201. Chiang Mai: Siam Ratana, 2008*a*.
———. "Territorial Planning in Burma during the Pagan Period, the Foundation of an Empire". In *From Homo Erectus to the Living Traditions, Choice of Papers from the 11th International Conference of the European Association of Southeast Asian Archaeologists, Bougon 25–30 September 2006*, edited by Jean-Pierre Pautreau, A. Coupey et al., pp. 203–5. Chiang Mai: Siam Ratana, 2008*b*.
———. *Territoires et Urbanisation en Birmanie des origins (IIe s. av J.-C.) à la fin du XIIIe siècle*. Paris: Brepols, 2011.
Bode, Mabel H. *The Pali Literature of Burma*. Rangoon: Burma Research Society, 1965.
Brac de la Perrière, Bénédicte. "L'Histoire des Neuf Karuin". *Journal Asiatique* 277 (1989), pts. 1–2, pp. 47–87; pts. 3–4, pp. 299–361.
Burma Gazetteer. Kyaukse District Rangoon: Superintendent Government Printing and Stationery, 1925.

Clarke, David. "Contemporary Asian Art and its Western Reception". *Third Text* 16, no. 3 (2002): 237–42.

Cooley, C.H. "The Theory of Transportation". In *Sociological Theory and Social Research*, pp. 17–118. New York: Augustus M. Kelley, [1894] 1969.

Cowell, E.B., ed. *The Jataka*, vol. 1, translated by Robert Chalmers. Cambridge: Cambridge University Press, 1898 <http://www.sacred-texts.com/bud/j1/index.htm>.

Harvey, G.E. *History of Burma*. London: Longmans, Green & Co., [1925] 1967.

Htun Yi. "She-haung Sa-pey thu-te-thi-ta-oo su-hsaung-byu su-thi-nan-hmu-nan-ya ah-hsin-tan-sa hnit thi-hmat-phweh-ya-mya ah-si-ah-nin, ah-baing 2" [Ancient records of royal conveyances (vehicles and shoes)]. Mimeographed. Yangon: Daw Kyi Baho-sa-ku, 1984.

Htwe Htwe Win. "Votive Tablets of Myanmar". PhD thesis, History Department, Yangon University, 2007.

Hudson, Bob, and Nyein Lwin N.D. "Earthenware from a Firing Site in Myanmar (Burma) Dates to More Than 4,500 Years Ago".

Luce, G.H. "Geography of Burma under the Pagan Dynasty". *Journal of the Burma Research Society* 42, no. 1 (1959): 37–51.

———. "Economic Life of the Early Burman". *Journal of the Burma Research Society* 30, no. 1 (1960): 283–335. Reprinted in Fiftieth Anniversary Publications No. 2, Burma Research Society, Rangoon, pp. 323–76.

Moore, Elizabeth. *Early Landscapes of Myanmar*. Bangkok: River Books, 2007.

Moore, E., and Win Maung (Tampawaddy). "The Social Dynamics of Pagoda Repair in Upper Myanmar". *Journal of Burma Studies* 20, no. 1 (2016): 149–98.

Moore, E., Win Maung (Tampawaddy), and Htwe Htwe Win. "Ta Mok Shwe-gu-gyi Temple: Local Art in Upper Myanmar 11th–17th Centuries AD". In *Connecting Empires and States: Selected Papers from the 13th International Conference of Southeast Asian Archaeologists*, vol. 2, edited by M.L. Tjoa-Bonatz, A. Reinecke, and D. Bonatz, pp. 150–55. Singapore, NUS Press, 2012.

Mya (Thiripiyanchi). *Votive Tablets of Burma*, vol. 1. Rangoon, Department of Archaeology, 1961.

Myanmar Language Commission. *Myanmar–English Dictionary*. Yangon: Department of the Myanmar Language Commission, Ministry of Education, 1993.

Myint Aung. "The Libation Jar in Asian History". *Working People's Daily*, 11 June 1986, pp. 5–6.

Pe Maung Tin and Luce. *The Glass Palace Chronicle of the Kings of Burma*. Rangoon: Rangoon University Press, 1960.

Phayre, Arthur. *History of Burma*. Bangkok: Orchid Press, Bibliotheca Orientalis, [1883] 1998.

Pichard, Pierre. "Les Monuments sur plan pentagone à Pagan". *Bulletin de l'École française d'Extrême Orient* 74 (1985): 305–68 <http://www.persee.fr/doc/

befeo_0336–1519_1985_num_74_1_1674#befeo_0336–1519_1985_num_74_1_
T1_0368_0031>.

———. *Inventory of Monuments at Pagan*, vol. 1 (Monuments 1–255), vol. 2
(Monuments 256–552), vol. 3 (Monuments 553–818), vol. 4 (Monuments
813–1136), vol. 5 (Monuments 1137–1439), vol. 6 (Monuments 1440–1736).
Paris: UNESCO; Gartmore: Kiscadale, 1992–96.

Pinney, Christopher. "Buddhist Photography". In *The Marshall Albums, Photography
and Archaeology*, edited by Sudeshna Guha, pp. 178–202. Delhi: The Alkazi
Collection of Photography in Association with Mapin Publishing, 2010.

Pranke, Patrick. "The 'Treatise on the Lineage of Elders' (Vamsadipani): Monastic
Reform and the Writing of Buddhist History in Eighteenth-Century Burma".
PhD Buddhist Studies, UMI No. 3122027, University of Michigan, 2004.

Reynolds, Craig. "New Look at Old Southeast Asia". *Journal of Asian Studies* 54,
no. 2 (May 1995): 419–46.

Roveda, Vittorio. *Sacred Angkor, the Carved Reliefs of Angkor Wat*. Bangkok: River
Books, 2002.

Rozenberg, Guillaume. *Renunciation and Power, the Quest for Sainthood in
Contemporary Burma*, translated by Jessica Hackett. New Haven: Yale Southeast
Asia Studies, 2010.

Siok-Hwa, Cheng. *The Rice Industry of Burma 1852–1940*. Kuala Lumpur: University
of Malaya Press, 1968.

Strong, John. *Relics of the Buddha*. Princeton: Princeton University Press, 2004.

Tambiah, Stanley. *Buddhism and the Spirit Cults in North-East Thailand*. Cambridge:
Cambridge University Press, 1970.

Than Swe. *Pu-gan Zei-di pu-htoe-mya* [Bagan period Zedi]. Yangon: Myawadi
Press, 1994.

Than Swe (Dawei). *Shin-ko-shin Tha-maing-win Dawei Hpaya-mya Ah-thein* [Nine
pagodas of Dawei]. Yangon: Ah-they Ah-waing Sabeh, 2004.

Than Tun. *Essays on the History and Buddhism of Burma*. Isle of Arran: Kiscadale,
1988.

Win Maung (Tampawaddy). "Myit-tha-11-ywa kwin-hsin-let-la-khyet-hmat-su"
[Field work notes on the leh-twin 11 khayaing]. Paper presented at the 84th
Birthday Commemoration (Mandalay), 4 December 2000.

———. *Pu-gan-shwe-nan-taw-gyi-twin hta-shi-myeh thi-ha-thana-palin-taw-gyi*
[The lion throne of Bagan Palace]. Mandalay: Myanmar Bithuka-ah-pwe,
2005.

———. *Shin Bin Shwe-gu-gyi Myet-swa-paya* [Ta Mok ancient city]. Ko Naing Min
Oo: Shwe-gu-gyi Monastery, 2010.

Yin Myo Thu. "The Role of Narapatisithu with Special Reference to the Selected
Stone Inscriptions of Bagan Period. Unpublished PhD paper, University of
Yangon: Department of Archaeology, 2011.

8

Silver Links! Bagan–Bengal and Shadowy Metal Corridors: 9th to 13th Centuries

Rila Mukherjee

This chapter isolates Bagan from its traditional moorings to Southeast Asian polities and highlights its westward links, particularly its relations with medieval Bengal, an expansive polity. The distinct geography and enigmatic history of Bagan — situated in an arid zone and driven by perennial cycles of conquest, expanding frontiers and growing exchange relations with small polities located between it and Bengal — illustrates how polities in the region responded to crisis and change. The region stretching from India's northeast into Burma experienced different trajectories of state formation, political legitimation and monetization; its nature can neither be studied within conventional paradigms of the state, nor by the "little kingdom" model (Schnepel and Berkemer 2003), the triad of time, change and linear evolution being irrelevant (Aung-Thwin 1991). Nor can its growth be analysed within a world-systems framework of cores and peripheries. Therefore, a different notion of political economy linked to time and change, distinct from the conventional notion of a sequential progression — from the prehistoric, through classical-ancient, to medieval, to the modern (Aung-Thwin 2002) — is necessary for our understanding of this region.

Enigma of Bagan

In its four-hundred–years-plus history (849 to ca. 1287 CE), Bagan displayed a state-driven religious policy, a state-directed labour system, a state-sponsored building programme and state-administered trading practices. There was a direct and circular relationship between spending on religion, increased agricultural production, proportional demographic expansion and state development (Aung-Thwin 1985, p. 27). In this distinctive political and social formation, how important was trade and what was the role of money in Bagan's economy? What connections were forged by Bagan, with its silver supplies, with neighbouring polities? What follows is a visualization of Bagan's international connections, through tracing exchanges between Bagan and Bengal, to explain the curious absence of silver circulation in Bengal at a time when Bagan was reportedly accessing silver deposits. Was this silver traded at all? Why was it not exported as done previously? And what prevented the silver from reaching Bengal?

A Brief History of Money

A new polity in the mid-9th century, Bagan faced challenges on land while struggling to create a space for itself (Lieberman 2009, pp. 16–17). It seems isolated, cut off from silver supplies to its north and from the bay trade to its south.[1] It had few international connections, but it apparently carried out an expedition against Nan Zhao to reopen routes to China, the precise date of this expedition being unknown (Stargardt 1971, pp. 51–53). An attack on Bagan by Sri Lanka in this century is referenced, the attack repelled with Nan Zhao's aid (Sun 1997, p. 23). Two regional forces, Tibet and Tang China, collapsed in the 10th century, which probably helped regional consolidation, but Tang decline also affected overland routes into China, as Bagan–Song interactions are recorded only from 1004 (Sun 1997, p. 17). The *Lingwai Daida* of 1178 is the earliest Chinese record containing the word *Pugan* (Sun 1997, p. 17). However, Sun mentions Tang notices on the overland route from China to India (possibly into Bengal) via northern Burma in 691 CE, in 807 or 810 CE, in 863, and again in 1060 (Sun 1997, pp. 13, 15–16). A Fatimid map of circa late 11th century showed a route from China running through northern India (Kanauj was mentioned; Rapoport and Savage-Smith 2004, p. 259; Johns and Savage-Smith 2003, p. 11). Athanasius Kircher's 17th-century map of China and South Asia depicted the same route bifurcating in north Burma, one portion coming down Bengal and into the Coromandel Coast.

Overland routes functioned again in the 11th century. We can only speculate as to whether this was an effect of the 11th-century "trade revolution" (Kulke 1999, pp. 17–35). From mid-century, Bagan accessed silver deposits through its campaign against Dali Yunnan, its conquest of Tagaung giving it access to routes into China, and also sources of silver, as it could now access the Bawdin and Yadanatheingyi mines at Namtu in and around Mogok via Tagaung.[2] Bagan was now also closer to the ruby mines at Mohnyin, a valuable diplomatic and commercial commodity. Amber was available, as was copper, tin, iron and some gold (Yule 1857, pp. 56, 67–68, 72, 99, 107; I do not know when these mines began to be worked). At this time, Bagan embarked on a series of conquests towards the bay, thereby greatly enlarging its southern limits and again bringing in silver (Aung-Thwin 1985, pp. 48, 58; Taylor 1999, p. 165; Hall and Whitmore 1976, pp. 306–7; Wade 2009, p. 246; Jacq-Hergoualc'h 2002; Mukherjee 2011, p. 205; Manatunga 2009, pp. 198–99). The 11th century, therefore, was a defining century for Bagan, but we still have little knowledge of its relations with its western neighbours.

The 12th century saw the need for monetization. The influence of Arab commerce in the lower reaches of the Bagan Empire became evident (the case of the Cambodian bazaar in Wicks 1992, p. 124 is one example). Trade was still conducted largely through barter, and large transactions became problematic (Wicks 1992, p. 125). A Chinese account of the late 12th century indicates that Bagan was still seen as a landlocked kingdom controlling neighbouring territory as far as Pattikera in Comilla, Bangladesh and not as a maritime polity with extensive commercial interests (Wicks 1992, p. 131). There is little record of Bagan's interactions with southeastern Bengal, except with the polity of Pattikera, possibly by way of the Buddhist complex of Mainamati-Lalmai (Frasch 2002; Wicks 1992, p. 131 suggests that Pattikera formed part of Narapatisithu's domains at the end of the 12th century) and the repairs of the monastery at Bodh Gaya (also in the 12th century) by Kyanzittha (Stargardt 1971, p. 60). Such connections suggest that land and fluvial routes between Bagan and southeastern Bengal were active.

Still typical of a redistributive economy with the monarch at its core, much gold and silver was diverted to meet the demands of the massive building works that Alaungsithu undertook towards the end of this century (Marco Polo noted that two towers of the mausoleum of a particular king of Bagan were covered with plates of gold and silver, each an inch thick; Wright [1854] 2002, p. 182). Alaungsithu also introduced standardized weights and measures throughout the kingdom, providing a much-needed impetus for monetization (Wicks 1992, p. 131). Narapatisithu's inscription of 1196 mentions the silver *klyap* as a measure of value and unit of exchange, and in the 12th century the *klyap* as unit extended to gold as well. But this did not presage coinage; the references indicate bars or ingots in circulation (Wicks 1992, p. 132).

Throughout its history, Southeast Asia has been plagued by a shortage of labour; Bagan was no exception. The issue of labour becomes important for Bagan, requiring fixed units of value. Although located in the dry zone, Bagan harnessed a system of perennial rivers by constructing dams, sluices, weirs and channels (Aung-Thwin 1985, p. 97). Raids into the southeastern Bengal delta were common from the 12th century; inscriptions frequently mention "Indians", probably from Assam and Bengal, settled in Bagan (Aung-Thwin 1985, p. 97; Wicks 1992, p. 125 mentions an inscription of 1164 where six "Indian" slaves were exchanged against one elephant, and forty slaves exchanged against one horse). Attacks brought in a large labour force. Chins, Kachin, Karen, Arakanese and "Indians" formed part of a labour force subordinate to Burmans, Mons and Shans, the latter group forming part of the elite labour force (Aung-Thwin 1985, p. 71). Some were used for constructing roadways and monasteries, and in digging canals. However, most of the people captured and resettled were skilled artisanal workers: spinners, weavers, bell-metal workers and washermen. Whether this was due to an 11th-century "trade revolution" in the Bay of Bengal remains to be seen, but questions arise: how was labour paid and did payment in kind unleash monetization? For example, payment in oil implies some kind of exchange relation (Wicks 1992, p. 127).

By the 13th century, silversmiths, potters, musicians, statue makers, painters, wood carvers, and even clothes washers were paid wages (Miksic 2002, p. 100). Increasing monetization from the 13th century modified the redistributive pattern and, consequently, specific weights of silver began to appear regularly in inscriptions (Wicks 1992, pp. 131–42), suggesting that the now extensive and monetized exchange network at Bagan used paddy as a measure of value and unit of exchange from the late 12th century, while copper and silver were used for larger transactions (Wicks 1992, p. 140). Bagan therefore used monetary units and values, but not coins as such. How far it approximated a "paddy state", whose authority was based on manpower rather than territory, is yet to be interrogated (Scott 2009).

The 13th century was significant for Bagan. Theravada Buddhism was declared the official religion, bringing Bagan into contact with commercially active Malay polities in the Bay of Bengal such as Tambralinga, which had moved away from the earlier Mahayanist tradition. This move also forged close contacts with Theravadin Sri Lanka, a dominant force in the Indian Ocean trade, although Bagan's immediate neighbours, Yunnan and Pala Bengal, and also the area to its west, followed Vajrayana or Tantric Buddhism (Wolters 1958, p. 600; Coedès 1918, p. 32; Majumdar 1933; Sastri 1940; Wade 2009; Sumio 2004; Hall 2010, pp. 111, 116–17; Hall 2004, pp. 217–18; Sen 2006; Frasch 2011).

How far did the new religious affiliation help Bagan's repositioning in the Indian Ocean economy? Did it bring into Bagan much needed metals, and how was circulation consequently affected? Between 1175 and 1250, donations to the sangha went up from 34,941.5 to 67,296.5 paddy lands, with a proportionate increase in silver donations from 1200 and labour from 1225 (Aung-Thwin 1985, p. 187, table 1). There are indications that gold was scarce or perhaps treated as a royal commodity, with Bagan prohibiting gold exports when Polo travelled in the region (Stargardt 1971, pp. 60–61). Bagan also needed silver, which maritime Arakan possessed, and a profitable Bagan–Arakan silver link was established. Arakan needed gold; 5 units of silver were worth 1 unit of gold from Bagan (Stargardt 1971, p. 60). The value of silver in Yunnan during the Yuan period can be seen from Polo's remarks at the end of the 1280s, when he was sent by Khubilai Khan through Yunnan to Burma. He mentioned that in the Kunming area, 8 taels of silver equalled 1 tael of gold. In the Gold Teeth area, where gold was relatively abundant, 5 taels of silver were exchanged for 1 tael of gold. This favourable rate lured merchants seeking great profits from their silver (Yang 2008, p. 8). Silver thus drained away from the coast to the uplands.

In the mid-13th century, overland routes were disturbed once again as the Mongols expanded westward, culminating in an attack on Bagan in 1287. Whether Bagan itself fell is debatable. Lieberman suggested that,

more than the Mongol invasions, it was the Martaban revolt preceding
the Mongol conquest and the Shan invasions in the 1350s–60s that finally
finished off Bagan (Lieberman 2003, pp. 119–20). As Bagan continued to be
a spiritual centre as late as 1393, buildings continued to be built, donations
accepted and sites occupied until the 15th century (Luce and Ba Shin 1961;
Grave and Barbetti 2002, p. 85; Frasch 2011), although public buildings were
now smaller, indicating dwindling economic resources (Hudson, Lwin and
Win Maung 2002, p. 52). It participated in the first "silver century" across
Eurasia when the Mongols created a financial, commercial, diplomatic and
military axis linking East with West, generating much silver and trade
through conquest and plunder (Kuroda 2009, p. 255). In 1244 the Mongols
invaded north Bengal, near Jalpaiguri, but did not proceed further south.
But the persistence of the place name *Tarap* (Trope) in southeastern Bengal,
a word supposedly referencing Mongols (Goh 2009, 2010), is significant.
In 1253 the Mongols conquered Dali Yunnan and by 1279 conquered
China. In 1257 they attacked Annam and destabilized Bagan in 1283 and
1287, Shan states appearing thereafter between Burma and Yunnan, while
Arakan declared independence from Bagan. Champa was conquered in
1283. Silver may have been drained away from the coast to the uplands
to facilitate the new Mongol axis.

Metals: Bagan and Bengal

Stories of stockpiling of precious metals dominate Bagan's history. Yet,
during its 450 years of life, Bagan seems to have opted for a non-monetized
economy. When repairing the monastery at Bodh Gaya in the 12th century,
although Kyanzittha accumulated funds through gold, silver and precious
stones, there was no mention of a measure of value or a medium of
exchange (Stargardt 1971, pp. 53–58, 60; Wicks 1992, p. 123). This changed
in the next century, with rice, oil, copper and silver appearing as values, as
we just noted. One 11th-century inscription says Kyanzittha's wealth was
80 *koti* (Wicks 1992). What precisely this quantity expressed is unknown.
It may perhaps have been a weight of silver, and if so one can speculate
that this metal had an exchange function in the early Bagan period (Miksic
2002, p. 99).

At inception, Bagan had no access to silver from overland routes,
due to severe political destabilization in the area. It is unclear how far
Bagan's emergence after the decline of Pyu and its relations with Nan

Zhao disturbed established relations and metal networks in the area, nor is it apparent how far the decline of Nan Zhao in 902 helped Bagan's expansion. Bagan's opting for a redistributive economy may have been due to an initial inability to link to the metal corridor, demonstrated by the fact that Bagan, although initially an upland state, moved southward to conduct diplomacy by sea routes (Stargardt 1971, p. 62). Although this brought in silver, Bagan still did not use a silver currency. Despite proximity to silver mines and being a copper-rich area, coins were generally not used at Bagan, although there is a tantalizing reference to the discovery of twenty-one metallic coins — of two sizes, one measuring an inch (2.5 cm) in circumference and the other a quarter of an inch (0.64 cm) — in an "elongated vase", which were deposited in the Bagan museum (Hudson 2004, p. 125).

Certain questions now arise. Why did Bagan opt for a redistributive non-currency economy in an area known for metal deposits? Was the action religious? The Burmese myth of the founding of Arimaddanapura (Bagan) in 849 CE mentions the Buddha cautioning the people of the city that they "shall not till the land but shall live by merchandise, selling and buying, and their speech shall not be the words of truth but of falsehood" (Wheatley 1971, p. 285). Was Bagan initially anti-trade? If so, this changed after 1136 when the *Ke shu* mentioned Bagan's commercial products. The *Yunlu manchao* of 1206 mentioned ships from Bagan at the ports of Fujian (Sun 1997, pp. 17–18). It is evident that Aniruddha's southward drive towards the Bay of Bengal was now paying off, but we find no evidence of Bagan–Bengal maritime links, unless they went through Arakan and Pattikera. Curiously, the absence of silver coinage at Bagan is reflected in a concurrent absence of silver currency circulation in Bengal. So let us now look at Bengal, whose largely monetized economy was so very different from Bagan's, but may perhaps have been closer to that of Sri Ksetra (Thirikittiya) and Halin.[3]

Bengal had a robust agricultural economy and a vibrant crafts industry dating from circa the 5th century. That silver and seashells should form the basis of exchange in medieval Bengal is remarkable in that neither of these commodities was a local product. So, while Bengal's monetary system was structured to meet the needs of a large domestic economy, it clearly depended for its existence on sustained linkages, both overland and maritime, with larger Asian/Indian Ocean trading networks. It also depended on the mediation of an active and growing financial industry. In the medieval period, Bengal supported a relatively dense rural population which consistently produced a surplus of agricultural commodities beyond the needs of self-sufficiency. This made possible a variety of handicraft industries, notably textiles, which produced an exportable surplus. Much of the economy was structured around the production of rural and semi-urban products and their domestic redistribution through processes of state revenue and expenditure and local marketing. Bengal also enjoyed a nodal geographic location, being both the delta of two great north Indian river systems as well as the apex of the Bay of Bengal, so it is no surprise that some of its surplus production fostered an active international trade (Deyell 2010, p. 64).

Until the 7th–8th centuries, silver came in by the maritime route from Pyu ports and overland from Lichhavi Nepal via Tibet, while gold coins came through the Tang–Sassanid silk trade. Tibet claimed to have conquered Bengal in the 7th–8th centuries, beyond the Karatoya to the Ganga. The early Pala kings may have been subordinate to Tibet; we hear of people of Tibetan or Yunnanese origin, the Khambojas, taking over Gaur in the 10th century (Gupta 1967, pp. 111, 132; Wink 1990, pp. 265–66). The Tibet–Bengal axis created favourable conditions for the transmission of metals. Over five hundred gold and silver coins from Mainamati (Wink 1990, pp. 270–71), including three hoards of 227 specimens, reveal two Gupta and a dozen post-Gupta "imitation" gold coins, a rare silver coin of Sasanka, a few Khadga and Early Deva gold coins, a large number of Arakanese and Arakan-type local (Harikela and Akara dynasties) silver coins, one gold and a few silver coins of Abbasid Caliphs.

Gold coins stopped circulating in deltaic Bengal after the Tang–Sassanid commercial collapse around the middle of the 7th century. Pundravardhana (Mahasthan), close to Burma, continued with a debased gold coinage (Rhodes 2011). Harikela, neighbouring Arakan, used its silver coinage to fill the gap, but this ceased from the early 10th century (Rhodes 2011), indicating diminishing silver supplies. The Tang–Abbasid network succeeded the earlier Sassanid link, which had brought in gold into deltaic Bengal, sidestepping the Bengal coast (Malekandathil 2010, p. 62; Mukherjee 2011b, p. 444). There was clearly a crisis in trade — and of silver — in Bengal during the 7th to 10th centuries; this was reflected in its overseas connections. Sailings to many southeastern ports tapered off; there are hardly any mentions of Bengali seafarers in inscriptions (Mukherjee 2011a, pp. 102–4). Yet, B.N. Mukherjee (in Sharma 2003, p. 129) and Wink (1990, p. 260) mention large numbers of silver and gold coins of Bengal and Kamarupa (later Assam) dating from between the 11th and 13th centuries, implying that the northeast metal corridor was still active. One entry point of silver flows from Tibet, China and Myanmar was Kamarupa. Two others were Tripura/Srihatta in the northeast (entry from Bagan via Manipur) and Chattagrama/Arakan in the southeast (the maritime route). Yule mentioned fluvial networks in this region, as well as mountain passes between India and China crossing the Bagan region (Yule 1857, pp. 67–68). Bagan possibly did not control the northern Chindwin passage, the boundary between Manipur and Myanmar. The southern course was under Bagan's control. Charney (2011) noted that "if we relied on Burmese state sources alone, we would note that from the early thirteenth century, during the Pagan period, only the southernmost extremities of the Chindwin are mentioned. These references are also largely made to monastic establishments in the area along the lower stretch of the river and these were forest-dwelling monasteries on the frontiers" (p. 165). And Yule (1857) wrote that "the lowest and largest mouth of the Kyendwen is traditionally said to have been an artificial cut made by one of the kings of Pagan" (p. 71).

Bengal's overseas trade and currency system recovered again only with the Islamic conquest of 1206; but silver stocks were still inadequate in Bengal (Deyell 1994, pp. 112–36). Were routes linking Bagan and Bengal obstructed, hampering silver flows and trade? If so, from which point(s)? In the pre-Bagan period, Nepal's Lichhavi kingdom was a silver transmission point, but from the middle of the 8th to the beginning of the 13th centuries, i.e., from the Lichhavi decline to the rise of the Mallas in Nepal, the appearance of transitional kingdoms in the Kathmandu Valley impeded flows. Tamralipta, an active port in the Bengal delta and site of much Chinese pilgrim passage to Bodh Gaya, recorded no sailings after the 7th century (N.R. Ray 1948, p. 199),[4] possibly reflecting a decline in the northern Bay of Bengal trade. By the 9th century, China dealt with the Malabar Coast, accessing the Indian Ocean trade directly by embarking at Kollam on small, fast boats to the Arabian ports (Hirth and Rockhill 1911, pp. 15, 24).

In 937 CE the Dali kingdom (937–1253) in Yunnan, succeeding Nan Zhao and coterminous with Bagan, appeared. And while silver supplies into Bengal dwindled, commercial, political, religious and artistic elements certainly flowed between Pala Bengal and Bagan.[5] During this period, Pala art forms also influenced Dali Yunnan, implying that the Bengal–Bagan–Yunnan link operated in the post–Nan Zhao period and continued into the Song period in China (Soper and Chapin 1970, 1971). These cultural routes may have been braided with the *kauri* route, Yunnan importing Maldivian *kauris* from Bengal (Yang 2004). At this time, Tagaung's strategic position on the Yunnan–Bagan frontier is evident from the array of Tagaung artefacts attributed to Aniruddha as part of his east-flank fortification (Association of Myanmar Archaeologists n.d.). And, soon after, Bagan–Song contacts, building upon previous Tang–Burma–India links (Sun 1997, pp. 13, 15, 17–18), are referenced. So it is unlikely that routes were in disarray in the 12th century.

Bagan became Angkor's dependency in the 12th century (Rispaud 1966, p. 222, quoting Chau Rugua), explaining Khmer influence on the Buddhist Candras of the southeastern delta. The second Bhatera plaque, dating from the late 11th to early 12th centuries, and containing thirty-two lines in Sanskrit in a proto-Bengali script, has a style similar to Khmer plaques from Cambodia (Boisselier 1971).

But did this factor mostly shift Bagan's networks more to the east? It is significant that Bengal became increasingly integrated into trans-regional trade routes emanating from the Ganga plains at this time, suggesting diversion of older networks between Bagan and Bengal. Was this due to collapse of former trading partners, troubled routes or some other, unspecified, crisis? Indication of network decay lies in the fact that the southeastern delta became progressively Hinduized from this time; the Hindu Varman dynasty was succeeded by the Vaisnavite Devas, who ruled for about a hundred years from around 1180 to 1281. Possibly Bengal now lapsed into feudalism (Thakur 1978, 1987), although the southeastern delta of Bengal continued to be commercially active, with a well-developed monetary system (Tarafdar 1978; Eaton 1993, chap. 4 and appendix "Mint Towns and Inscription Sites under Muslim Rulers"; Deyell 1983, 2011).

So, what happened to silver supplies from Yunnan that came into Bengal via Bagan? Did supplies fall? Did links suddenly snap? How far did Dali Yunnan's decline in 1253 enable Bagan to retain its hegemony in the region until the Mongol attack of 1287? We need more information on the various networks spanning the region. This is difficult, since the inevitable outcome of area studies classifications into "South" and "Southeast" Asia makes it difficult to trace routes. We turn to the region's geography to understand Bagan–Bengal links.

Constituting a Region: Fault Lines, Rivers, Polities

Although, like southeastern Bengal, Bagan lies in Monsoon Asia, it is nevertheless positioned in an arid zone on the Ayeyarwady River (Lieberman 2003, pp. 88, 107–10). It has been argued that the division between Arid and Monsoon Asia lies between the western and southeastern deltas of Bengal (Gommans 2002); hence, traditionally, polities on the Southeast Asian mainland were deemed Bagan's immediate neighbours (Rispaud 1966, p. 215; Daniels 2012; Griffiths and Lepoutre 2013).

The conventional line of demarcation between the historiography of South and Southeast Asia is, however, erased once the southeastern Bengal delta becomes focal. How far this erasure applies to arid Bagan awaits research (Lieberman 2009, p. 17 notes that Bagan experienced a drier climate from ca. 1250 to 1470), but we are told that the king of Bagan was also called the king of Mien and Bengala, suggesting that the two were seen as a political and cultural unit by China (Wade 2009*b*, pp. 40, 42).

The geographic bond between Bengal and Bagan was echoed in maps. One of the earliest to depict the region, the *Catalan Atlas* of 1375,[6] showed the Indus (mistaken for the Ganga) linking the northern Bay of Bengal to the uplands. Abraham Ortelius' "Asia" in *Theatrum Orbis Terrarum* (1570), using information from Marco Polo's *Travels*, showcases this regional unit again by way of a river uniting the region. This putative unit contains the area between Bengal, Bagan and Yunnan. The river is the Ganga and the map has the Ganga flowing southward via Tacan, Mezu and Cangigu (Polo's Cangigu, identified most likely with Katha) becoming the "Cantan fl." and flowing into the China Sea at "Cantan". The same map also shows Polo's Cardandan, Carazan and Caraian (Yunnan), Toloman (Bagan/Ava, Polo's Tholoman), suggesting that these were significant areas forming a coherent unit (Ortelius [1572] 2006, plate 3). While its flow into China was corrected in Ortelius's map kept at the Vatican Library, *Tavola XVIII* nevertheless shows the Ganga rising in the Imaus Mons, but as a separate stream; the bifurcation occurs above, beyond and to the right of Tenduch or present-day Beijing (Almagia 1944, vol. 2). The correction therefore still portrayed the region as one.

Mercator's nephew, Gerhard Mercator or Gerard Jr., followed the same strategy of constituting a region through a river as commons. He published a map of Asia in 1595 where the Ganga flowed through the northeast of India then turned southeast and ultimately flowed into

the sea at the same stretch of the Chinese coast highlighted earlier by
Ortelius and called by Fra Mauro "Cantan fl. olim Ganges" (Falchetta
2006, p. 88). Gerard Jr. attempted to bridge the space between the Indus
and the Ganga by introducing a third river, the Mandus, which passed
Ava, "Pochang" (Polo's Vochang or Bagan), "Kasma" (Cosmin), "Paigu"
(Pegu) and "Marthaban" (Falchetta 2006). Rughesi in 1597 followed the
same model; in his *Tavola XXII* the Ganga was depicted as rising in this
upland region, issuing from "Cardandan" (Yunnan), possibly a reference
to it rising in Mansarowar in Tibet ("Carta dell'asia di Fausto Rughesi,
Roma, 1597, *Tavola XXII*" in Almagia 1944, vol. 2). The imaginary Ganga
therefore united Bengal with China through Bagan.

Now, back to Ortelius's map of 1570. At Cangigu or Katha the river
bisected — one stream flowing into China, the other into Bengal (Pendua)
via Mien (Burma), Ausun (Assam), Tipura (Tripura) and Rachang (Arakan)
(Ortelius 2006, plate 48; Skelton 1964). The course of his Ganga obviously
incorporated the Ayeyarwady. The region of Toloman or Bagan is shown as
contiguous to Tripura, Srihatta and the Khen and Kamta zones to Bengal's
northeast. To the northwest of Toloman lay Macin or Mahachin; this was
the name used for Ava, and it is curious that both Bagan and Ava as Macin
are depicted on the same map.

These formulations suggest that Bagan and the southeastern Bengal
delta were regarded as ecologically and culturally compatible, the
compatibility enforced through active connections facilitated through
rivers, interspersed with overland laps (Coryton 1875; Christie 1957,
pp. 159–66). The *Tripura Vaṁsavali*, referencing the invasions of Srihatta and
Suvarnagrama (in Bangladesh) by Bijoymanikya of Tripura, mentions the
southeastern delta's 16th-century riverine network: the Gomati, Meghna,
Brahmaputra, Dhaleswari, Kirtinasa and the Jamuna (Kali Prasanna
Sen 2003, pp. 1, 189). It is likely that some of them linked up with the
Ayeyarwady through routes yet to be traced. Bagan's fluvial networks
prior to the 16th century are unknown. Tagaung and Bagan are closer to
the Ayeyarwady than Halin, Maingmaw, Waddi or Beikthano. While the
west wall of both is currently the Ayeyarwady, each may once have been
further from the bank and the threat of flood. At Bagan, Daw Thin Gyi
concluded from aerial photographs that the west wall was gradually lost
to the Ayeyarwady through erosion and flood. A jutting out of the river
at the village of Myit Khe ("lower portion") north of Bagan also supports
its gradual eastward shift. Bagan's setting may have obviated the need

for fortification on the immediate east, while the ecology and location of Tagaung, on the Yunnan frontier, may have required it (Association of Myanmar Archaeologists n.d.).

Political Economy, Routes, Clusters

Bagan is visualized here functioning independently of, and as pivot between, two *kauri*-using (cowrie shell) Vajrayana Buddhist polities: Yunnan and Bengal. Being known by three names in Marco Polo's account — Tholoman, Vochang and Mien — suggests that Bagan's boundaries, and networks, were unclear. Polities here show no clear capital or core area, a characteristic shared by Bagan and Pala Bengal (Frasch 2003, p. 109). This regional unit, the northern Bay of Bengal world, comprised a coherent unit composed of parts of what are now four nation states: India, Bangladesh, Myanmar and China. Historically, the northern bay showed no visible economic centre; rather, what Hall calls "a poly-centric networked realm" prevailed — "there was no hierarchical trade structure corresponding to markets with a single clearing house or a single core with peripheries with which it traded on terms of unequal exchange" (Hall 2010, p. 113). There was no one dominant power either; rather, it was multi-centred. In this multi-centred world of the northern bay, Bengal became a minor player in the larger game for control of the bay trade between the 9th and 13th centuries. We do not know how far this contributed to the rise of Bagan. Traditional scholarship emphasizes instead the vacuum in the southern Bay of Bengal caused by Chola raids (Lieberman 2003, p. 93).

Kauri networks connected the landlocked states in the northern bay with the Maldive Islands in the Arabian Sea by way of the southern Bay of Bengal (Yang 2004; Mukherjee 2011*b*). These, however, participated only marginally in the medieval Indian Ocean economy (Heiman 1980). Polo shows, at the end of the 13th century, how the economy was structured in the uplands of the Bay of Bengal, in the Shan states and at Bagan. In the inland states of Cangigu, Bhamo and Tholoman (also Ava), *kauris* (sent from Bengal via Srihatta) circulated as money, although gold was found in great quantities at Yunnan, Cangigu and Tholoman, and gold and silver jewellery was plentiful at Bhamo (Wright 1854, pp. 175, 184–86). In Vochang and at Yungchang-fu, men and women had gold-plated teeth (Wright 1854, p. 177). In Tibet, too, although gold was plentiful, coral — rather than *kauris*, gold or the paper money of the khan — was used as money (Wright 1854, p. 169). Smuggled gold from Bagan was exchanged for silver from Arakan at a ratio of 1:5 (Stargardt 1971, p. 60; Yang 2004, p. 8) in Yunnan-fu (Polo's Vochang, also identified as Bagan) and in the shadowy area between Yunnan and Mien (Latham 1958, pp. 181–82, 187). The Marsden and Wright editions[7] mention that the natives who brought in the gold came from the mountains between Yunnan and Mien. This was possibly the Shan area.

The *kauri* trade did not unleash the 11th-century "trade revolution" here (Kulke 1999; Mukherjee 2011a, 2011b). However, unlike Lieberman's charter polities of the 9th to the 14th centuries on the Southeast Asian mainland, the fluid *kauri*-using zone between Bagan and Bengal did see an unprecedented level of state formation and demise between the 11th and 13th centuries. How far this activity was the result of the metal hunger in Bagan is yet to be seen. There were only closed economies between Bagan and Bengal, with few, if any, outlets to the bay when Polo travelled in the region. The Hedamba kingdom, known also as the Cachar polity, emerged around 1086 CE; the Khen dynasty rose circa 1185; and the older Srihatta polity declined by the 12th century by splitting up partly into the Cachari state and partly into a new, and smaller, Hindu polity. Many of these Buddhist states were peopled by Indo-Mongoloid Bodos. More states rose in the 13th century: the Shan states to Bagan's north and the Ahom state to Bengal's immediate northeast in 1231, the latter partly dislocating the older Tripuri state southward.[8] It is significant that few coins have been found for these polities. Did the absence of a single large and stable political unit in this region obstruct route formation or continuity?

It seems that not just Bengal and Bagan but the entire northern bay region experienced a coinage decline in the 9th–10th centuries. There were "no local coins from the rest of mainland southeast Asia after the fall of Funan and Dvaravati, their function being replaced by barter, cowrie shells and standardized metal bars or lumps" (Gutman 1978, citing R. le May 1932, p. 9). Twelfth century Bengal expressed valuation units in "kapardaka (*kauris*) Purana" (Wicks 1992, p. 107) and did not use coins as such. Thirteenth-century Bengal expressed value in both *kauri* units and the new Muslim silver *tankas*, carrying, among other elements, weights and size standards of Burmese coins of the first millennium (Deyell 2010, p. 66), thus commemorating old trading practices and market relations. Political and economic destabilization must have been the reason for the disappearance of coins at centres such as Bagan, Sukhothai and Angkor

— the last Arakan coinage hoards date to the 9th–10th centuries, as do coins from Mon sites (Gutman 1978, p. 9).

The thirst for metals in Bagan and interdiction on gold exports now profited Arakan. Instead of exporting silver to Bengal, Arakan sent silver up to Bagan. Merchants who made the long journey into this area made profits of up to a hundred per cent (Wright 1854, p. 175). The trade was lawful and not a smuggling trade; merchants met local traders at a designated market held three days a week in a particular plain (Wright 1854, p. 181), indicating this upland area was becoming active in the Bay of Bengal metal trade. Arab and Persian networks had appeared on the eastern coast, noticeably at Samandar and Chattagrama. It is likely that these merchants connected the coast with the uplands through the many rivers of the region; the kingdoms of Muja and Ma'id, whose locations remain debated, were certainly located around this region, being probably Shan states (Tibbetts 1979, p. 89) or upper and lower Tibet (Akasoy 2011, p. 22).

There were two routes from Yunnan to Bengal: a southern one from Dali to Yongchang, through the Pyu Kingdom, Prome, the Arakan Range, Kamarupa, and into Assam; and the western one crossing the Ayeyarwady, the Mogaung and the Chindwin rivers to Bengal and beyond (Yang 2004, p. 28). The western route (for routes, see Stargardt 1971, pp. 43–44), with its variations, concerns us:

> The first went from Yung Chang to Momien, crossed the Irrawaddy to Mogaung, went north through the Hukong Valley, across passes in the Patkai Range, to the upper Brahmaputra Valley. This was the eastern frontier of Kamarupa. The second route followed the Shweli River, crossing the Irrawaddy at Tagaung, followed the Chindwin River north and crossed via the Imole pass to Manipur. This was the eastern approach to Bangala via Tripura. The third route embarked on the Irrawaddy at Tagaung, Ava or Pagan, and then passed from Prome over the Arakan Range to Arakan. A variation of this went directly from Pagan to Arakan via the Aeng pass. This gave access to either a land route northwards to Chatigaon, or embarkation on the coastal trading boats to Bengal. (Deyell 1994, p. 128)

Bhamo and, somewhat lower down, Katha, were privileged points on the route between north Burma, the Shan states and China (Sladen 1870), but these do not enter our story of routes between Bagan and Bengal. Rather, Kale in the southern Kabo valley, contiguous to both present Mizoram and Manipur in India, must be emphasized (Stargardt 1971, pp. 61–62 also suggests this), connecting the Chindwin and Ayeyarwady valleys through what the British called the "Munipoor river", the lower Chindwin being important to Bagan as already noted. Yule wrote:

> Kale is much the most populous part of the valley, and it has an exit for its teak by the Narenjara or Munnipur river which passes through it into the Kyendwen. It also produces rice and cotton, with wax and ivory. Kale is one of the sites in which Burman history or legend places the dynasty of ancient Hindoo immigrants into their country. The classic name of the Kubo valley is Mauriya. (Yule 1857, p. 73)

He added:

> Myeengyan, on a low plain opposite the little Delta of the Kyendwen, is at present one of the largest provincial towns in Burma. It is a great mart for rice, both from the adjoining districts and from Pegu, and exhibited more of business and bustle than any other town which we saw in Burma. The population is probably 8000 or 10000. Nyoungoo and Pagan-myo, 3 miles apart, are both embraced in the space, thickly spotted with the ruined temples of the ancient Burmese capital, Pagan. (Yule 1857, p. 76)

Kale gave Bagan access to the area south of Ahom territory, to Cachar and Srihatta in the north and to Tripura and Comilla in the south. But we remain ignorant about the nature of riverine navigation between Bagan and Manipur, Tripura and Assam. The *Sri Rajmala* of Tripura and the *Tripura Vaṁsavali* are not geographically precise when referencing bullion routes. When Ratna Manikya succeeded to the Tripuri throne in 1279 (or in 1282 or 1464 CE) with the Bengal sultan's help, the *Rajmala* recorded that the Bengal sultans got to know of the mountain routes and fluvial networks of the region (K.P. Sen 2003, vol. 1, p. 189). These were routes through which bullion came into Bengal, and such a route was shown in Kircher's map of 1667: "Tabula Geodorica Itinerum a varijs in Cataium", or "Roads to China", taken from his encyclopedia *China Illustrata*.

This area was a corridor of cultural and technological transmissions, with nodes and clusters of trade outposts and smelting works along the overland route. Nal Rajar Garh (Garh Mendabari), a military outpost dating from late Gupta times in Jalpaiguri district in north Bengal, is one such; its ruins display plans similar to Chang 'añ, the capital of the Sui and Tang in China, suggesting the antiquity of the complex as well as cultural contiguity between India and China. A sophisticated system of waterways, harbours, canals and culverts, as well as kiln-fired bricks used in construction, and numerous iron-smelting works in the complex indicate it was not just an outpost but a fortified township to ward off aggression from neighbouring China, Tibet and Nepal (Santra 2005, pp. 29–36; Dasgupta 2005). Excavations suggest that this late Gupta site may have been continuously occupied from the Pala period until the 13th century (Deshpande 1975, p. 46; Chakrabarti 2001, p. 62). The same is true for Bhitargarh, ten miles away, in Bangladesh, whose strategic position on the trade routes between Sikkim, Nepal, Bhutan, Tibet, Assam, Koch Behar, and the middle and lower Ganga valleys cannot be ignored (Jahan 2006, 2010). The discovery of Nal Rajar Garh and Bhitargarh and similar other mud forts and fortified cities in the Tista-Karatoya valley testify to the region's role as transmitter of goods and technology. Smelting works in Nal Rajar Garh support the hypothesis of clusters in the northeastern corridor for the transmission of metals from southwest China through north Burma into Bengal (Mandal, Datta and Chattopadhyay 2010, pp. 224–27). Further support comes from archaeological finds of numerous copper and bronze idols in this Zomian wasteland, evidence of a sophisticated material culture that once prevailed here (Santra 2005, pp. 22, 41–42).

Conclusion

This essay about Bagan's connections and compulsions shows that its history cannot be studied merely through its territorial frames or its Southeast Asian linkages. It highlights Bagan's physical and cultural compatibilities with Bengal, affirming the necessity of further research on the Bagan–Kale–eastern South Asia route. The histories of Tripura, Comilla and other polities the route crossed await further research, as does fluvial route tracking through GIS.

Our main question was, why did these metal-abundant states opt for a non-cash economy? The means whereby trade was conducted therefore assumes great importance for the region. Earlier, surplus wealth had been redistributed through leadership strategies to vassals, as in the case of the Pyu chiefs, but now these were redistributed, in a more refined fiscal strategy, to monastic and temple complexes. Fairly standardized lumps of silver and gold served for transactions in Bagan. Therefore, shortage of metals is not the issue here, nor its use or non-use as currency; rather, its value as circulating media is significant, and the means whereby this was undertaken and sustained deserves our attention.

But there could be other reasons as well. Was the general move away from minted coinage in the northern bay world between the 7th and 13th centuries a reflection of the emergence of a different political economy? Did the nature of urban structures change? Which came earlier: urbanity or economy? We introduce here the concept of orthogenetic cities, which — as opposed to heterogenetic cities dependent on external relations, change and mobile entrepreneurship — are marked by stability, ritualized behaviour, monumental architecture and fewer coins (Miksic 2002, p. 94). An urgent subject for further study concerns the nature and functions of the Myanmar urban sites: Were they largely ceremonial? Were they built for defensive purposes? To what extent were they commercially oriented (Miksic 2002, p. 91)?

We must also consider the impact of a Mongol financial axis that drained much of the silver away (Kuroda 2009) by the end of the 13th century. The Mongol "silver century" united the uplands, less so the northern bay, and it would be interesting to speculate how far trade was affected there. There was a similar drainage of metals from China from 1074, leading to interdictions on coin export and attempts at floating a paper currency by the later Song (for early and mid-Song financial initiatives and constraints, see Lamouroux 2000) and then by the Yuan (Rockhill 1915, pp. 420–21). It is not yet clear whether the drain, and consequent shortage, started at the Chinese end.

There could be yet another reason. Bagan is invariably linked with stasis and mechanical reproduction because Western training assumes that there is an inviolable link between a linear, progressive view of history and the concept of change. This assumes a single temporalizing possibility, and the mere passage of such a time becomes the criterion for change; we automatically assume change simply if a great deal of time has elapsed (Aung-Thwin 1991, pp. 579, 584). However, cross-temporal arcs cut across multiple, interacting, and partially open temporal systems that through their complex interactions participate in the emergent processes we identify as history (Born 2015, p. 381). Spirals, not cycles or straight lines, may have characterized Bagan's development (Aung-Thwin 1991), obviating the need for immediate cash to lubricate everyday life and transactions, and encouraging stockpiling of metals as circulating media instead. The latter action made the region an attractive target for metals; a drain, acquiring alarming proportions from the 13th century, appeared. We really need more information on silver links in the region, since use of metals as coined currency came back only from the 14th century, with the disappearance of the Mongol realm and the appearance of the Bengal Sultanate and Ming China, at opposite ends of what had once been Bagan.

Notes

1. Bagan had no access to the bay. Sen mentions armed conflicts along the Taklimakan and the Yunnan–Burma areas resulting in the decline of land routes and the rise of maritime trade between China and India from the 9th century (Sen 2003, pp. 211, 213). Elisseeff, quoting the *Biographies of Eminent Monks*, remarks that prior to 644 CE some 710 monks used the Buddhist Route, and only 633 used this route between 645 CE and 988 (Elisseeff 2000, p. 5). However, Sun (1997, pp. 13–16) notes several Tang notices on the overland route from China to India via northern Burma. The disturbances probably occurred in the early part of the 7th century, and fit the picture of lessened maritime trade from Bengal, fewer sailings from Tamralipta and the decline of gold coinage, all reflections of the collapse of the Tang–Sassanian maritime silk trade (Rhodes 2011).
2. The Bawdingyi mines were worked from the 10th century, but Wicks (1992, pp. 133–34) suggests that large amounts of silver only became accessible from the end of the 12th and the beginning of the 13th century. Was this through access to new technology because of commercialization, or by way of conquests opening up new routes?
3. Comment by John Miksic, 3 December 2015.
4. Both Faxian (414 CE) and Yijing (695 CE) used this port — Yijing returning to China from Tamralipta via Kedah. In any case, the overland route we are talking of is not referenced in this period. Yijing, who remained in Tamralipta for five months, mentions two routes to India from China; one a land route by way of Khotan and Northern India, and the other the southern sea route from Canton to Condore (Kun-lun) and thence to the Straits of Malacca, Kedah, Pegu and Tamralipta. Three routes radiated from Tamralipta: one to Burma and beyond via the Arakan coast, a second route to the Malaya Peninsula and the Far East via Paloura near Chicacole, and a third route which passed along Kalinga and the Coromandel coasts to Sri Lanka. See Ramachandran (1951, pp. 226, 228). Obviously, the overland route from Bagan to Bengal was not known, or perhaps not used, in the 7th century.
5. For Bagan's Buddhism impacting on Mainamati, see Bautze-Picron 2008–9, p. 7. For diplomatic and matrimonial relations, see Frasch 2002. For musical instruments (notably the harp), see Becker 1967. For art, see Strachan 1996, p. 21.

6. <http://cartographic-images.net/Cartographic_Images/235_Catalan_Atlas. html> (accessed 21 January 2012).
7. *The Travels of Marco Polo the Venetian*, translated and edited by William Marsden, re-edited by Wright, 1854, pp. 181, 267–68.
8. According to Mong Mao (Pong) legend, Sukampha became the King of Pong in 777 CE and his brother Samlongpha invaded Cachar, Tripura, Manipur and Assam. The foundation myth of the Tai Ahom in Assam mentions the founder's name as Sukhapa, who marched into the area about 1228–29 and conquered Kamarupa around 1231. The similarity with Sukampha is obvious: "[T]he obvious links between the Ahom and the Möng Mao polity of Lu-chuan need to be studied far more deeply. The marked similarity of the list of Ahom rulers with those of the Tai Mao cannot be coincidental" (Wade 2005).

References

Akasoy, Anna. "Tibet in Islamic Geography and Cartography: A Survey of Arabic and Persian Sources". In *Islam and Tibet: Interactions Along the Musk Routes*, edited by Anna Akasoy, Charles Burnett, Ronit Yoeli-Tlalim, pp. 17–42. Farnham: Ashgate, 2011.

Almagia, Roberto. "Carta dell'Asia: Asiae Orbis partium maximae nova descriptio di Abramo Ortelio". In *Planisferi Carte Navtiche e Affini dal Secolo XIV al XVII esistenti nella Biblioteca Apostolica Vaticana*, 4 vols. Vatican City, 1944.

Association of Myanmar Archaeologists. n.d. <http://aomar.wordpress.com/> (accessed 24 January 2012).

Aung-Thwin, Michael A. *Pagan: The Origins of Modern Burma*. Honolulu: University of Hawai'i Press, 1985.

———. "Spirals in Early Southeast Asian and Burmese History". *Journal of Interdisciplinary History* 21, no. 4 (1991): 575–602.

———. "Origins and Development of the Field of Prehistory in Burma". *Asian Perspectives* 40, no. 1 (2002): 6–34.

Bautze-Picron, Claudine. Review article, *Journal of Bengal Art* 13–14 (2008–9): 65–88.

Becker, Judith. "The Migration of the Arched Harp from India to Burma". *Galpin Society Journal* 20 (1967): 17–23.

Boisselier, Jean. *Review of Copper-Plates of Sylhet*, vol. 1, *7th–11th Century A.D.* by Kamalakanta Gupta. *Journal of the Economic and Social History of the Orient* 14, no. 1 (1971): 90–94.

Born, Georgina. "Making Time: Temporality, History and the Cultural Object". *New Literary History* 46, no. 3 (2015): 361–86.

Chakrabarti, Dilip K. *Archaeological Geography of the Ganga Plain: The Middle and Lower Ganga*. New Delhi: Permanent Black, 2001.

Charney, Michael W. "Literary Culture on the Burma–Manipur Frontier in the

Eighteenth and Nineteenth Centuries". *Medieval History Journal* 14, no. 2 (2011): 159–81.

Christie, Anthony. "Ta-ch'in p'o-lo-men". *Bulletin of the School of Oriental and African Studies, University of London* 20, no. 1 (1957): 159–66.

Coedès, George. "Le royaume de Çrivijaya". *Bulletin de l'École française d'Extrême Orient* 18, no. 1 (1918): 1–36.

Coryton, J. "Trade Routes between British Burmah and Western China". *Journal of the Royal Geographical Society of London* 45 (1875): 229–49.

Daniels, Christian. "Script without Buddhism: Burmese Influence on the Tay (Shan) Script of mäng maaw as Seen in a Chinese Scroll Painting of 1407". *International Journal of Asian Studies* 9, no. 2 (2012): 147–76.

Dasgupta, Pareshchandra. "Tarapada Santra", appendix. In *Jalpaiguri Jelar Purakirti* (in Bangla), pp. 65–81. Kolkata: West Bengal State Archaeology Department, 2005.

Deshpande, M.N., ed. *Indian Archaeology 1966–67: A Review*. New Delhi: Archaeological Survey of India, Government of India, 1975.

Deyell, John S. "The China Connection: Problems of Silver Supply in Medieval Bengal". In *Precious Metals in the Later Medieval and Early Modern Worlds*, edited by John F. Richards, pp. 207–27. Durham: Carolina Academic Press, 1983. Reprinted in Sanjay Subrahmanyam, ed., *Money and the Market in India 1100–1700*, pp. 112–36. Delhi: Oxford University Press, 1994.

———. "Cowries and Coins: The Dual Monetary System of the Bengal Sultanate". *Indian Economic and Social History Review* 47 (2010): 63–106.

———. "Monetary and Financial Webs: The Regional and International Influence of Pre-modern Bengali Coinage. In *Pelagic Passageways: The Northern Bay of Bengal before Colonialism*, edited by Rila Mukherjee, pp. 279–314. Delhi: Primus Books, 2011.

Eaton, R.M. *The Rise of Islam, and the Bengal Frontier, 1204–1760*. Berkeley: University of California Press, 1993.

Elisseeff, Vadime. "Introduction". In *The Silk Roads: Highways of Culture and Commerce*, pp. 1–26. New York: Berghahn Books, 2000.

Falchetta, Piero, ed. *Fra Mauro's World Map*, Terrarum Orbis 5. Venice: Brepols, 2006.

Frasch, Tilman. "Coastal Peripheries during the Pagan Period". In *The Maritime Frontier of Burma: Exploring Political, Cultural and Commercial Interaction in the Indian Ocean World, 1200–1800*, edited by Jos Gommans and Jacques P. Leider, pp. 59–78. Amsterdam: KITLV Press, 2002.

———. "In an Octopussy's Garden: Of Chakravartins, Little Kings and a New Model of the Early State in South and Southeast Asia". In *Sharing Sovereignty: The Little Kingdom in South Asia*, edited by Georg Berkemer and Margret Frenz, pp. 93–114. Berlin: Klaus Schwartz, 2003.

———. "1456: The Making of a Buddhist Ecumene in the Bay of Bengal". In *Pelagic*

Passageways: The Northern Bay of Bengal World before Colonialism, edited by Rila Mukherjee, pp. 383–405. Delhi: Primus Books, 2011.

Goh Geok Yian. "Myanmar's Relations with China from Tagaung through Hanthawati-Taunggu Periods". In *Connecting and Distancing: Southeast Asia and China*, edited by Ho Khai Leong, pp. 115–33. Singapore: Institute of Southeast Asian Studies, 2009.

———. "The Question of 'China' in Burmese Chronicles". *Journal of Southeast Asian Studies* 41, no. 1 (2010): 125–52.

Gommans, Jos. "Burma at the Frontier of South, East and Southeast Asia: A Geographic Perspective. In *The Maritime Frontier of Burma: Exploring Political, Cultural and Commercial Interaction in the Indian Ocean World, 1200–1800*, edited by Jos Gommans and Jacques P. Leider, pp. 1–7. Amsterdam: KITLV Press, 2002.

Grave, Peter, and Mike Barbetti. "Dating the City Wall, Fortifications, and the Palace Site at Pagan. *Asian Perspectives* 40, no. 1 (2002): 75–87.

Griffiths, Arlo, and Amandine Lepoutre. "Campa Epigraphical Data on Polities and Peoples of Ancient Myanmar". *Journal of Burma Studies* 17, no. 2 (2013): 373–90.

Gupta, Kamalakanta. *Copper-Plates of Sylhet*, vol. 1. Sylhet: Lipika Enterprises, 1967.

Gutman, Pamela. "The Ancient Coinage of Southeast Asia". *Journal of the Siam Society* 66, no. 1 (1978): 8–21.

Hall, Kenneth R. "Local and International Trade and Traders in the Straits of Melaka Region: 600–1500". *Journal of the Economic and Social History of the Orient* 47, no. 2 (2004): 213–60.

———. "Ports-of-Trade, Maritime Diasporas, and Networks of Trade and Cultural Integration in the Bay of Bengal Region of the Indian Ocean: *c*.1300–1500". *Journal of the Economic and Social History of the Orient* 53 (2010): 109–45.

Hall, Kenneth R., and John K. Whitmore. *Explorations in Southeast Asian History: The Origins of Southeast Asian Statecraft*. Ann Arbor: Centre for South and Southeast Asian Studies, University of Michigan, 1976.

Heimann, James. "Small Change and Ballast: Cowry Trade and Usage as an Example of Indian Ocean Economic History". *South Asia: Journal of South Asian Studies* 3, no. 1 (1980): 48–69.

Hirth, Friedrich, and W.W. Rockhill. *Chau Ju-kua: His Work on the Chinese and Arab Trade in the Twelfth and Thirteenth Centuries: Entitled Chu-fan-chi*, translated from the Chinese and annotated. St. Petersburg: Academy of Science, 1911.

Hudson, Bob. "The Origins of Bagan: The Archaeological Landscape of Upper Burma to AD 1300". PhD Dissertation, University of Sydney, 2004 <http://acl.arts.usyd.edu.au/~hudson/bobhpage.htm> (accessed 11 August 2010).

Hudson, Bob, Nyein Lwin, and Win Maung (Tampawady). "The Origins of Bagan: New Dates and Old Inhabitants". *Asian Perspectives* 40, no. 1 (2002): 48–74.

Jacq-Hergoualc'h, Michel. *The Malay Peninsula: Crossroads of the Maritime Silk Road.* Leiden: Brill, 2002.

Jahan, Shanaj Husne. *Excavating Waves and Winds of (Ex)change: A Study of Maritime Trade in Early Bengal.* Oxford: British Archaeological Reports International Series, 2006.

———. "Archaeological Investigations at Bhitargarh in Panchagarh District". *Journal of Bengal Art* 15 (2010): 173–200.

Johns, Jeremy, and Emilie Savage-Smith. "The Book of Curiosities: A Newly Discovered Series of Islamic Maps". *Imago Mundi* 55, no. 1 (2003): 7–24.

Kulke, Hermann. "Rivalry and Competition in the Bay of Bengal and its Bearing on Indian Ocean Studies". In *Commerce and Culture in the Bay of Bengal 1500–1800*, edited by Om Prakash and Denys Lombard, pp. 17–35. New Delhi: Manohar/ICHR, 1999.

Kuroda, Akinobu. "The Eurasian Silver Century, 1276–1359: Commensurability and Multiplicity". *Journal of Global History* 4 (2009): 245–69.

Lamouroux, Christian. "Militaires et financiers dans la Chine des Song". *Bulletin de l'École française d'Extrême-Orient* 87, no. 1 (2000): 283–300.

Latham, Ronald, trans. *The Travels of Marco Polo.* London: Penguin, 1958.

Le May, R. *The Coinage of Siam.* Bangkok: Siam Society, 1932.

Lieberman, Victor B. *Strange Parallels: Southeast Asia in Global Context c.800–1830*, vol. 1, *Integration on the Mainland*. New York: Cambridge University Press, 2003.

———. *Strange Parallels: Southeast Asia in Global Context c.800–1830*, vol. 2, *Mainland Mirrors: Europe, Japan, China, South Asia and the Islands*. New York: Cambridge University Press, 2009.

Luce, G.H., and Ba Shin. "A Chieng Mai Mahathera Visits Pagán (1393 A.D.)". *Artibus Asiae* 24, nos. 3–4 (1961): 330–37.

Majumdar, R.C. "Les rois Šailendra de Suvarnadvîpa". *Bulletin de l'École française d'Extrême-Orient* 33, no. 1 (1933): 121–41.

Malekandathil, Pius. *Maritime India: Trade, Religion and Polity in the Indian Ocean.* Delhi: Primus Books, 2010.

Manatunga, Anura. "Sri Lanka and Southeast Asia during the Period of the Polonnaruva Kingdom". In *Nagapattinam to Suvarnadwipa, Reflections on the Chola Naval Expeditions to Southeast Asia*, edited by Hermann Kulke, K. Kesavapany, and Vijay Sakhuja, pp. 193–207. Singapore: Institute of Southeast Asian Studies, 2009.

Mandal, Barnali, Prasanta K. Datta, and Pranab K. Chattopadhyay. "Ancient Hot-Mould Casting Technology of Eastern India in Comparison with Chinese Bronze Technology. *Pratna Samiksha: A Journal of Archaeology* (2010): 213–29.

Miksic, John N. "Early Burmese Urbanization: Research and Conservation". *Asian Perspectives* 40, no. 1 (2002): 88–107.

Mukherjee, Rila. "A Dynamic Eastern Indian Ocean: Review Article". *Archipel* 82 (2011*a*): 201–12.

———. "Introduction: Bengal and the Northern Bay of Bengal". In *Pelagic Passageways: The Northern Bay of Bengal before Colonialism*, edited by Rila Mukherjee, pp. 1–260. Delhi: Primus Books, 2011*b*.

———. "Conclusion: Time, Space and Region in the Northern Bay of Bengal". In *Pelagic Passageways: The Northern Bay of Bengal before Colonialism*, edited by Rila Mukherjee, pp. 443–72. Delhi: Primus Books, 2011*c*.

Ortelius, Abraham. *Indiae Orientalis, Gedruckt zu Nuermberg Durch Johann Koler, Anno MDLXXII*. Darmstadt: WBG, 2006.

Ramachandran, T.N. "Tamralipta (Tamluk)". *Artibus Asiae* 14, no. 3 (1951): 226–39.

Rapoport, Yossef, and Emilie Savage-Smith. "Medieval Islamic View of the Cosmos: The Newly Discovered Book of Curiosities". *Cartographic Journal* 41, no. 3 (2004): 253–59.

Ray, N.R. *Bangalir Itihas (Adi Parva)*. Calcutta: Dey's, 1948.

Rhodes, Nicholas G. "Trade in South-East Bengal in the First Millennium CE, the Numismatic Evidence". In *Pelagic Passageways: The Northern Bay of Bengal before Colonialism*, edited by Rila Mukherjee, pp. 263–75. Delhi: Primus Books, 2011.

Rispaud, Jean. "Contribution à la géographie Historique de la haute Birmanie (Mien, Pong, Kosambi et Kamboja)" [Essays offered to G.H. Luce by his colleagues and friends in honour of his seventy-fifth birthday, vol. 1, Papers on Asian history, religion, languages, literature, music folklore, and anthropology]. *Artibus Asiae, Supplementum* 23 (1996).

Rockhill, W.W. "Notes on the Relations and Trade of China with the Eastern Archipelago and the Coast of the Indian Ocean during the Fourteenth Century", pt. 4. *T'oung Pao*, 2nd ser., 16, no. 4 (1915): 435–67.

Santra, Tarapada. *Jalpaiguri Jelar Purakirti* (in Bangla). Kolkata: West Bengal State Archaeology Department, 2005.

Sastri, K.A.N. "Sri Vijaya". *Bulletin de l'École française d'Extrême-Orient* 40, no. 2 (1940): 239–313.

Schnepel, Burhard, and Georg Berkemer. "History of the Model". In *Sharing Sovereignty, The Little Kingdom in South Asia*, edited by Georg Berkemer and Margret Frenz, pp. 11–20. Berlin: Klaus Schwartz, 2003.

Scott, James C. *The Art of Not Being Governed: An Anarchist History of Upland South East Asia*. New Haven: Yale University Press, 2009.

Sharma, R.S. *Early Medieval Indian Society*. Hyderabad: Orient Longman, 2003.

Soper, Alexander C., and Helen B. Chapin. "A Long Roll of Buddhist Images", pts. 1–3. *Artibus Asiae* 32, nos. 1–4 (1970): 5–41, 157–99, 259–89, 291–306.

———. "A Long Roll of Buddhist Images", pt. 4. *Artibus Asiae* 33, nos. 1–2 (1971): 75–140.

Sen, Kali Prasanna, ed. *Sri Rajmala*, 4 vols. Agartala: Tribal Research Centre, 2003.

Sen, Tansen. *Buddhism, Diplomacy, and Trade: The Realignment of Sino-Indian Relations, 600–1400*. Honolulu: University of Hawai'i Press, Association for Asian Studies, 2003.

———. "The Formation of Chinese Maritime Networks to Southern Asia, 1200–1450". *Journal of the Economic and Social History of the Orient* 49, no. 4 (2006): 421–53.

Skelton, R.A. "Introduction". In *Abraham Ortelius, Theatrum Orbis Terrarum, Antwerp 1570*. Amsterdam: Meridian, 1964.

Sladen, Edward Bosc. "Trade through Burma to China: An Address Read to the Glasgow Chamber of Commerce 14th Nov., 1870". *Foreign and Commonwealth Office Collection*, 1870.

Stargardt, Janice. "Burma's Economic and Diplomatic Relations with India and China from Early Medieval Sources. *Journal of Economic and Social History of the Orient* 14, no. 1 (1971): 38–62, 51–53.

Strachan, Paul. *Pagan: Art and Architecture of Old Burma*. Oxford: Kiscadale, 1996.

Sumio, Fukami. "The Long Thirteenth Century of Tambralinga: From Javaka to Siam". *Memoirs of the Research Department of the Toyo Bunko* 62 (2004): 45–79.

Sun Laichen. "Chinese Historical Sources on Burma". Special issue, *Journal of Burma Studies* 2 (1997): 1–53.

Tarafdar, M.R. "Trade and Society in Early Medieval Bengal". *Indian Historical Review* 4, no. 2 (1978): 275–84.

Taylor, Keith W. "The Early Kingdoms". In *The Cambridge History of Southeast Asia*, vol. 1, edited by Nicholas Tarling, pp. 137–82. Cambridge: Cambridge University Press, 1999.

Thakur, Vijay Kumar. "Beginnings of Feudalism in Bengal". *Social Scientist* 6, nos. 6–7 (1978): 68–82.

———. "Trade and Towns in Early Medieval Bengal (c. A.D. 600–1200)." *Journal of the Economic and Social History of the Orient* 30, no. 2 (1987): 196–220.

Tibbetts, G.R. *A Study of the Arabic Texts Containing Material on South East Asia*. Leiden: Brill, 1979.

Wade, Geoff, trans. *Southeast Asia in the Ming Shi-Lu: An Open Access Resource*. Singapore: Asia Research Institute and the Singapore E-Press, National University of Singapore, 2005 <http://epress.nus.edu.sg/msl/entry/>.

———. "An Early Age of Commerce in Southeast Asia, 900–1300 CE". *Journal of Southeast Asian Studies* 40, no. 2 (2009*a*): 221–65.

———. "An Annotated Translation of the *Yuan Shi* Account of Mian (Burma)". In *The Scholar's Mind: Essays in Honor of Frederick W. Mote*, edited by Perry Link, pp. 17–49. Hong Kong: Chinese University of Hong Kong, 2009*b*.

Wheatley, Paul. *Pivot of the Four Quarters: A Preliminary Enquiry into the Origins and Character of the Ancient Chinese City*. Chicago: Aldine, 1971.

Wicks, Robert S. *Money, Markets and Trade in Early Southeast Asia: The Development of Indigenous Monetary Systems to* AD *1400.* Ithaca: SEAP Publications, 1992.

Wink, André. *Al-Hind: The Making of the Indo Islamic World*, vol. 1, *Early Medieval India and the Expansion of Islam, Seventh to Eleventh Centuries.* Delhi: Oxford University Press, 1990.

Wolters, O.W. "Tāmbralinga". *Bulletin of the School of Oriental and African Studies* 21, nos. 1–3 (1958): 587–607.

Wright, Thomas. *The Travels of Marco Polo, the Venetian.* Blackmask Online, [1854] 2002 <http://www.blackmask.com> (accessed 11 August 2010).

Yang Bin. "Horses, Silver, and Cowries: Yunnan in Global Perspective". *Journal of World History* 15, no. 3 (2004): 281–322.

———. *Between Winds and Clouds, The Making of Yunnan (Second Century* BCE *– Twentieth Century* BCE.*)* New York: Columbia University Press, 2008.

Yule, Henry. "On the Geography of Burma and its Tributary States, in Illustration of a New Map of Those Regions". *Journal of the Royal Geographical Society of London* 27 (1857): 54–108.

9

Positioning Bagan in the Buddhist *Ecumene*: Myanmar's Trans-Polity Connections

Goh Geok Yian

This chapter starts with the assumption that Bagan of the 11th through the 14th centuries was a religious hub for monks and pilgrims and constituted one of three important nodes in a Buddhist common world or commonwealth, or what I have elected to call "Buddhist *ecumene*". The Buddhist *ecumene* demarks a common world within which exchanges and interactions between the different nodes shared a religion: Buddhism. Buddhism represents an overarching principle for all the polities which belonged to the same *ecumene*, but it is by no means the only linking principle. Within this *ecumene*, ideas, texts and items travelled and were exchanged among the different nodes of the same network that were also connected via commercial trade. Polities waged wars, sometimes on the pretext of religion, but in other times to obtain more people, more resources and to assert supremacy over another. The *ecumene* refers to a network of centres which is marked by a common shared religion under the "one house" (*oikos*) of Buddhism.

Bagan represents one of the three key nodes of this Buddhist *ecumene*. The Buddhist *ecumene* begins with the reign of Anawrahta, an 11th-century king of Bagan whose exploits are recorded in the Burmese chronicles of the 18th and 19th centuries, the northern Thai chronicle(s) of the 15th century and the Sri Lankan chronicle, *Cūlavaṁsa*. The *Cūlavaṁsa* dates from the 13th century but contains updates through the 19th century. The chronicles present the view that Bagan, northern Thailand and Sri Lanka had close interactions with one another, which began as early as the 11th century. These accounts emphasize the king's importance and the position of the kingdom's capital, Bagan, within the context of a regional Buddhist commonwealth or network, characterized by the idea of a Buddhist *ecumene* (for detailed discussions, see Goh 2007 and 2014).

Chronicle Accounts

Textual accounts of Anawrahta and Bagan characterize the king making great efforts to obtain Buddhist texts and relics. His endeavours to take religious texts and relics to Bagan resulted in the sending of a number of expeditions to foreign countries such as Tarup-China,[1] Sri Lanka and India. According to the textual accounts, most of these missions were carried out without the outbreak of wars. Textual accounts such as U Kala's *Mahayazawingyi* (ca. 1720s), Twinthin Taikwun Mahasitthu's *Yazawinthit* (ca. 1798), and the *Hmannan Yazawindawgyi* (1829) provide detailed descriptions of King Anawrahta's exploits, but when it comes to the description of Bagan itself, information is lacking. The descriptions pertain mainly to the enshrining of Buddha's relics in several locations, where stupas were erected; the most significant being the four shrines or *zedis* associated with the Buddha's tooth relic that came from Sri Lanka (Theingho). These four shrines are the stupas at Shwezigon, Tangyidaung, Lokananda and Tuywindaung. The account of how the single tooth relic grew to five can be found in Burmese chronicles (see, for example, U Kala 1960, pp. 195–96). According to the chronicle tradition, a fifth tooth grew from the fourth, and this was borne by a white elephant to a place on the eastern slope of the mountain ranges to the southeast of Bagan; at the top of Thalyaung peak, the elephant stopped and prostrated for a brief moment, before it climbed Khaywe peak, and eventually took the relic to Pyek peak, where the king ordered the establishment of a *zedi*. Anawrahta also ordered the building of *zedis* on the other two peaks that the elephant journeyed to (U Kala 1960, p. 195). This would account for the number of monuments found at the summits of the mountains to the southeast of Bagan, with Tuywindaung being the highest peak.

The *Mahayazawingyi*, for instance, states that Anawrahta ordered the building of numerous *hpaya* (temples which comprise stupas and pagodas), *gu* (cave-like single-storied temples), *kyaung* (monasteries) and irrigation canals throughout the *nainngan* (country/kingdom) (U Kala 1960, p. 201); one of these was in Taungbyon village, which was named Hsutaungpyi. The latter description comes under the section which describes what the king did for the people he conquered and captured (U Kala 1960, p. 189). The text also provides the names of irrigation works established by Anawrahta and the eleven villages he "founded" (U Kala 1960, p. 202).

Chronicle accounts also describe the extent of Anawrahta's kingdom by listing the countries with which Anawrahta's Bagan shared borders. The *Mahayazawingyi* (U Kala 1960, p. 204)[2] presents an idea of the geographical boundaries of Anawrahta's Bagan by stating, for instance, that to the west is Kala Pyi (India), to the northwest corner is Kutungana water body, to the north is Gandharaj-Tarup (China), to the northeast corner is Kadhanti Muslim country, to the east is Satissa-Pankar (Bengal?), and in the southeast corner is Yawsa-Gywan country (Cambodia). There is, however, no description of the capital of Bagan (Arimaddanapura/Arimaddana-Paukkarama naypyidaw), its people or their activities. For these, one has to use other contemporary sources, namely Chinese descriptions of Bagan (see Goh 2007 and Goh 2014). Another category of textual source is inscriptions. Inscriptions generally provide an additional layer of information, particularly on individual donors or types of donors, and people and services dedicated to certain temple-building projects and monasteries. However, when trying to use them as an unequivocal source of evidence to reconstruct everyday life in Bagan during the 11th through 14th centuries, they present a problematic dataset.

What Do the Inscriptions Say about Bagan?

Inscriptions list long lists of donations of land, people, goods and other things to the temples and monasteries:

> Thus in AD 1190 a donor named *Singhasura* dedicated musicians such as *cansan* — drummers, and *pantya* — nautches, for the enjoyment of music.

Old Burmans apparently thought the Buddha was a living deity.... Slaves dedicated to him were of various professions. Such musicians as *pasasan* — side drummers, *saro san* — violinist, *nhan san* — trumpeters, *candra san* — dulcimer players, *sikran san* — singers, and *kakhriy san* — dancers, were also mentioned in the inscriptions of our period as slaves for the Buddha. The wife of *Kankasu* gave the services of such persons as *panpwat* — turners, *panpu* — sculptors, *pankhi* — painters, *puran* — masons, *cariy* — secretaries, *nwathin* — cowherds, *panthin* — goldsmiths, *uyan san* — gardeners, and *kuha san* — launderers, when she dedicated them to the Buddha in AD 1242. In the same year *Cuiw Man* gave to the Buddha slaves such as *sanryan san* — palanquin bearers, *kuha san* — launderers, *thi san* — umbrella bearers, and *yan san* — weavers. (Than Tun 1978, pp. 68–69)

He added that "Such slaves[3] as *muchit rip* — barbers, *han san thaman san amay san* — cooks, and *kwam san* — servers of betel, were also dedicated to the Buddha" (Than Tun 1978, p. 69). Than Tun (1978, p. 158) listed the five categories of *kywan*: (1) agriculturalists, (2) food suppliers, (3) craftsmen, (4) musicians and (5) miscellaneous. Others mentioned in inscriptions include: *laksma* (carpenters), *tacan san* (plane men?), *panran* (masons), *panpin* (woodcarvers), *pankhi* (painters), *panpwat* (woodturners), *tankyat san* (canopy makers), *ut san* (brick makers), *panphay* (blacksmiths), *athusan* and *purhan san* (image makers), *thisan* (umbrella makers), *panthin* (goldsmiths), *uiwthin* (potters), *karasan* (jug makers), *lanpansan* (tray makers), *khran nay* (spinners), *pukhran san* (loincloth makers), *yan san* (weavers) and *sanaphway* (chair makers? cushion makers?) (Than Tun 1978, p. 159).[4]

Inscriptions suggest a fair degree of specialization of labour. The key to understanding what all these mean is to determine what the presence of these occupational groups signifies. A possible variable which could be used as an indication of an urban centre is occupational specialization. The presence of different occupational groups may be indicative of a differentiated population; the manufacturing of different types of products suggests the settlement may be a city or urban centre, perhaps of the heterogenetic variety. A heterogenetic city has a dense population (see the models of cities proposed by Redfield and Singer [1954] and modified for Southeast Asia by Miksic [2000]).

According to Fox (1971) there are two types of societies: "monument-building militaristic kingdoms inland and trading ports on coasts and margins of hinterland empires" (Miksic 2000, p. 107). Redfield and Singer (1954) also propose two different models of urban society, but refer to them instead as orthogenetic (stability and ritual) and heterogenetic (change and entrepreneurship). In Miksic's (2000) adaptation of Redfield and Singer's model to Southeast Asia, the orthogenetic city is characterized by manufacturing activities, which are not centralized in the monumental area; they are scattered around the periphery at some distance away from the centre, and they specialize in one specific product. Dense population clusters are absent in orthogenetic cities; the permanent population comprises nobles, civil, religious and military bureaucrats and their staff (Miksic 2000, p. 107). Heterogenetic cities, on the other hand, produced few monuments, are usually found on the borders of ecological zones rather than at their centres, used money, produced many types of commodities in the same settlement, and had dense populations (Miksic 2000, p. 107).

Inscriptional evidence suggests that occupation specialization appears to have been highly variegated in early Bagan. But caution must be exercised here: it is important for us to note that a list of varied occupational groups and individuals does not necessarily mean that the services rendered by these individuals were made available to other persons in the same society, especially the non-elite. As these individuals of various occupational specializations were often mentioned in inscriptions as individuals who were donated or dedicated to temples, et cetera, and as little evidence was presented which could provide us with absolute numbers in terms of how many of these individuals were brick makers versus blacksmiths versus weavers, it is difficult to obtain a clear idea of the diversity of early Bagan society. The vocations of the people donated indicate that a great number of these individuals' occupations were related to monument building and activities associated with Buddhism and the monastic order, as well as with the royal palace. The inscriptional evidence points to an orthogenetic and redistributive economy, with elite control of craft production.

Inscriptional evidence suggests royal control of resources and possible applicability of Polanyi's redistributive model for early Bagan (11th through 14th centuries). Polanyi argues in his substantivist model (1944; Polanyi et al. 1957) that ancient state economies (Bagan, Angkor, and even central Javanese Mataram, for instance, representing Southeast Asian examples) were non-capitalist and largely organized around the exchange mechanism of reciprocity and redistribution, and not like the capitalist model of market exchange, but this is problematic (Smith 2004, p. 75). It does not provide enough scope for variation in ancient "non-capitalist" economies. Brumfiel and Earle (1987) identify three alternatives to Polyani's model which can be utilized to examine the phenomenon of elite control of craft production: (1) adaptationist, (2) commercial, and (3) political.

The adaptationist approach "focuses on the adaptation of human groups to their environment" (Smith 2004, p. 75; examples include Redman 1978 and Sanders et al. 1979). This is in essence a functionalist approach to understanding elite control over the economy. In this model, scholars undertake regional settlement pattern surveys and use their results to reconstruct regional demography and agricultural practices. They focus primarily on local adaptations and downplay the significance of long-distance trade and exchanges (Feinman and Nicholas 1991, cited in Smith 2004, p. 76). This approach is functionalist because Brumfiel and Earle argue that the political elites assume control over the economy in order to run it more efficiently. One of the approach's central arguments is that population pressure leads to the rise of states by generating agricultural change (see Cohen 1977 and Netting 1993).

In the commercial model, Brumfiel and Earle assert that "increases in specialization and exchange are seen as an integral part of the spontaneous process of economic growth" (1987, p. 1; cited in Smith 2004, p. 76). However, they (Brumfield and Earle 1987, p. 2) argue that they could identify few cases of ancient state economies which originated through commercial development, mainly because they are only considering profits which have accumulated in the hands of private individuals (an indication that they are attempting to apply strictly the commercial capitalist model to early examples, which is problematic; Smith 2004, p. 77).

The last model is the political model, which Brumfiel and Earle favour. In this model the "local elites assume control of the economy" by taking "a more self-centered stance by strategically controlling aspects of the economy for their own economic and political ends" (Smith 2004, p. 77). Two approaches emerged from this model: one which focuses on the role of the individual actor, and the other, which is more relevant to studies pertaining to ancient state economies in Myanmar as well as in the Southeast Asian region, is archaeological political economy. The broad themes associated with the study of archaeological political economy are: (1) a global perspective on economies as open systems, (2) attention to the economic dimensions and implications of political behaviour and institutions, (3) a concern with inequality and social classes, and (4) a focus on processes of local historical change rather than broad processes of cultural evolution (see works by Wolf 1982, Roseberry 1988, Stein 2001). Gil Stein's work (2001), in particular, is highly relevant to future research on the study of ancient state economies in Myanmar and Southeast Asia. Stein focuses on four themes characterizing the political economy of old world states: (1) a shift from models of states as highly centralized to notions of variability and limits of state power, (2) a focus on the economic organization of states, (3) research on rural areas and centre–hinterland interactions, and (4) attention to inter-regional interaction at diverse spatial scales (Stein 2001, p. 356). Examining these themes for ancient Southeast Asian polities and their interactions with each other within the pre-modern context provides a more nuanced perspective on the factors that influenced Myanmar's relations with its neighbouring polities and the process of urbanization in early Myanmar "states" such as Bagan.

Bagan as an Urban Centre

Most authors see Bagan as a centralized agrarian state that established its suzerainty over a swath of territory which approximated that of modern Myanmar. The issue of whether Bagan was a city or urban site has not been seriously discussed, except in Miksic's work on heterogenetic and orthogenetic cities (1996, 2000). Bagan was probably not a densely populated capital and kingdom. It was not an example of an extreme case of agrarian centralized state and orthogenetic society: it possesses features characterizing both orthogenetic and heterogenetic societies. However, one would argue that it was probably much closer to the orthogenetic end of the spectrum than the heterogenetic end. This assertion remains largely speculative until more work can be undertaken, especially excavations of sites believed to contain dense layers of pottery. This section of this chapter takes an initial look at how archaeological data provides important insight into the distribution of artefacts and hence activities within the archaeological zone. The materials come from preliminary random surveys of the vicinity of Bagan (2008–11) and an initial examination of a small sample of ceramic artefacts excavated from the Anawrahta and Kyanzittha Palace sites, which are now stored in the Bagan Archaeological Museum's store (December 2013 – January 2014). The preliminary survey of surface ceramic finds at various sites in Bagan and the initial examination of the Anawrahta and Kyanzittha Palace sites' artefacts support the hypothesis that Bagan was a ceremonial administrative centre closer to the orthogenetic end of the spectrum, but the capital city's population also engaged in market exchange to a certain extent. The population's involvement in some form of privatized exchange is suggested from the range of porcelain sherds found distributed throughout the Bagan archaeological zone. Blue and white, green and white porcelains of Chinese origins of varying quality are found in surface scatter together with indigenous glazed stoneware (produced in Myanmar but possibly in different parts of the country) and locally made earthenware sherds.

As textual sources are limited, in the sense that even if one can prove that the accounts are accurate reflections of 11th-century Bagan they provide no information on the actual sectors of activities in the capital and kingdom, archaeological research becomes important. Archaeology in Bagan has largely focused on the excavations of building sites; other types of research, such as a study of ceramic distribution, are needed to refine the characterization of ancient Bagan's economy.

Further understanding of early Bagan can also be achieved by undertaking comparative studies of the sites outside and within the elite zone, such as the palace site complexes or sites within and outside the "city" wall. Some scholars (see Aung-Thwin, Hudson, Miksic, Grave and Barbetti in *Asian Perspectives* 2001) have proposed that Bagan was either a centralized agrarian polity, an orthogenetic city, or a ceremonial centre (Wheatley's model), but little is known about everyday life in 11th- through 14th-century Bagan. The thousands of temples and stupas and inscriptions do not provide information on habitation sites or economic facets of daily life in monastic complexes. Similar questions can be asked regarding habitation sites for commoners. Here, ceramic distribution patterns are fundamental in identifying habitation sites as opposed to other activity areas. By examining both the horizontal and vertical density of pottery scatter throughout the entire Bagan archaeological zone, it may be possible to identify likely habitation areas or different activity sites.

The proportion of Chinese and other foreign ceramics to indigenously produced ceramics is an important form of quantitative data which has not been collected. A more detailed typology of indigenous ceramics will also provide a much-needed understanding of the dynamics of internal trade; some of the glazed ceramics found around Bagan appear to have been produced somewhere else, very likely further upriver and north of Bagan, perhaps in kilns near Shwebo and Mandalay, where many modern glazed ceramics come from. Another possible site is down south in the Twante region, but that appears to have functioned as a producer of glazed ceramics only in the 15th and 16th centuries. We have barely scratched the surface in terms of research on Myanmar ceramics. Much can be learned from explorations, not only of Bagan but of other sites throughout Myanmar. Chinese ceramics are present in Bagan; most date to the Song and Yuan dynasties, and many are of high quality. However, there are also examples of lower-quality green porcelain, some of which likely came from Southern Chinese kilns in Fujian and Guangdong.

Importance of Ceramic and Pottery Distribution Studies

Data on the density, distribution and extent of ceramics throughout a site such as Bagan can provide information on the types of activities undertaken at specific sites. The density of ceramics is indicative of many aspects of human activity. People rarely travel long distances to throw away things — dense concentrations of ceramic sherds suggest the presence of human habitation sites. Furthermore, the types of ceramics excavated from monastic complexes give researchers ideas of the functions of types of ceramics within a monastery: how monastic communities used these ceramics can reveal much about the daily lives of the members of monastic orders; it can also reveal much about the people who performed services for the monastic complexes, such as the people who were donated to the monastic communities.

A study of ceramics and ceramic distribution should utilize a four-stage approach: (1) creating a typology of ceramics found in Bagan, (2) developing a seriation of local earthenware pottery, (3) recording the density of ceramic scatter within Bagan, and (4) identifying patterns in the distribution of ceramic densities.

The following section presents summaries and preliminary discussions on the ceramics found during the 2008–11 random and opportunistic surveys and a sampling of the Bagan Archaeological Museum's collection of ceramic sherds excavated from the Anawrahta and Kyanzittha Palace sites examined from December 2013 to January 2014. Discussions on the artefacts suggest the importance of undertaking further research, especially surveys and excavations of areas in the archaeological zone, not restricted to areas near the Anawrahta and Kyanzittha Palace sites. If the surface artefacts are any indication of the complexity of the Bagan urban site, future archaeological research will provide interesting information on site usage in the Bagan site complex, which extends over and beyond the Bagan archaeological zone.

Artefacts from the Random Surveys

This section examines the artefacts found at sites within the old Bagan city wall and outside the old wall. The surfaces around these sites contain a large quantity of broken sherds, the greater percentage of which comprise the most common type of pottery, earthenware, which is not as useful as Chinese ceramics in providing chronology for archaeological sites. In this work I will focus on Chinese ceramic finds and other unusual artefacts.

A preliminary survey of the area to the northwest of 1589 Shwegugyi temple reveals a number of surface finds. These include Chinese porcelain: two sherds of Song dynasty white porcelain, possibly from Jiangxi province; four green porcelain sherds dating from the Song–Yuan period: two Longquan-type bowls and two green porcelain sherds which likely came from southern Chinese kilns, one of which has an olive green crackling glaze. Another interesting surface find is a Yuan dynasty blue and white porcelain sherd; the dating of the sherd is based on its cobalt blue, bluish-tinge *qingbai* glaze, thin body, whiteness of clay, pinholes on the glaze surface, et cetera. Other surface finds include two Burmese glazed stoneware sherds: one white glazed ware (pinkish clay, glaze flakes off easily, potholes in glaze, crackling, etc.) and a black-glazed stoneware jar/big bowl rim (glaze on the exterior, rim unglazed, interior unglazed, thick body, reddish clay typical of Burmese glazed stoneware). There were also three Burmese earthenware sherds: red polished fine paste ware, earthenware rim polished on the interior, and a stamped earthenware body sherd. The red polished fine paste ware is representative of the types of surface sherds.

Outside the old Bagan wall, several sites were surveyed. The first is the north sector of the archaeological zone in the vicinity of Upali Thein. The area surveyed is west of 2136 Catur Mukha, which forms one of the Upali Thein group of temples. A dense scatter of ceramics was found between Upali Thein and Myazigon, close to the river. Three examples of Chinese ceramics were found. Two are green porcelain sherds; one of these sherds has a rim with incised design which has an almost dark olive-greyish green glaze, which likely came from a southern Chinese kiln. The third sherd is a light green glazed porcelain, which also likely came from one of the southern Chinese kilns. Beautiful white Song porcelain with incised decoration on the interior was also found in this location.

East of Upali Thein is another area where surface finds of Chinese porcelain are noted. The Chinese porcelain found *in situ* includes an incised Song–Yuan dynasty green porcelain bowl, most likely a product from a southern Chinese kiln. There are also two white porcelain sherds: a *qingbai* glaze base and a slip-moulded body sherd; both sherds dating to the Song dynasty. Both sherds are characteristic of white porcelain from Jiangxi province.

Surface finds were also found near temple number 2102 between Upali Thein and Ta Kya Hi Hpaya. A green porcelain sherd was found in a ditch east of the temple. There were also four other Chinese green porcelain sherds. They include one of the Longquan variety and three sherds (one base and two sherds with incised designs on their interior) that likely came from a southern Chinese kiln. All these ceramics are typical of the Song–Yuan period. A Burmese black glazed rim stoneware sherd was also found; an interesting characteristic of this sherd is that the rim is thicker than the body.

An incised white porcelain sherd was found near temple number 2053 in Taung Bi village, east of the Yinmana group of temples. To the south of temple number 0213, a dense pottery scatter was noted; the area is located between Wetkyī In and Nyaung U.

Several sites of ceramic scatter are recorded in the eastern sector of old Bagan. In particular, a dense accumulation of ceramics was noted in the vicinity of the earthen mound, Otein Taung ("Potters' Mound"). The author found no sherds of Chinese or foreign origins in the vicinity of the mound. Several Burmese or local pottery were found during the random surveys, which include a Burmese glazed ware base that has a whitish glaze, pinkish clay bisque and a thick profile; a high-fired Burmese earthenware with perforations on the rim and stamped designs on the interior of the rim; and a burnished or polished orange earthenware. The only non-Burmese sherds found in the vicinity of the mound were four white sherds (see Hudson 2004). Based on Hudson's images of these sherds, they are most likely Chinese white porcelain rather than Burmese glazed ware. This observation is made on the basis of the type of rims, bases and colour of the glaze observable from the photos.

Another location which was surveyed is 0664 Ma La Phyit Hpaya, which is situated to the north of Hsinbyushin monastic complex.

A preliminary survey of the ground yielded green celadon and blue and white porcelain sherds. In December 2011, more Chinese porcelain sherds were observed in the big field. There were four blue and white sherds of the Yuan dynasty period. Two Burmese white glazed stoneware sherds with pinkish clay bisque were also found; one is a rim sherd and the other a plain body sherd.

The last area surveyed in the east sector is a temple located to the northwest of Minnanthu and west of 447 Le Myet Hna. Examples of ceramics found comprise a Song dynasty white spur-marked porcelain sherd and one gray stoneware Burmese rim with incised decor on the interior.

The author surveyed five sites in the southeastern sector of old Bagan. One of these is the area near Shwe Hsan Daw. One Chinese green porcelain base was found together with four Burmese glazed stoneware sherds; of the latter, two were bases (one of a large jar and another of a bowl) and two were body sherds. Two red burnished earthenware sherds were also found, and these include one spout and a neck of a *kendi*. There was also a fragment of a stone pipe (16th–17th century Burmese).

Other sites surveyed in this area are: (1) temple number 1521, which is part of the Mye Kin Tha group, north of Shwe Hsan Daw. A Song white porcelain sherd, a green porcelain sherd and much earthenware were found in the vicinity. (2) A soya bean field located approximately 120 degrees southeast of Mye Bon Tha and due east of temple 1514 has a dense scatter of local pottery. The wares include tiles, bricks, stoneware, high-fired earthenware (some with stamped motifs and paddle-marked designs) and reddish *kendi* necks. (3) Temple number 0862 is located to the north of Dhammayazika. Chinese ceramics found include a green porcelain body sherd, albeit not of the Longquan variety. There was also a Burmese earthenware rim sherd which is high-fired, burnished/polished and bears a punctate stamped design on its surface. (4) Temple 0889 Hman Si Hpaya is situated east of Dhammayazika. Chinese porcelain samples include two green porcelain sherds, one of which is Longquan ware and the other is a very light green glazed rim, possibly from one of the southern Chinese kilns. There were also Burmese glazed stoneware sherds found *in situ*; these include a dark green stoneware sherd (from a large jar) with moulded designs (tail of a fish?) — the glaze used was very likely copper (oxidization process). Another sherd is an example of green glazed plaques used as decoration on the exterior of temples.

The plaque sherd is a fragment of a glazed plaque used as decoration on the exterior of the little structure, 889.

The last area surveyed between 2009 and 2011 is the southern sector of old Bagan. One area in which Chinese and indigenous ceramics were found is in the vicinity of 1145 Somingyi and 1147 Somingyi Okkyaung. An example of Chinese porcelain found here is a green porcelain base of the Longquan type. Burmese glazed stoneware sherds were also found: one black glazed stoneware rim and one dirty green and reddish brown glazed base. The author identified two types of Burmese earthenware pottery. Group 1 comprises red burnished fine paste ware: one kendi neck and two carinations, two orange-coloured fine paste lids, and one orange fine paste ware part of neck and carination with jabbed designs. Group 2 consists of tempered earthenware: brown or buff ware (two handles of lids) and one rim of a jar (water jar?). There was also a stamped paddle-marked earthenware body sherd.

Other sites which were surveyed in the vicinity include a field near 1155, which is a strange stupa abutting a wall near Somingyi Okkyaung and northeast of Kyauk Mye Mo Zedi Gyi (1158). This three-hundred-metre-long field is full of sherds. Temple 1048, north of Thiripyitsaya, is another site where there were lots of red burnished sherds; examples include one spout found together with a small bronze bell. Temple 1905, northeast of Min O Chan Tar complex, is a stupa within a stupa. A green glazed stoneware base was found nearby. This base has a thick body, low foot, a ring marking on the bottom of the base, and a green crackling glaze. The sherd is Burmese, not Chinese, and likely came from Twante. Dark brown glazed stoneware was also found at this site, the clay of which is dark chocolate brown in colour; from the profile, coarse temper was used in the clay. The sherd is Burmese with an uneven brown glaze.

Other surface finds from the random surveys include nine green porcelain sherds, three white porcelain sherds, two blue and white porcelain, four Burmese glazed stoneware sherds, and numerous Burmese earthenware types. Of the green porcelain, one is a beautiful Longquan-type base, one good quality celadon rim of a large bowl (Longquan type), two body sherds of which one is of the Longquan variety, two rims of medium-sized bowls of Southern Chinese origins, and three sherds of large porcelain bowls (from different southern Chinese kilns — rim of a very light-coloured green and two body sherds). For the two blue and white bases, one is a Yuan dynasty sherd and the smaller base dates to the early Ming period. The white porcelain comprises a bowl base, one rim (unglazed on the interior) which suggests that it forms part of a vase or flask, probably Dehua, and a rim with an unglazed edge on the interior, likely indicative of a Song-dynasty bowl.

The Burmese glazed stoneware sherds comprise one turquoise glazed sherd with thick reddish clay bisque and no glaze on the interior, one dark bluish-green glazed plaque (architectural decoration), one white glazed sherd, one large base with olive-green glaze, and a thick dark-brown glazed stoneware rim. Among the numerous Burmese earthenware sherds found here are two more unusual examples: one orange fine paste earthenware with stamped designs, grey earthenware bearing scratched and incised design, and two black polished high-fired earthenware. The interior of one of these examples bears a horizontal "ladder" motif near the rim.

Two unusual artefacts are two sherds with reddish-orange clay body and a greyish-pinkish glaze. The glaze is opaque with an almost metallic shine to it. One of them bears a pattern of two incised bands with a zigzagged design beneath them. These two sherds may be of Persian origin.

During the survey the author also noted recent pottery types, such as Japanese transferred-print blue and white porcelain, a modern pink glazed stoneware sherd, brown and yellow glazed modern Burmese stoneware from Shwebo, white glazed stoneware sherds, a fragment of a stone pipe, and paddle-marked earthenware sherds.

Preliminary Note on a Sampling of Ceramics Excavated from the Bagan Palace Sites

Between December 2013 and January 2014, a team comprising the author, her co-primary investigator John Miksic, and ten Burmese participants from the Directorate of Historical Research and Directorate of Archaeology, Ministry of Culture, University of Yangon's Department of Archaeology, Monywa University, General Administration of Home Affairs, and Mon State sorted and completed a preliminary analysis of approximately forty kilograms of artefacts which were excavated from the Anawrahta and Kyanzittha Palace sites, Bagan. A total of approximately eight hundred artefacts were sorted during the project. Preliminarily, the artefacts from the palace excavations show a similar ratio of a larger percentage of indigenous ceramics over a smaller percentage of imported ceramic items as observed from the initial estimation of ceramics encountered during the random opportunistic surveys. This suggests that there is a greater proportion of locally produced ceramics to imported Chinese ware both within and outside the palace site complex. Whether this is the result of a preference for locally produced wares, accessibility or some other factor cannot be determined until more research has been undertaken. The variety of artefacts in the palace assemblages — in terms of diversity of decorative motifs in the earthenware, vessel types, range in terms of quality and the proportionate difference between fine paste earthenware and tempered earthenware, for instance, and glazed stoneware and earthenware, for another example — suggests observable and substantial differences between the artefacts in the palace sites and outside the palace. There may also be discernible differences between the range of artefacts found in sites within and outside the Bagan city wall and probably in different sectors. The random surveys indicate differences, but without systematic surveys or planned excavations within the Bagan site complex, it is impossible to draw any major conclusions.

Conclusion

The surveys yielded little evidence to suggest that Bagan was a densely populated urban centre. The Pyu sites and Bagan likely differ from each other in terms of the form, shape, size and characteristic features of their city walls and the period of occupation (see Hudson 2004, Shah Alam's unfinished dissertation and Miksic's chapter in this volume). If Sriksetra and Bagan were urban centres, they represent two different forms. Bagan was a ceremonial capital with certain heterogenetic characteristics, denoted by surface finds of Chinese sherds. The idea that Bagan was involved in internal trade is based on surface finds of glazed Myanmar stoneware. However, it is very likely that Bagan did not support a large population.

Perhaps the reason why there is little evidence of a large population residing in Bagan is connected with the idea of having to feed a large population. Most of the fields where land was donated are not within the immediate vicinity of the capital, but are distributed over a large area. The greater number of Bagan's population probably resided in the outer areas, possibly in satellite towns. In times of need the kings carried out *sasana* (religious) reforms (see Aung-Thwin 1979; Aung-Thwin 1985; Lieberman 1976; Lieberman 1980) to regain the labour lost to the sangha in order to construct or repair weirs, canals, new pagodas, or to recruit men for their wars. The Kyaukse district was probably home to a larger population than Bagan. Future archaeological research may be able to verify this hypothesis.

There are two reasons for suggesting the above hypothesis:

1. Other than the remains of temples, pagodas and supposed palaces, there is no conclusive evidence of habitation sites within or beyond the wall. No systematic reports of pottery distribution around Bagan have been published.
2. It would have been difficult to produce enough food in the Bagan vicinity to support a large population. The closest rice-growing area is the Kyaukse district to the northeast. "Of the land that surrounds Pagan, the Mon gave it the name of Tattadesa — the parched land, which is the Dry Zone of Upper Burma". This suggests that "Pagan and its neighbourhood were, just as they are today, semi desert land of thorny scrubs." (Than Tun 1978, p. 3)

However, population size is only one criterion for an urban environment. One should also consider other criteria.

The Chinese ceramics found in Bagan suggest that the ceremonial and administrative centre at Bagan was involved to some degree in commercial exchanges with China, as demonstrated in the Chinese ceramic finds. The range of ceramic types observed in the limited survey indicates that exchange was not limited to the "tributary" kind, as the sherds include a number of pottery types produced in Southern Chinese kilns. These were likely used in everyday life and are characteristic of the utilitarian variety. The materials presented in this chapter represent only a small portion of artefacts with potential to be documented. In any case, the archaeological evidence supports the argument that Bagan was a ritual and urban centre in a Buddhist *ecumene* which facilitated not only fluid exchanges of monks, pilgrims, relics and texts, but also goods of commercial importance, like ceramics.

Notes

1. For detailed discussions of the identity of Tarup-China at various periods in Burmese history and on Tarup-China's relations with Myanmar, see Goh 2010 and 2009, respectively.

2. For convenience, I am using U Kala's chronicle as the basis for looking at the textual descriptions. Even though the *Hmannan* differs from U Kala's chronicle in a number of areas (for detailed discussion on the differences, see Goh 2007 and Goh 2015), the two are very similar as *Hmannan* derives much of its information on pre-18th-century Myanmar polities from U Kala's text. The *Yazawinthit* contains more abbreviated information regarding Bagan, and has been described as more critical (see U Thaw Kaung 2005 and Charney 2006, pp. 94–95).
3. Even though Dr Than Tun defined *kywan* as slaves, their status did not correspond to slaves in the Western sense of the word.
4. Various other vocations also include "*alay san* (brokers), *uphway san* (coiffeurs), *ka san* (harness makers), *kuha san* (launderers), *cakhi* or *cariy* (clerks), *cicon* (keepers of the granary), *chasan* (salt makers), *chan chaum san* (oil producers), *than san* (wood cutters), *naga kran san* (armourers), *pi san* (salted fish makers), *phara san* or *bhameda san* (stewards), *muchit rip* (barbers), *mlon mliy san* (canal diggers), *rakan san* (poets), *riy san* (water carriers), *lak san* (midwives), *lak san thuiw* (manicurists), *lhan san* (cartmen), *lhawka san* (boatmen), *samkok san* (blacksmiths) and *sanryan san* (palanquin bearers)" (see Than Tun 1978).

References

Aung-Thwin, Michael. "The Role of Sasana Reform in Burmese History: Economic Dimensions of a Religious Purification". *Journal of Asian Studies* 38, no. 4 (1979): 671–88.

———. *Pagan: The Origins of Modern Burma*. Honolulu: University of Hawai'i Press, 1985.

Aung-Thwin, Michael, and M. Stark. "Recent Developments in the Archaeology of Myanma Pyay (Burma): An Introduction". *Asian Perspectives* 40, no. 1 (2001): 1–5.

Brumfiel, E.M., and T.K. Earle. "Specialization, Exchange, and Complex Societies: An Introduction". In *Specialization, Exchange, and Complex Societies*, edited by E.M. Brumfiel and T.K. Earle, pp. 1–9. New York: Cambridge University Press, 1987.

Cohen, M.N. *The Food Crisis in Prehistory: Overpopulation and the Origins of Agriculture*. New Haven: Yale University Press, 1977.

Feinman, G.M., and L.M. Nicholas. "New Perspectives on Prehispanic Highland Mesoamerica: A Macroregional Approach". *Comparative Civilization Review* 24 (1991): 13–33.

Fox, E.W. *History in Geographic Perspective*. New York: Norton, 1971.

Goh Geok Yian. "Cakkravatiy Anuruddha and the Buddhist Oikoumene: Historical Narratives of Kingship and Religious Networks in Burma, Northern Thailand,

and Sri Lanka (11th–14th Centuries)". Doctoral Dissertation, University of
    Hawai'i at Manoa, 2007.
———. "Myanmar's Relations with China from Tagaung through Hanthawati-
    Taungngu Periods". In *Connecting and Distancing*, edited by Ho Khai Leong,
    pp. 115–33. Singapore: Institute of Southeast Asian Studies, 2009.
———. "The Question of 'China' in Burmese Chronicles". *Journal of Southeast Asian
    Studies* 41, no. 1 (2010): 125–52.
———. *The Wheel-Turner and His House: Kingship in a Buddhist Ecumene*. Dekalb:
    Northern Illinois University Press, 2014.
Grave, Peter, and M. Barbetti. "Dating the City Wall, Fortifications, and the Palace
    Site at Pagan". *Asian Perspectives* 40, no. 1 (2001): 75–87.
Hudson, Bob. "The Origins of Burma: The Archaeological Landscape of Upper
    Burma to AD 1300". PhD dissertation, University of Sydney, 2004.
Hudson, Bob, Nyein Lwin, and Win Maung (Tampawaddy). "The Origins of Bagan:
    New Dates and Old Inhabitants". *Asian Perspectives* 40, no. 1 (2001): 48–74.
Kala, U. *Mahayazawingyi.* ဦးကုလား၏မဟာရာဇဝင်ကြီး", 3 vols., edited by Saya Pwa.
    Yangon: Burma Research Society, 1980.
Lieberman, Victor. "A New Look at the Sāsanavamsa". *Bulletin of the School of
    Oriental and African Studies* 39, no. 1 (1976): 137–49.
———. "The Political Significance of Religious Wealth in Burmese History: Some
    Further Thoughts". *Journal of Asian Studies* 39, no. 4 (1980): 753–69.
Miksic, John. "Heterogenetic Cities in Premodern Southeast Asia". *World Archaeology*
    32, no. 1 (2000): 106–20.
———. "Early Burmese Urbanization: Research and Conservation". *Asian
    Perspectives* 40, no. 1 (2001): 88–107.
Netting, R.M. *Smallholders, Householders: Farm Families and the Ecology of Intensive,
    Sustainable Agriculture*. Stanford: Stanford University Press, 1993.
Polanyi, Karl. *The Great Transformation*. Boston: Beacon Hill, 1994.
Polanyi, Karl, C.M. Arensburg, and H.W. Pearson, eds. *Trade and Market in the Early
    Empires*. Chicago: Regnery, 1957.
Redfield, R., and R. Singer. "The Cultural Role of Cities". *Economic Development
    and Social Change* 3 (1954): 335–73.
Redman, Charles L. *The Rise of Civilization*. San Francisco: Freeman, 1978.
Roseberry, W. "Political Economy". *Annual Review of Anthropology* 17 (1988): 161–85.
Sanders, W.T., J.R. Parsons, and R.S. Santley. *The Basin of Mexico: Ecological Processes
    in the Evolution of a Civilization*. New York: Academic, 1979.
Smith, Michael. "The Archaeology of Ancient State Economies". *Annual Review of
    Anthropology* 33 (2004): 73–102.
Stein, Gill J. "Understanding Ancient State Societies in the Old World". In *Archaeology
    at the Millennium: A Sourcebook*, edited by G.M. Feinman and T.D. Price,
    pp. 353–80. New York: Kluwer, 2001.

Than Tun. "History of Buddhism in Burma AD 1000–1300". *Journal of the Burma Research Society* 61, nos. 1–2 (1978): 1–267.

Twinthin Taikwun Mahasitthu. *Twin: Thin: Myanmar Yazawinthit (Tvaṅ`"saṅ`" Mran`mā Rājavaṅ`sac`).* တွင်းသင်းတိုက်ဝန်မဟာစည်သူ။မြန်မာရာဇဝင်သစ်။ရန်ကုန်၊မင်္ဂလာပုံနှိပ်တိုက်၊၁၉၆၈။, vol. 1. Yangon: Mingala Printing Press, 1968.

Various. Hmannan Yazawindawgyi (Mhan`nan`" Mahārājavaṅ`to`krī"). မှန်နန်းရာဇဝင်တော်ကြီး။ရန်ကုန်၊၁၉၉၂။, 2nd ed., 3 vols. Yangon: Myui" Khyac` Sit`dhāt` Thak`san`re", 1992.

Wheatley, Paul. *Nagara and Commandery: Origins of the Southeast Asian Urban Traditions*, research paper nos. 207–8. Chicago: University of Chicago, Department of Geography, 1983.

Wolf, Eric R. *Europe and the People without History*. Berkeley: University of California Press, 1982.

10

Orthogeneity, Settlement Patterns and Earthenware Pottery Distribution in Bagan

John N. Miksic

On the surface, Southeast Asian archaeology presents an extreme example of the dichotomy between the theoretical extremes of the orthogenetic and heterogenetic types of city. The remains of major monumental complexes such as Angkor, Borobudur/Prambanan and Bagan contrast sharply with the remains of trading port-cities such as Palembang, Barus and Singapore. This apparently simple picture, however, begins to display more shades of grey the more one peers beneath the surface, as further exploration begins to provide more detailed information about the lives of these ancient cities. Research at the site of Trowulan, east Java, in the early 1990s necessitated a revision of the previous assumption that Majapahit's 14th-century capital was merely a complex of royal and religious buildings. Surface survey in the wake of large-scale looting of bricks for modern construction revealed dense scatters of pottery, both local and foreign. This pottery demonstrated the existence of numerous occupations and a dense population.

Archaeological observation at the sites of Bagan and Sriksetra (Pyay, Prome) is beginning to shed light on the distribution of population and range of economic activity at these sites. The occupations at the two sites overlap to a considerable extent, indicating that for a period of time they were linked in a complex economic relationship which written materials hint at but do not describe in detail.

Data obtained from the study of pottery distribution patterns is capable of measuring the degree of socio-economic complexity at a site. Preliminary analysis of recent discoveries indicates that Sriksetra and Bagan, like Trowulan, may have been hinterland capitals with some heterogenetic as well as orthogenetic characteristics. Preliminary pottery data indicates that Sriksetra and Bagan were similar but differed in several significant aspects, including internal settlement patterns and presence or absence of Chinese ceramics.

*****

While our knowledge of pre-modern interaction between Southeast Asia and its neighbours to the east and west is increasing, we still know little of the interaction between Southeast Asian societies during this period. Stylistic studies of art suggest that Southeast Asian societies interacted and exchanged cultural and artistic traits to a relatively high degree, as well as economic commodities (Brown 1994). Gradually increasing data suggest that Myanmar interacted with the eastern mainland of Southeast Asia during the late prehistoric (Bronze–Iron) period. Bronze spearheads from surface collections in Upper Burma, mainly the Dry Zone, are similar to those from Ban Chiang (Aung-Thwin 2001, p. 28), but the precise nature of this interaction is still obscure. Myanmar is still largely excluded from archaeological syntheses of the region, due to the relative scarcity of data published in English (e.g., Higham 1996, 2002).

Some of the earliest urban centres in mainland Southeast Asia emerged in the Dry Zone of Myanmar during the early centuries of the first millennium CE. Five major walled sites of three hundred hectares or more are commonly attributed to an Indianized, Tibeto-Burman speaking group called the Pyu, who are thought to have constituted the main population of this area during the first millennium CE (Aung Thaw 1968, 1972; Aung-Thwin 1982–83, 2006; Brown 2001; Gutman and Hudson 2004; Hudson 2004; Moore 2007; Luce 1960; Stadtner 1998). A paradigm based on interpretation of Chinese texts, which was long popular and is still found in much secondary literature, infers that the sites of Beikthano, Halin and Sriksetra formed successive capitals of a Pyu kingdom encompassing the Dry Zone and areas in southern Myanmar (Luce 1960). While Luce generally treated the Pyu as a homogenous group, he also acknowledged that Chinese sources from the 4th and 9th centuries mentioned 298 tribes (*bulou*; recent scholars prefer to translate this word as "settlements", according to Sun 1997, p. 16) and eighteen dependent kingdoms in Pyu territory (1985, pp. 68–71).

Discovery of new archaeological sites at Mongmao (Maingmaw) and Wadi, and the application of radiocarbon dating techniques, have shown that there were more than three Pyu-type urban sites, and that the occupations of these sites overlapped, leading to reconsiderations of earlier theories according to which successive Pyu capitals were abandoned as new ones arose (Hudson 2001, 2004; Moore 2004, 2007; Shah Alam 2002, 2006, n.d.; Stadtner 1998). Beikthano has yielded four dates ranging from the 2nd century BCE to the 5th century CE; carbon samples from Halin date between the 1st and 9th centuries CE (Gutman and Hudson 2004, p. 160). Stone ornaments in the form of rings have been found at Nyaung-gan, Halin and Taungthaman, believed to date from the Neolithic, Bronze and Iron Ages, respectively. Similar rings have been found at sites in western Thailand (Moore 2001, p. 40). As Moore notes, "the labels Pyu and Mon [imply] that inscriptions related to linguistic groups may be used to define cultures [is] a problematic procedure" (Moore 2001, p. 44). It is necessary to be aware that archaeological cultures are defined by artefact styles and patterns of distribution, and it cannot be assumed that the boundaries of their distribution correspond to linguistic boundaries. This assumption is probably often the case, but the level of confidence one can assign to this correlation is less than perfect. The loss of many items with stylistic complexity such as bronze and gold jewellery to looting is a particular hindrance.

Bob Hudson and Pamela Gutman (2004) proposed an evolutionary framework whereby earlier bronze–iron culture evolved in the Chindwin Valley, followed by the Bronze Age Samon Valley culture. In the Iron Age, new artefact types appeared in Halin and Samon, but not in the Chindwin area (Hudson 2004, p. 91). Hudson views the Samon valley as the region where Pyu culture originated (Hudson 2004, pp. 19, 260–63) and spread over the Dry Zone; the late formation of Sriksetra is therefore logical because it is the Pyu centre furthest from the Samon Valley.

Hudson writes that the Pyu "radiated outward from Binnaka/ Pyawbwe" (Hudson 2004, p. 149), and that Pyu urban centres emerged due to the formation of an elite group who desired access to resources. The latter aspect of his theory derives considerable support from comparative studies of other early complex societies, but the migration hypothesis has yet to be widely accepted. Several scholars now believe that the Pyu centres were probably politically autonomous (e.g., Hudson 2004, p. 121; Lieberman 2003, p. 83; Shah Alam 2002, n.d.). Elizabeth Moore asks whether the Pyu were culturally homogeneous or whether the centres now called Pyu were created by related but distinct Tibeto-Burman sub-cultural groups (Moore 2004, p. 2). Artefacts of both Bronze–Iron Age and Pyu style have been found in Halin and Mongmao, but systematic excavations have been insufficient to confirm that development was continuous between the two eras (Moore 2003, p. 26).

Shah Alam (n.d.) suggests an analogy between the Pyu-era sites and the emergence of Malay ethnicity in the Straits of Melaka. The extensive distribution of this ethnic identity was not the result of an outward migration of people from a single origin, but was disseminated by various means and adopted by various groups in various sequences over an extended period (Andaya 2001). Hudson's expression that "If the pattern of establishment of settlements is taken to have radiated outward from the Samon Valley" (Hudson 2004, p. 263) is probably acceptable to most, but to say that *people* did so is difficult to prove. One of the major hurdles facing archaeological reasoning is the difficulty of distinguishing between the diffusion of ideas through communication, as opposed to migration.

What is Meant by Pyu and Myanmar?

Archaeology cannot identify linguistic groups. Archaeological units are based on the identification of the distribution of artefacts of similar style; assumptions that these artefacts can be correlated with any ethno-linguistic groups can never be directly proven. Correlations between ancient distributions of artefact types and modern cultures are indicative but not conclusive of such continuity. Thus the term Pyu in archaeology may not necessarily have the same meaning as it does in history.

In archaeological terms, the artefact assemblage known as Pyu comprises finger-marked bricks of large dimensions, burial urns, beads and coins. Artefacts of these types with similar styles are found at a number of sites such as Beikthano and Sriksetra. Historically, "Pyu" is equated with the "Piao" of Chinese historical sources (Aung-Thwin 2005, pp. 20–21 for discussion on P'iao, and chap. 2 for discussion on "Pyu" and "Pyu" cities).

Pyu Sites and Their Dates

Chronicles date the foundation of Sriksetra, the southernmost of the major Pyu cities, as early as 443 BCE. A radiocarbon date from Beikthano yielded an age of 1950 ± 90 BP, which when calibrated at ninety-five per cent probability gives a date during the period from 180 BCE to 260 CE (Aung Thaw 1968, p. 61; Bronson 1969, p. 142). Bellwood (1992) and Bronson (1992) noted that the sample dated was found below the foundations of a brick structure and, therefore, predates the structure. Bellwood and Bronson also noted that the samples tested could have been from the inner parts of a tree trunk used as a pillar in a structure, thus giving a significantly older date than that of the structure's construction. Bronson (1992) suggested that a date during the 2nd or 3rd centuries CE is most logical and argues that the height of activity at Beikthano was probably in the 7th and 8th centuries. Similar caveats on the interpretation of radiocarbon dates pertain to Halin. This revised chronology would assign early urbanization and brick architecture in the Dry Zone to a similar period as is attested for eastern mainland Southeast Asia.

Pyu Trade

The Pyu formed trading relationships with southern China to the northeast and Arabo-Persian traders to the south (Luce [1937] 1960). Very probably they also exchanged goods and ideas with neighbouring highland groups. Sriksetra was ideally located to form a gateway connecting the Dry Zone in the north and the Ayeyarwady Delta to the south; the site assumed this role during the Pyu period, and continued to do so during the Bagan era.

Sun Laichen (1997, p. 9) noted that Sima Qian in his *Shi Ji*, written before 91 BCE, already mentioned an overland route from Sichuan via Yunnan and Myanmar to India, thus passing through the Dry Zone. People of the Dry Zone probably participated actively in the trade network. The term *Panyue* according to Sun is derived from Brahma-vatthu, a Sanskrit name for the Pyu (Sun 1997, p. 10); this term appears as early as the 3rd century. *Piaoyue* appears in a quotation from a 1st-century CE text, in a context which Sun believes "indicates that in the 1st century, China, Burma, and

India maintained a very active intercourse, most likely of a commercial kind" (Sun 1997, p. 11). Tang dynasty sources describe the use of this route by Buddhist pilgrims. A mission from *Piao* reached the Tang capital in 802, bringing thirty-five musicians, who made a great impression on the court. Two more missions arrived from *Piao* in 806 and 862 (Bielenstein 2005, p. 69). Sources from the 9th century mentioned trade relations between the Pyu and Nanzhao; the commodities mentioned, however, are primarily exports from the Dry Zone, including river pigs (possibly Ayeyarwady dolphins), cloth and ceramics (Luce 1960).

The main archaeological evidence for trade in the Samon, Chindwin and Ayeyarwady valleys in the late centuries BCE comes from beads of carnelian, agate and glass. They are common in Samon sites (Hudson 2004; Moore 2007; Nyunt Han et al. 2002; Pautreau et al. 2006, 2007) and unfortunately attract the attention of looters. These were imported from South Asia either as raw material or in finished form (Bellina-Pryce and Praon Silapanth 2006; Glover 1990; Francis 2002).

Sriksetra: Dates and Functions

Sriksetra, the largest and southernmost of the sites identified with the Pyu, lies eight kilometres east of the modern town of Prome and the Ayeyarwady River. There is no concrete evidence that this is the Pyu capital mentioned in Chinese sources, which sent a mission around 802. Luce (1960) based his assumption that this was the site's name on his interpretations of distances from Pyu capitals to the kingdom of Nanzhao. Visible archaeological remains include elliptical main walls, seven fully restored temples and stupas, and a rectangular enclosure commonly referred to as the palace. Brick remains and ceramic shreds can be found at depths of up to 3.5 metres in well shafts.

The florescent period of this site has been conventionally dated to the period between the 5th and 9th centuries, based on Indian art styles, palaeography and dated inscriptions. Early researchers noted abundant remains from the period after the 9th century (e.g., ASB 1925), but subsequent scholars have paid little attention to them. These include Mahayana statuary stylistically dated later than the 9th century, and Bagan-period art and architecture (Ray 1936, p. 45). Material from the post-Pyu period at Sriksetra has largely been considered irrelevant to Burmese archaeology (see Aung Thaw 1968). Luce (1969, pp. 19, 55) suggested that

Sriksetra was still an important site for the early kings of Pagan, given the fact that Kyanzittha (1084–1113) claimed to be a descendant of the kings of Sriksetra. Hudson (2004, p. 283) obtained two thermoluminescence (TL) dates from Sriksetra, the first calibrated to 710 CE, the second to 1410 CE. The first date is within the date range adopted for the period of florescence in Sriksetra, while the second falls within the late Bagan period. However, these samples were dated in 1975, when TL dating was in an experimental stage and errors were common.

Sriksetra is generally considered a Pyu site due to the following criteria:

1. A layout with an outer wall and inner enclosure generally considered the palace (Kan Hla 1979);
2. Epigraphy using a common South Indian script (e.g., ASB 1916, p. 21);
3. Ceremonial architecture with specific ground plans (Aung-Thwin 1982–83; Aung Myint 1999; Aung Thaw 1968, 1972; Myint Aung 1970; Hudson 2004);
4. Secondary burials in terracotta funerary urns (e.g., ASB 1925; Aung Thaw 1968);
5. Standardized coinage (Wicks 1991, pp. 114–21);
6. Bricks of standardized dimensions with finger markings (Aung Myint and Moore 1991).

According to conventional historiography, Sriksetra should have declined after it was replaced as the capital of Dry Zone Myanmar in the Bagan period. However, archaeological data show that the settlement was an important urban centre as late as the 13th century. Numerous monuments on the site display features typical of the Bagan rather than Pyu architectural styles. Shah Alam (n.d.) argues that Sriksetra was a major urban centre from the 5th to 13th centuries. Some Bagan-style buildings overlie a layer of white pebbles, a feature typical of early Pyu practice. Shah Alam suspects that this practice may indicate some degree of resistance to Pagan rule, but it may simply have been continued for religious reasons by the local population who continued to live at the site.

Sriksetra's location is ideal for a role as intermediary between the Dry Zone and the delta region. The fact that the site continued to function as an urban centre in the Bagan period suggests that its population was occupied in a range of economic activities which were independent of its position in a political hierarchy. Bagan's ascendancy to the status of regional hegemon may not have affected Sriksetra's economic status to any appreciable extent. The major Pyu sites may well have been autonomous polities.

Sriksetra is in a geographically strategic position; it sits on a narrow strip of land that links the Dry Zone and areas to the south, areas which provide the northern regions of Burma with commodities needed for their sociocultural development. There is little evidence of silver- or gold-working in Samon sites (Gutman and Hudson 2004; Hudson 2004; Luce 1960; Moore 2007). In the Pyu period, demand for tin, copper, iron, gold and silver increased; the Pyu were adept at working these metals. Artefacts of all these metals have been found in Sriksetra, but none of the raw material is found nearby. The closest source of iron is the Pegu Yoma, a mountain range 150 kilometres to the east. Copper, gold and silver may have been mined in the Shan hills, more than five hundred kilometres to the northeast. Tin probably came from the Isthmus of Kra and the Malay Peninsula. Precious stones found in Sriksetra probably originated in northern Myanmar.

The date when Prome replaced Sriksetra as the major centre in the region is unknown. While settlement in the Sriksetra area continued into the post-Pagan period, the 13th century marks a watershed after which the frequency of features and artefacts decreases substantially, according to surveys undertaken by Shah Alam. The shift to Prome may have occurred in the immediate post-Pagan period.

Sriksetra's Settlement Pattern

Like the other major sites grouped under the term Pyu, Sriksetra consists of a roughly circular outer wall of brick enclosing a very large area including a second enclosure with a rectangular outline. About fifty per cent of the area within the main walls is used for wet rice agriculture (Shah Alam n.d., chap. 4, p. 10). The inner enclosures of Pyu sites are usually assumed to represent elite areas such as palaces, but Hudson (2004, p. 128) thinks that the rectangular inner wall at Sriksetra, which encloses forty-four hectares, is an early occupation phase, not an elite building.

At Sriksetra the main walled area encloses about twenty square kilometres. Shah Alam found that, while the main walls may have formed a boundary in the early phase of the site, settlement and the building of monuments and burials soon spread beyond it, particularly to the south, where he detected, using aerial photography, rectangular enclosures more than five hundred metres beyond the southern walls. The total additional area where related structures and remains were found covered another twenty square kilometres, effectively doubling the size of the inhabited area.

Surveys from 2001 to 2004 indicated that about eighty per cent of an area of twenty square kilometres of the site had been looted, mainly by local people in search of gold; in these areas, subsurface deposits are now part of the surface scatter (Shah Alam n.d., fig. 8). The densest concentration of surface finds lay within five hundred metres of the "palace" site, although dense clusters were also found in western, southwestern and southeastern sections. In areas now used for rice cultivation, including almost the entire northern half of the site within the walls and much of the southeast, no remains were found either on or below the surface.

Shah Alam's 2001–4 field research sought to test the hypothesis that Sriksetra had initially consisted of several discrete sites with linked functions which together formed an urban centre that gradually coalesced into a unit. It is often assumed that urban centres invariably form as small settlements which gradually become larger. At Jenne Jeno, in the Niger River, western Africa, during the late 1st to early 2nd millennium CE, several discrete communities each performed one or more of the functions associated with a city (McIntosh 1991, 1999). The distribution of Hindu and Buddhist remains of various specialized patterns of belief at Sriksetra could be interpreted as indicating the presence of discrete communities. In the early stages of settlement growth, Sriksetra may have been a group of communities which gradually grew together to form a single urban centre, not unlike the "mythical" nineteen villages of Bagan (GPC 1960; Hudson 2004, p. 236).

While Shah Alam's data was insufficient to confirm the existence of a pattern associated with the urban cluster model, he concluded that the pattern of surface finds was not inconsistent with the hypothesis that Sriksetra was a "multi-nucleated center". His initial procedure was to plot the distribution of ceramic types assumed to belong to discrete time periods in order to detect the pattern of settlement growth, but it was found to be impossible to identify distinct cultural horizons using ceramics from excavations. Whereas brick structures and religious statuary can be assigned to phases termed "Pyu" and "Bagan", the ceramic assemblage from Shah Alam's main excavation site, SR 3, displayed no evolution. The most that could be observed was that dense surface remains of pottery clustered around structures in a way which could be consistent with a multi-nucleated urban site. Surface remains were densely distributed over an area within seven hundred metres of the "palace" enclosure.

Shah Alam found 62 brick features, 27 from the Bagan period, 23 from the Pyu period, 2 from the early 19th century, and 10 which could not be dated (Shah Alam n.d., chap. 4, p. 16). Hudson et al. (2008) recorded 277 buildings, of which 65 are made from Bagan-type bricks. Bagan-phase bricks are generally smaller compared to Pyu bricks. Bagan-period structures were found throughout Shah Alam's survey area. Some Bagan-period structures formed part of complexes built in the Pyu period which continued to be used during the Bagan period; for instance, the Payataung cluster, which includes a Bagan-phase stupa and platform. As Hudson et al. note (2001, p. 49), "the 'fall of the Pyu/rise of Bagan' hypothesis is therefore debatable".

Surface remains were also concentrated around brick features south of the main wall. The Department of Archaeology excavated mound HM 36 west of the Bebe temple and discovered a brick platform, the lower portion of which is constructed of Pyu-size bricks and the upper platform of Bagan bricks (Shah Alam n.d.). Two sets of *sima* stones were found around the platform, one set probably associated with the Pyu-period structure and the other with the Bagan period. White pebbles were found below floors made of Bagan-period bricks and in a funerary urn dated to the 7th century CE. White pebbles were also associated with burials. No such white pebbles have been reported at other sites, whether Pyu or Bagan phase.

The continuity of Sriksetra as a major urban centre and of Pyu culture after the 9th century bears implications for the function of the site and for social, economic and political organization in the Dry Zone. Aung Thaw believed that Bagan-period material in Beikthano indicated a second, less important phase, between the 11th and 13th centuries. Aung Thaw (1968, p. 62) also believed that Sriksetra's emergence in the 5th century led to Beikthano's downfall. This perception is directly related to the assumption that the Dry Zone was always dominated by a single political centre. Moore (2003) mentions that a number of sites in the Samon Valley at Halin have remains from the Iron Age, Pyu and Bagan phases.

The Bawbawgyi contained votive tablets bearing the seal of Anawrahta. In a Mon inscription found in the Shwesandaw pagoda in what is now modern Prome, Kyanzittha (1084–1112) traced his origin to the kings of Sriksetra (Luce 1969, p. 55). Archaeological remains at Sriksetra suggest a degree of continuity with sites after the 9th century. The lack of stylistic change in the ceramic assemblage suggests cultural continuity. Although art and architecture at Sriksetra of the Bagan phase is discernibly different from the Pyu phase, structures built with Pyu bricks in Pyu style, including the four major stupas, continued in use during the Bagan period.

Bagan-period material has also been found in Halin (Moore 2007). Nihar-Ranjan Ray (1936) noted that votive tablets in a style associated with Bagan have been found in Sriksetra (Thiripyanchi U Mya 1961). Stadtner suggests that East Zegu and Lemyethna may have been built after the 9th century; Strachan (1989), however, believes these temples provided the prototype for some Bagan temples. Guy (1999, p. 17) noted that some architectural features in Sriksetra suggest Bagan-period construction, including doorjambs, mouldings and the use of arches and stucco.

Ceramics from Sriksetra

Shah Alam dated many of the ceramics recovered at Sriksetra to the Bagan period, although his basis for this dating is unclear. These included both slipped and unslipped ware with textures ranging from fine to coarse. Slip is generally reddish orange, with either orange or whitish-pink paste. Unslipped wares are generally orange in colour, though there are some dark grey, medium-textured buff and whitish-pink coarse wares. Whether the colours were produced intentionally or the result of firing conditions is still unknown. Non-destructive EDXRF analysis on twenty samples of slipped and unslipped fine, medium and coarse ware from surface collections showed very tight clustering compared to ceramics from other parts of Southeast Asia. Most decoration consisted of cord-marking, paddle impressions and incision. Some of the decorative motifs used are similar to those from Beikthano. A type of roof tile associated with Chinese origin (late first millennium BCE) was found in Sriksetra. Shah Alam did not find any glazed ceramics in his survey. A small greyish-green jar has been reported (Gutman 2001, p. 109) but not dated. No Chinese ceramics are displayed in the site museum in Sriksetra, and none have been reported in excavations. The present author, however, found a sherd of white porcelain of Song age as a surface find.

Cultural complexity is often correlated with specialized craft production (e.g., Pool 1992). Shah Alam analysed major rim forms collected during excavations in a standardization study to infer organization of production. He collected 1033 kilogrammes of ceramics, 125 kilogrammes from excavations, basing his classification on ceramics from SR 3, which yielded more material than SR 1 and 2 and in a more secure context. SR 1 consisted of rubble from a collapsed structure; SR 2 was obtained near the foundation of a structure. He identified nine types: three of fine ware, one fine slipped ware, medium ware, medium slipped ware, coarse ware, coarse slipped ware, and high-fired medium ware.

Shah Alam identified 106 rim forms, which were correlated with paste texture but were independent of ceramic types. Two different types of temper were used — sand and grog — in almost all ceramic types and rim forms. Ceramics used for grog temper were finely ground and are only visible under microscopic examination.

Decorative Motifs

The most common decorative motifs are cord and paddle marking. More than ninety per cent of the decorated sherds from the excavation at SR 3 were decorated in this manner. Anthropomorphic, zoomorphic and abstract motifs similar to Beikthano were also observed. Sherds with sunburst motifs — such as found in Sriksetra — have not been reported at Beikthano, but Hudson (2004, chart 4) found them in excavations at Otein Taung, Bagan, between 400 and 450 centimetres below the surface. Analysis of the organization, production and craft specialization based on rim form suggested a high degree of standardization, despite the possibility that these were produced in multiple workshops. It would seem that consumer demand for specific vessel forms influenced labour investment by potters. Such intensive labour investment is usually associated with full-time craft specialists (Shah Alam 2002, 2004). He also recovered a large number of ceramic ring stands during the survey.

A restudy of diagnostic earthenware sherds collected by Shah Alam during his excavation of SR 3 is now in progress. Another attempt will be made to search for correlations between decorative forms and stratigraphic position.

Ceramics at Other Pyu Sites

Beikthano

At Beikthano, almost ninety per cent of pottery is a red ware of medium fabric and texture, rarely decorated with slip or wash. Shapes include funerary urns and domestic wares classified as storage jars, spouted vessels, cooking vessels and shallow bowls. A small percentage — mainly bowls, sprinkler vessels (*kendi*) and miniature pots — are made of fine clay covered with red slip. A small quantity of sherds bear stamped and incised patterns and figures (Aung Thaw 1968, p. 28).

Some types of domestic wares continued to be used during the second phase of occupation in Beikthano, which Aung Thaw (1968, p. 29) dated between the 11th and 13th century. This is consistent with reports of Bagan-period material in other Pyu sites such as Halin.

Tagaung

Tharehkettara (Sriksetra) was described as Burma's first Buddhist kingdom in earlier chronicles, but in 1829 the *Hmannanyazawindawgyi* gave this honour to Tagaung. Goh Geok Yian has discussed possible reasons for this development (Goh 2010). Earlier authors such as Aung Thaw believed that Tharehkettara was older. Excavations at Tagaung in 1993 yielded Buddhist reliefs, sculpture and Bagan-period votive tablets, with "Pyu" artefacts as surface finds (Khyit San Win 2004, 2005). Further excavations in 2004 and 2005 yielded much additional pottery with stamped designs.

A type of artefact known as roof end tiles discovered at Tagaung resemble those found at Go Cam and Tra Kieu, central Vietnam (Moore and U Win Maung 2006) and at the Thanh Long Citadel in Hanoi. Parallels to these exist as far away as Nanjing, where tiles called *wadang* in Chinese appeared during the Zhou and were elaborated during the Han dynasty. They were also made at kiln sites in the Angkor area of Cambodia, including Tanei and Thnal Mrech.

Khyit San Win characterized early Tagaung as Pyu and dated this phase to the period 700 to 300 BCE, based on the presence of Pyu burial urns and other artefacts; this compares with proposed dates for Halin as 100 CE and Sriksetra as 500 CE (Goh 2010). Goh argues that Tagaung should be assigned to the transitional period when the occupations of Sriksetra and Bagan overlapped.

Bagan, Sriksetra and the Pyu

Burmese chronicles say that nineteen villages existed east of the present site of Bagan by 107 CE (Pe Ming Tin and Luce 1923). Several hundred iron-making furnaces have in fact been identified east of Bagan (Hudson et al. 2001, 2002; Hudson 2004, p. 200), but radiocarbon samples from these have not yet yielded very early dates.

Traditional sources date the construction of the walled city to 849 by King Pyinba, who came from near Beikthano. The oldest chronometric dating yet obtained for the eastern wall ranges over a long period (990–1230 CE; Grave and Barbetti 2001). Bagan is first mentioned in a Cham inscription of 1050 (Aung-Thwin 1985, p. 21), whereas the oldest dated inscription at the site (from the Kubyauk-gyi temple, Myinkaba) gives the date 1113. Monuments attributed to the 11th century in the *Inventory of Monuments at Pagan* (Pichard 1992–2001) covered a length of over nine kilometres from north to south; "This pattern of local rather than centralized construction suggests that several communities may have been involved" (Hudson et al. 2001, p. 51).

Paul Strachan (1989) believed that the temples of Sriksetra were prototypes for the later temples of Bagan. Guy (1999, p. 16), however, noted that many of the Bagan-type structures in Sriksetra may date from the Bagan period. Stadtner (1998, p. 46) has a similar opinion of these various structures, although he considers the Bebe and the major stupas to have Pyu origins. It is also possible that structures built in the first millennium were altered during the Pagan period. Matijagon (designated Gwebindet in earlier reports by the survey), south of the main wall, is the only known structure in Sriksetra with a ground plan that resembles brick structures in other major Pyu sites. There is a circular central structure, circa three metres in diameter, with four steps on each of the cardinal points. A number of terracotta plaques were recovered close to the structure (ASI 1930).

A site provisionally termed Kyanzittha's Palace, where excavations began in the early 1990s, has yielded dates from 980 to 1440 CE (Grave and Barbetti 2001, p. 81, table 1). The presence of foundations for larger timber columns is "consistent with a large palatial building" (Grave and Barbetti 2001, p. 81). Sherds of Chinese ceramics observed on the site during a visit in 2002 support this inference. Hudson identified at least three construction levels there (Hudson 2004, p. 224). Further study and publication of the ceramics from this site would well repay the effort.

Another site know known as "Anawrahta's Palace" was excavated 120 metres west of Kyanzittha's Palace in 2003 and several occupation levels were detected there as well. Hudson inferred that the upper layers of this site date from the "post-empire" period. This excavation yielded a *kendi* with green-on-white decoration and a cover of a Vietnamese ceramic box with cobalt-blue decoration, both typical of the 15th century (Hudson 2004, p. 303). The lowest levels of the site have not yet been exposed.

The Bagan site with the most radiocarbon dates is Otein Taung ("pottery mound"). The site has yielded a range of dates given as 760–1410 (Hudson et al. 2001) or 650–1370 (Hudson et al. 2002, p. 20n3). One date (OZE 770, 650–830) is out of sequence; lower dates are younger (Hudson 2004, pp. 210–11). Hudson argues that this may have been a reused piece of old wood. Until more dates are available to resolve this question, it is safer to conclude that there is limited evidence for use of the site before the 11th century. Sample 769 (760–980 CE) was found a hundred metres from the site, and may or may not relate to the Otein Taung mounds. It does however suggest a pre-11th-century occupation of this general area.

The clustering of ceramic production implied by the size of these mounds of pottery indicates centralized control over the craft during this period. Although Hudson properly notes that the mounds may have been middens rather than pottery production sites (animal bones and teeth were found in one trench; Hudson et al. 2001, p. 54), the presence of anvils used in pottery making seems strong confirmation of the pottery-workshop hypothesis (Hudson et al. 2001, p. 56).

Some finger-marked bricks of Pyu type have been found at Bagan, but the shapes of spouts for *kendis* at Otein Taung are straight, whereas those at Beikthano are all curved (Hudson et al. 2001, p. 58). An early 20th-century report, however, noted the presence at Bagan of earthenwares identified as Pyu (ASB 1917, p. 42). Some votive tablets with Pyu script have been found in Bagan relic chambers (Luce 1969, plates 443–44; Gutman 1996). Further evidence of Pyu presence at Bagan comes from structure 996 (Paw-daw-mu or Gu-byauk), where an 11th-century structure encases a Pyu building, and the use of finger-marked bricks in at least fifty-five sites (Hudson et al. 2001, pp. 67, 77n5).

Layout of Bagan

Hudson (2004, pp. 221, 266) proposed that the development of Bagan did not represent an evolution from Pyu culture. Bagan can be differentiated from Bagan by walls significantly smaller than those of the major Pyu sites, and the site's location on the Ayeyarwady. The location of the major Pyu sites suggests that the river was not an important determinant of their location, and thus not a principal means of communication. Pyu sites are located a considerable distance from the Ayeyarwady; Sriksetra is the closest Pyu site to this river.

Bagan's position on the main river system enabled its residents to take advantage of developments in the water transport infrastructure. Hudson (2004, p. 266) believes that the development of Bagan and the expansion of its territory led to the diminishing importance of early urban centres; in his opinion they became provincial branches of a new administration. "Bagan, which would have been able to develop away from the shadow of these central places" — what is the literal meaning of "shadow"? Such metaphors should be used sparingly if at all, since they obscure rather than clarify meaning. One cannot merely assume that a "shadow" would be created by a central place; one must give evidence for such an effect. A general model of urbanization should be utilized here, either adopted from other authorities or created by the author himself. If "shadows" exist, they should be detected in other parts of the world where data is more complete.

The internal layout of Bagan differs from Pyu sites in that it has no outer wall enclosing much of the monumental zone, just an enceinte with three walls, open on the riverbank side. Hudson (2004, p. 221) wrote that "The walled centre of Bagan appears to have been an administrative and residential complex for the elite and the rulers of the city. Structurally, it cannot be linked to the early urban system. It does not fit the physical or landscape model proposed as typically Pyu."

There are, however, three sites which have three walls and are open on the river side: Dounyazit (65 hectares, three-walled irregular shape, on the bank of the Sittaung River); Sampanago (259 hectares, on the Thanlwin River) and Tagaung (about 204 hectares) (Hudson 2004, p. 145; Goh 2012; Aung Myint 1998). Thus there are precedents for this form in Burmese settlement history. It has been suggested that a fourth wall once existed at these sites but was eroded by the river, but no evidence for this has been found. It is worth considering the possibility that this was in fact the original shape which the builders contemplated. Thus Bagan's layout does not necessarily constitute a departure from Pyu forms. Hudson (2004, p. 245) noted that in the early phase of Bagan there seem to have been four monumental clusters, each possibly connected with separate settlements, another facet of Bagan's settlement pattern which parallels Pyu convention.

Pottery from Bagan

Unlike Pyu sites, little has yet been published on Bagan pottery. Motifs on some sherds Hudson (2004, chart 4) recovered from the Otein Taung excavations bear some resemblance to motifs seen on sherds from Beikthano, and also from the survey and excavation phases in Sriksetra. Other motifs on ceramics from Bagan have yet to be found or reported in Pyu sites. This may be due to sampling bias or restricted distribution of some motifs outside of the immediate Bagan area. One particularly distinctive pottery type found on the surface around several Bagan-period sites is typified by red slip and elaborate burnishing. These seem to have formed parts of *kendis*.

The late great scholar Than Tun noted that "The Myanma Archaeological Survey Department has done only conservation works at Bagan and so we cannot have the usual archaeological data on pottery as we have acquired on other sites" (Than Tun 2003, p. 19; English translation). He records the information that at Tagaung, 12th-century pottery stamps were applied in isolated circular, rectangular or elliptical frames, whereas in earlier periods such decorations normally formed belts around the entire body of the pot. At Bagan he observed similar designs, also enclosed in circular or elliptical rings (Than Tun 2003, p. 20).

Conclusion

Many scholars, including Paul Wheatley (1983) and K.R. Hall (1985), have argued that Southeast Asian urbanization arose as a result of foreign contact. Early heterogenetic cities in coastal areas of Indonesia such as Kota Cina, northeast Sumatra, seem to have formed around nuclei of foreign merchants. Research at the site of Trowulan, a hinterland site of the 14th century believed to have been the capital of a large kingdom known as Majapahit, superficially appeared to have been an orthogenetic city without evidence of a large foreign community during its formative period. Subsequent archaeological survey, however, suggested that Trowulan had possessed important heterogenetic characteristics, and may have had an important foreign component at some stage of its development (Miksic 1994). Research at early urban sites of the Pyu type does not support the presence of a substantial population of foreign merchants. These sites may have lain close to the orthogenetic end of the scale. The discovery of imported porcelain (Goh, this volume) and possibly a high level of specialized pottery production at Bagan yield a contrasting preliminary impression of an urban society with significant heterogeneity but without an appreciable foreign component in its population. Further archaeological survey and analysis aimed at the elucidation of the complexity of pottery production at Bagan will contribute significant new information to the endeavour to clarify the various processes by which urban life evolved in Southeast Asia (cf. Miksic 2001).

References

Andaya, L. "The Search for the Origins of Melayu". *Journal of Southeast Asian Studies* 32, no. 3 (2001): 315–30.

ASB. *Annual Reports of the Archaeological Survey of Burma*. Government Press, Rangoon, 1908–25; 1936–42.

ASI. *Annual Reports of the Archaeological Survey of India*. Calcutta, 1905–37.

Aung Myint. *Ancient Myanmar Cities in Aerial Photographs*. Yangon: Ministry of Culture, 1998.

Aung Myint and E. Moore. "Finger-Marked Designs on Ancient Bricks in Myanmar". *Journal of the Siam Society* 72, no. 2 (1991): 81–102.

Aung Thaw. *Report of the Excavations at Beikthano*. Rangoon: The Ministry of Union Culture, 1968.

⸻. *Historical Sites in Burma*. Rangoon: Ministry of Union Culture, 1972.

Aung-Thwin, M. "Burma before Pagan: The Status of Archaeology Today". *Asian Perspectives* 25, no. 2 (1982–83): 1–22.

⸻. *Pagan: The Origins of Modern Burma*. Honolulu: University of Hawai'i Press, 1985.

⸻. *Irrigation in the Heartland of Burma: Foundations of the Pre-Colonial Burmese State*. DeKalb: Center for Southeast Asian Studies, University of Northern Illinois, 1990.

⸻. "Origins and Development of the Field of Prehistory in Burma". *Asian Perspectives* 40, no. 1 (2001): 6–34.

⸻. *The Mists of Rmanna: The Legend That Was Lower Burma*. Honolulu: University of Hawai'i Press, 2005.

Bellina, B., and I. Glover. "The Archaeology of Early Contact with Indian and the Mediterranean World, from the Fourth Century BC to the Fourth Century AD". In *Southeast Asia from Prehistory to History*, edited by I. Glover and P. Bellwood, pp. 68–88. London: Routledge Curzon, 2004.

Bellina-Pryce, B., and Praon Silapanth. "Khao Sam Kaeo and the Upper Thai Peninsula: Understanding the Mechanism of Early Trans-Asiatic Trade and

Cultural Exchange". In *Uncovering Southeast Asia's Past — Selected Papers from the Tenth Biennial Conference of the European Association of Southeast Asian Archaeologists, London, 14th–17th September 2004*, edited by E.A. Bacus, I.C. Glover, and V.C. Pigott, pp. 379–92. Singapore: National University of Singapore Press, 2006.

Bellwood, P. "Early Burmese Urbanisation: Inspired Independence or External Stimulus?" *Review of Archaeology* 13, no. 2 (1992): 1–7.

Bielenstein, Hans. *Diplomacy and Trade in the Chinese World 589–1276*, Handbuch der Orientalistik, sec. 4, vol. 18. Leiden: Brill, 2005.

Blagden, C.O. "The Pyu Inscriptions". *Journal of the Burma Research Society* 7, no. 1 (1917): 37–44.

Bronson, B. "Report on the Excavations at Beikthano (A Review)". *Asian Perspectives* 12 (1969): 142–43.

———. "Exchange at the Upstream and Downstream Ends: Notes toward a Functional Model of the Coastal State in Southeast Asia". In *Economic Exchange and Social Interaction in Southeast Asia*, edited by K. Hutterer, Papers on South and Southeast Asia no. 13, pp. 39–54. Ann Arbor: Center for South and Southeast Asian Studies, University of Michigan, 1977.

———. "The Late Prehistory and Early History of Central Thailand with Special Reference to Chansen". In *Early Southeast Asia: Essays in Archaeology, History and Historical Geography*, edited by R.B. Smith and W. Watson, pp. 315–36. New York, Kuala Lumpur: Oxford University Press, 1979.

———. "Review of 'The Ancient Pyu of Burma'". *Journal of Southeast Asian Studies* 23, no. 2 (1992a): 435–38.

———. "Patterns in the Early Southeast Asian Metals Trade". In *Early Metallurgy, Trade and Urban Centres in Thailand and Southeast Asia*, edited by I.C. Glover, P. Suchitta, and J. Villiers, pp. 63–114. Bangkok: White Lotus, 1992b.

Brown, R.L. "Rules for Change in the Transfer of Indian Art to Southeast Asia". In *Ancient Indonesian Sculpture*, edited by M.J. Klokke and P.L. Scheurleer, pp. 10–32. Leiden: KITLV Press, 1994.

Çoedès, G. *The Indianized States of Southeast Asia*, translated by S.B. Cowing. Honolulu: University of Hawai'i Press, 1968.

Fletcher, R. *The Limits of Settlement Growth: A Theoretical Outline*. Cambridge: Cambridge University Press, 1995.

Glover, I.C. *Early Trade between India and Southeast Asia: A Link in the Development of a World Trading System*, Occasional Papers no. 16. Hull: Centre for Southeast Asian Studies, University of Hull, 1989.

———. "The Archaeological Evidence for Early Trade between India and Southeast Asia". In *The Indian Ocean in Antiquity*, edited by J. Reade, pp. 365–400. London: Kegan Paul International and the British Museum, 1999.

Goh Geok Yian. "Writing Tagaung into Burmese History: The Fabula of the

First 'Myanmar' Kingdom". Conference of the International Association of Historians of Asia, Singapore, 2010.

———. "Settlement Hierarchies of the 5th to 16th Centuries in Myanmar". In *Connecting Empires and States*, edited by Mai Lin Tjoa-Bonatz, Andreas Reinecke, and Dominic Bonatz, pp. 349–61. Berlin: European Association of Southeast Asian Archaeologists, 2012.

Grave, P., and M. Barbetti. "Dating the City Wall, Fortification and the Palace Site at Pagan". *Asian Perspectives* 40, no. 1 (2001): 75–87.

Gutman, P. "The Pyu Maitreyas". In *Tradition in Current Perspectives: Proceedings of the Conference on Myanmar and Southeast Asia*, pp. 165–78. Yangon: Universities Historical Research Centre, 1996.

———. *Burma's Lost Kingdoms: Splendours of Arakan*. Bangkok: Orchid Press, 2001.

Gutman, P., and B. Hudson. "The Archaeology of Myanmar (Burma) from Neolithic to Pagan". In *Southeast Asia from Prehistory to History*, edited by I. Glover and P. Bellwood, pp. 149–76. London: RoutledgeCurzon, 2004.

———. "Pyu Stucco at Pagan". *TAASA Review* 14, no. 4 (2005): 20–22.

Hall, K.R. *Maritime Trade and State Development in Early Southeast Asia*. Honolulu: University of Hawai'i Press, 1985.

Higham, C.F.W. *The Archaeology of Mainland Southeast Asia*. Cambridge: Cambridge University Press, 1988.

———. *The Bronze Age of Southeast Asia*. Cambridge: Cambridge University Press, 1996.

———. "Archaeology in Myanmar: Past, Present, and Future". *Asian Perspectives* 40, no. 1 (2001): 127–38.

———. *Early Cultures of Mainland Southeast Asia*. Bangkok: River Books, 2002.

Hudson, B. *The Origins of Pagan: The Archaeological Landscape of Upper Burma to AD 1300*. PhD dissertation, University of Sydney, 2004.

Hudson, B., and T. Lustig (with an introduction by Michael Aung-Thwin). "Communities of the Past: A New View of the Old Walls and Hydraulic System at Sriksetra, Myanmar". *Journal of Southeast Asian Studies* 39, no. 2 (2008): 269–96.

Hudson, B., Nyein Lwin, and Win Maung (Tampawaddy). "The Origins of Pagan: New Dates and Old Inhabitants". *Asian Perspectives* 40, no. 1 (2001): 48–74.

———. "Digging for Myths — Archaeological Excavations and Surveys of the Legendary Nineteenth Founding Villages of Pagan". In *Burma: Art and Archaeology*, edited by A. Green and T.R. Blurton, pp. 9–22. London: British Museum, 2002.

Kan Hla. "Ancient Cities in Burma". *Journal of the Society of Architectural Historians* 38, no. 2 (1979): 95–102.

Khyit San Win. *Tagaung hma Athit thwe shi hmu Pyu Ahtauk Ahtar myar* [Newly discovered Pyu finds from Tagaung]. Yangon: Pan Myo Thityar Cape, 2004.

―――. *Tagaung hma Pyu A Yo O Myar* [Burial urns from Tagaung]. Yangon: Pan Myo Thityar Cape, 2005.

Luce, G.H. "The Ancient Pyu". In *Fiftieth Anniversary Publications No. 2: Selection of Articles from the Journal of the Burma Research Society (History and Literature)*, pp. 307–22. Rangoon: Burma Research Society, [1937] 1960.

―――. *Old Burma–Early Pagan*, 3 vols. Ascona and New York: Artibus Asiae and Institute of Fine Arts, New York University, 1969.

McIntosh, R.J. "Early Urban Clusters in China and Africa: The Arbitration of Social Ambiguity". *Journal of Field Archaeology* 18, no. 2 (1991): 199–212.

―――. "Clustered Cities and Alternative Courses to Authority in Prehistory". *Journal of East Asian Archaeology* 1, nos. 1–4 (1999): 63–86.

Miksic, J.N. "Settlement Patterns and Sub-regions in Southeast Asian History". *Review of Indonesian and Malaysian Affairs* 24 (1990): 86–144.

―――. "Survei permukaan situs Trowulan dan perkotaan di Indonesia pada zaman kelasik [Recent research at Trowulan: Implications for early urbanization in Indonesia]. *Pertemuan Ilmiah Arkeologi* 6 (1994): 357–66.

―――. "Evolving Archaeological Perspectives on Southeast Asia". *Journal of Southeast Asian Studies* 26, no. 1 (1995): 46–62.

―――. "Heterogenetic Cities in Premodern Southeast Asia". *World Archaeology* 32, no. 1 (2000): 106–20.

―――. "Early Burmese Urbanization: Research and Conservation". *Asian Perspectives* 40, no. 1 (2001): 88–107.

Moore, E. "Bronze and Iron Age Sites in Upper Myanma: Chindwin, Samon and Pyu". *SOAS Bulletin of Burma Research* 1, no. 1 (2003): 24–39.

―――. "Interpreting Pyu Material Culture: Royal Chronologies and Finger-marked Bricks". *Myanmar Historical Research Journal* 13 (2004): 1–58.

―――. *Early Landscapes of Myanmar*. Bangkok: River Books, 2007.

Moore, E., and Aung Myint. "Line Decorated Beads amongst the Pyu and Chin". *Journal of Siam Society* 81, no. 1 (1993): 57–87.

Moore, E., and Pauk Pauk. "Nyaung-gan: A Preliminary Note on a Bronze Age Cemetery near Mandalay, Myanmar (Burma)". *Asian Perspectives* 40, no. 1 (2001): 35–47.

Moore, E., and Win Maung (Tampawaddy). "Change in the Landscape of First Millennium AD Myanmar". *SOAS Bulletin of Burma Research* 4, no. 2 (2006): 2–26.

Myint Aung. "The Excavations at Halin". *Journal of the Burma Research Society* 53, no. 2 (1970): 55–64.

Nyunt Han, Win Maung, and E. Moore. "Prehistoric Grave Goods from the Chindwin and Samon River Regions". In *Burma: Art and Archaeology*, edited by A. Green and R. Burton, pp. 1–8. London: British Museum, 2002.

Pautreau, J.-P., ed. *Ywa Htin. Iron Age Burials in the Samon Valley, Upper Burma*. Chiang Mai: French Archaeological Mission in Myanmar, 2007.

Pautreau, J.-P., A.-S. Coupey, P. Mornais, and Aung Aung Kyaw. "Tombes des ages du Bronze et du Fer dans le basin de la Samon [Bronze and Iron Age burials in the Samon river valley]. In *Selected Papers from the 10th International Conference of the European Association of Southeast Asian Archaeologists*, edited by E.A. Bacus, I.C. Glover, and V.C. Pigott, pp. 128–36. Singapore: NUS Press, 2006.

Pichard, Pierre. *Inventory of Monuments at Pagan*, 8 vols. Arran: Kiscadale/Paris: UNESCO/EFEO, 1992–2001.

Pool, C. "Interpreting Ceramic Production and Distribution". In *Ceramic Production and Distribution: An Integrated Approach*, edited by G.J. Bey III and C.A. Pool, pp. 275–314. Boulder, CO: Westview, 1992.

Ray, N. *Sanskrit Buddhism in Burma*. Amsterdam: H.J. Paris, 1936.

Shah Alam Mohamed Zaini. "Urbanisation in the Dry Zone of Burma: The Pyu Site of Sriksetra, ca 1st to 13th century". Unpublished manuscript, n.d.

———. "Recent Research at the Pyu Settlement of Sriksetra". Taipei: Indo-Pacific Prehistory Association, 2002.

Stadtner, D. "The Art of Burma". In *Art of Southeast Asia*, edited by M. Girard-Geslen, pp. 39–91. New York: Abrams, 1998.

Strachan, P. *Pagan: Art and Architecture of Old Burma*. Arran: Kiscadale, 1989.

Sun Laichen. "Chinese Historical Sources on Burma: A Bibliography of Primary and Secondary Works". Special issue, *Journal of Burma Studies* 2 (1997): 1–116.

Than Tun. *Myanma Terracottas: Pottery in Myanma and Votive Tablets of Myanma*. Yangon: Khyit Saya Sape, 2003.

Wheatley, Paul. *Nagara and Commandery: Origins of the Southeast Asian Urban Traditions*, Department of Geography, Research Papers 207–8. Chicago: University of Chicago, 1983.

Wicks, R.S. *Money, Markets, and Trade in Early Southeast Asia: The Development of Indigenous Money Systems to* A.D. *1400*. Ithaca: Southeast Asia Program, Cornell University, 1991.

Index

Note: Page numbers followed by "n" denote endnotes.

Nalanda-Sriwijaya Series